CH01466254

DIALECTICAL RESEARCH METHODS
in the CLASSICAL MARXIST TRADITION

critical qualitative research

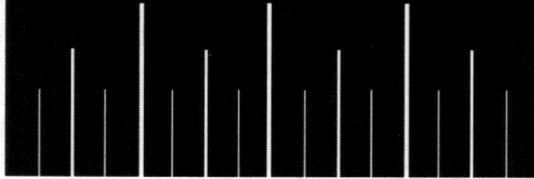

CRITICAL ISSUES FOR LEARNING AND TEACHING

Shirley R. Steinberg and Gaile S. Cannella
Series Editors

Vol. 6

The Critical Qualitative Research series
is part of the Peter Lang Education list.
Every volume is peer reviewed and meets
the highest quality standards for content and production.

PETER LANG
New York • Washington, D.C./Baltimore • Bern
Frankfurt • Berlin • Brussels • Vienna • Oxford

FAITH AGOSTINONE-WILSON

DIALECTICAL RESEARCH METHODS
in the CLASSICAL MARXIST TRADITION

PETER LANG
New York • Washington, D.C./Baltimore • Bern
Frankfurt • Berlin • Brussels • Vienna • Oxford

Library of Congress Cataloging-in-Publication Data

Agostinone-Wilson, Faith.
Dialectical research methods in the classical Marxist tradition /
Faith Agostinone-Wilson.
pages cm. — (Critical qualitative research; v. 6)
Includes bibliographical references.
1. Education—Research. 2. Education—Research—Methodology.
3. Communism and education. I. Title.
LB1028.A333   370.72—dc23   2013003316
ISBN 978-1-4331-1713-8 (hardcover)
ISBN 978-1-4331-1712-1 (paperback)
ISBN 978-1-4539-1100-6 (e-book)
ISSN 1947-5993

Bibliographic information published by **Die Deutsche Nationalbibliothek**.
Die Deutsche Nationalbibliothek lists this publication in the "Deutsche
Nationalbibliografie"; detailed bibliographic data is available
on the Internet at http://dnb.d-nb.de/.

The paper in this book meets the guidelines for permanence and durability
of the Committee on Production Guidelines for Book Longevity
of the Council of Library Resources.

© 2013 Peter Lang Publishing, Inc., New York
29 Broadway, 18th floor, New York, NY 10006
www.peterlang.com

All rights reserved.
Reprint or reproduction, even partially, in all forms such as microfilm,
xerography, microfiche, microcard, and offset strictly prohibited.

Printed in the United States of America

Table of Contents

Introduction

If one spends any time on social media or consuming reality television, the phrase "it is what it is" will be familiar. Originally a part of the urban lexicon, meant to express an "f-this" attitude, "it is what it is" has become a form of cyber shoulder-shrugging or a way to end a discussion that has gone on too long or that might be politically uncomfortable. Educational research is currently mired in "it is what it is" thinking. A variation on the mantra of neoliberalism's "there is no alternative" (TINA), "it is what it is" thinking is intellectual corralling at its best. The implication is that if one even attempts to investigate the legitimacy of existing practices—such as high-stakes standardized testing—one is not being practical enough and should instead be busy accepting reality as "it is."

For educational researchers, the hopes of obtaining tenure, promotion, or grant funding are dependent on following the mantra of "it is what it is." So year after year, there appear dissertations, journal articles, reports, and summaries focused on pragmatic topics, "doable" topics. In the wake of No Child Left Behind (NCLB), the theoretical framing (if one could call it that) of published research was limited to how schools could meet annual yearly progress (AYP). Now that NCLB is old news, researchers have moved on to Race to the Top, Common Core, Positive Behavioral Intervention (PBI), Response to Intervention (RtI), Professional Learning Communities (PLCs), 21st Century Skills, and other reforms that have emerged in the wake of the accountability era of the early 1980s. These are only slightly different topics, which are likely to change after five to ten years—but after all, "it is what it is."

The unmentioned deal often proposed to researchers is that if they put in their time on these topics now, they will be free later on to do the kind of research they like. Even better, the lure is that they can "contribute to the conversation" and have a part in shaping policy in positive directions. Of course, to participate, one has to accept "it is what it is" as the starting point of research. It is also key that one dismisses the work of those who don't play along with "it is what it is," lest others confuse one's work with that camp. The idea is that going along to get along will be much more productive in the long run than wasting time resisting. Yet, this practical approach has not resulted in putting a stop to the most egregious practices such as tying teacher employment to student test scores; indeed, the pace of these reforms has only accelerated. "It is what it is" research has *enabled*—not halted or even slowed—existing educational conditions, with no sign of abating. Followers of "it is what it is" don't realize that the conversation was over long before the research ever began.

In many ways, educational research faces the same constraints of the possible that often are leveled at the political philosophy of Marxism. All criticisms of Marxism boil down to the stubbornness of dialectical materialists in rejecting the framework of "it is what it is." Eagleton (2011) outlines and responds to common critiques of Marxism after presenting a hefty case for debunking its oft-reported demise. Marxism, including dialectical materialist educational research, appears to be "dead" because it is often outnumbered by other theoretical paradigms supported by the ruling elites. As with governments, "the political odds will always be on the system in power, if only because it has more tanks than you do" (p. 7, loc. 130). Instead of conventional weaponry, however, the prevailing research paradigms have the big grants and the media to communicate study findings.

Rather than expecting Marxism to justify itself, Eagleton turns the tables on capitalism's own dismal record of meeting human needs:

> How long are we prepared to wait for it to come up with the goods? Why do we continue to indulge the myth that the fabulous wealth generated by this mode of production will in the fullness of time become available to all? Would the world treat similar claims by the far left with such genial, let's-wait-and-see forbearance? (p. 10, loc. 167–169)

One could also make the same demands of "it is what it is" research. How long are we supposed to wait for it to close the achievement gap, reduce educational inequality, create engaging and creative curricula, empower teachers and administrators? . . . the list goes on and on.

Capitalism has had close to 500 years to prove itself and has not done so with any degree of success, other than for the wealthy and for elements of the middle class who have been tossed some paltry scraps to convince them that they were not "working class." Additionally, as an economic system, capitalism was given an unheard-of head start with the "investment" of appropriated lands, resources, and slave labor under colonialism. Nevertheless, instead of the benefits of capitalist production leading to a shorter work week, engaging and meaningful labor, better health, and sustained infrastructure for all, "what used to be apocalyptic fantasy is today no more than sober realism" (Eagleton, 2011, p. 8, loc. 146). The ultimate in "it is what it is."

Likewise, we have run out of time to wait for traditional educational research to turn things around. People are in dire straits while we wait around discussing the merits of assessment systems and teacher evaluation. Dialectical materialist inquiry is the only research methodology that is capable of making the connections between increased militarism and the security state, a declining social safety net, the rise in fascist discourse, and capitalism. No other research approach is willing to take the steps to directly name the culprit of this totalizing economic system. Instead, to varying degrees, educational research, whether empirical or constructivist or postmodern, accepts capitalism as "it is what it is."

The purpose of this book is to provide a starting point for those interested in leaving behind "it is what it is" research, in order not only to describe the world, but also to change it. Each of the chapters addresses a facet of dialectical materialist inquiry, with Chapters One through Three addressing foundational philosophy/critique, Four through Six focusing on examples of existing research in the dialectical tradition, and the final chapters presenting methodological considerations.

Chapter One, "Against Pragmatism," engages the reader in a sustained critique of mainstream educational research. The limits of both pragmatism and postmodernism are explored, including their tacit support for imperialism and capitalism. This chapter will demonstrate that rather than moving things forward, these research approaches have emboldened the continued attack on the poor and working class, from education to labor sectors.

Chapter Two, "Research in the Service of Empire," presents a historical and current overview of how mainstream inquiry, including educational research, has been used to support the most egregious policies of the ruling elite. Research projects such as the military's Human Terrain System are described, along with discussion of how quantitative inquiry is used to fight environmental and health regulations. Additionally, educational research's role in advancing the dominance of assessment-driven policies and practices is discussed.

Chapter Three, "What Makes Marxist Research 'Marxist,'" presents several key tenets common to most dialectical research studies. A presentation of dialectical materialism begins the chapter, followed by essential factors of Marxist research. It is hoped that the reader will walk away with a better sense of the nature of dialectical materialist inquiry and a clear vision of what it entails.

Chapter Four, "Dialectical Empiricist Research," presents the scope and type of work of those scholars who conduct quantitative research in a Marxist tradition. The purpose of the chapter is to dispel the myth that empirical research is automatically opposed to issues of social justice by virtue of method alone. Examples of work from the areas of social policy, public health, and education are presented.

Chapter Five, "Dialectical Materialist Ethnographers," presents qualitative researchers who use classic ethnographic methods of gathering data from a Marxist (or methods and framing compatible with Marxism) perspective. As with Chapter Four, the purpose of this chapter is to introduce readers to possibly unfamiliar faces (or to reintroduce readers to familiar ones)—scholars who use dialectical principles to engage in research that sides with the oppressed rather than collaborating with the oppressors.

Chapter Six, "Theoretical Research in the Dialectical Tradition," presents examples of basic research, also known as theoretical research, criticalist research, or pure inquiry. Scholarship that falls into this category includes work that seeks to build on existing knowledge—in this case, dialectical materialism—by analysis and examination alone, rather than through data collection or testing theory. As with ethnography, theoretical research is interdisciplinary in nature and works across a diversity of fields such as politics, technology, law, medicine, history, psychology, physics, and education.

Chapter Seven, "People," addresses aspects of working with human beings in research contexts. This includes a discussion of the history and purpose of institutional review boards (IRBs), problems with traditional limits of ethics and consent/privacy, and the principle of reciprocity in light of Marxist philosophy.

Chapter Eight, "Places," considers environmental factors in dialectical materialist research. More than simply a "setting," place involves social contexts that have a specific history and trajectory. Marxist geography is introduced as a way to frame the environment, followed by a presentation of the limits of individualism as a method of interpretation. A critique of localism is also included.

Chapter Nine, "Things," deals with material culture and its significance in shaping capitalist social relations. Cultural Marxism is presented as one way to approach the study of artifacts. Several examples of these approaches applied to mass media products are provided.

Chapter Ten, "Interpretation," will hopefully assist researchers with using dialectical materialism to shape analysis of data. Foundational data collection methods are addressed, including interviews, observations, and text analysis. Problematic situations such as researching those in power are also presented.

Chapter Eleven, "Technology," uses Marxist analysis to examine the cyber world, which reflects the same inequalities as face-to-face society. Special considerations in terms of ethics and privacy are presented for consideration for those contemplating conducting online research of their own. The knowledge commons is also included as a potential embodiment of Marxian principles applied to technological worlds.

Chapter One

Against Pragmatism

Overview: Problems with Mainstream Educational Research

There are two primary questions that dialectical research addresses: How did things get this way? What are we going to do about it? "Things" can refer to a wide range of phenomena, from the use of standardized testing to the unpaid labor of women. "Get," because the way things are is not natural or enduring; things become the way they are through a combination of historical forces, under the constant shadow of capitalist social relations. "We" is deliberately invoked because individual, narrow solutions do not work for the kinds of things we are now facing, including environmental disaster.

In this chapter, the term *pragmatic* refers to a narrow, instrumentalist research philosophy that seems, on the surface, to address the need to take action and solve problems, but in reality seeks to never offend prominent stakeholders. This is a different use than the traditional "pragmatism" of notable philosophers such as Peirce (1878), Dewey (1998), and James (1904). Their form of pragmatism broke from the more restrictive traditions of top-down empiricism applied to social science research, and viewed knowledge as the result of human activity, not as existing in an unchanging, eternal state. The pragmatic research referred to in this chapter may allude to this heritage of social constructivism, but remains mired in plodding along the path of localized solutions, which only entrenches the status quo. It should be considered a "false pragmatism" (xynz, 2010), where "the main changes are centered on the change of words and not in changing the world" (Torres & Reyes, 2011, pp. 38–39).

Because false pragmatism often uses a catch-all of philosophical approaches in the pursuit of "whatever works," postmodernism is included in this critique of mainstream educational research. Following Jameson (1991), postmodernism can be considered the philosophy of late-stage capitalism, which made its appearance during the 1970s. According to Torres and Reyes (2011), "educational institutions have fallen into a stronghold of postmodern discussions, while the corporatization of education is advancing in making these institutions work toward their interests" (p. 37). Allman (2007) explains further:

> During this period of almost continuous capitalist growth and relative weakening of the class struggle, many Marxists began to think that Marx had got it wrong and it was possible, after all, to reform capitalism. As a result some abandoned Marxism altogether, while others looked to the theories of political economies who were trying to rework Marxist theory in terms of what they thought was a changed reality...[T]here has been a mounting predilection to integrate or merge Marxism with other intellectual theories, such as existentialism and phenomenology, or other theorists. (p. 55)

This echoes parallel academic developments during the 1980s and 1990s that saw the rejection of Marx and the acceptance of false pragmatism/postmodernism, alongside the growth of right-wing and reactionary ideologies; this is what happened with the transformation of feminism from materialist to cultural interpretations (Di Leonardo & Lancaster, 2002; Holmstrom, 2002a; Kushner, 2012).

It is interesting how pragmatists claim that they go with "what works," often pointing to their methods as the only realistic option. This mirrors the TINA defense of capitalism: "there is no alternative." Yet, capitalism definitely does *not* work for the majority of people, including people in the United States, one of the wealthiest nations on the planet. If by "what works" one means 37 million people in the United States living below the poverty line, soaring debt, lack of health care, out-of-reach college tuition, eroding pensions, stagnant wages, expensive child care, and having to hold down two or three jobs in order to squeak by, that is hardly a rousing endorsement of the status quo (Grande, 2010). In fact, the economies of more than 100 nations have worsened since the implementation of pragmatic structural adjustment policies in the 1970s (Hawkesworth, 2002). As Hedges (2011a) remarks, "The timidity and silencing of the left fuels the steady impoverishment of a dispossessed working class and a beleaguered middle class. It solidifies corporate oligarchy that is dismantling the anemic regulatory agencies that once protected citizens from predatory corporations" (para. 16). Instead of the economic crisis of 2008 endangering the corporate sector, the historical partnering of banks with government culminated in the massive taxpayer-funded bailout and immediate profits for Wall Street—in many ways, capitalism has emerged from the crisis stronger, not weaker (Albo, Gindin, & Panitch, 2010). This is the result of the "realistic," pragmatic alternative to fully nationalizing the banks.

At the same time, pragmatic research does not "work" for the majority of people. Lingard (2010) explains that the problem-solving approach often touted in pragmatic research "accepts the world as it finds it, including existing power relations, inequalities, and oppressions... accepting the status quo as a framework for action" (p. 382). By casting class as simply one of several equally influential factors, thereby downplaying its importance (i.e., class can be overcome), pragmatism "mistakes the problem for a solution, and an obstacle for an opportunity" (Wood, 2002, p. 290). Postmodern research can also employ what Denzin (2009) calls "qualitative ethicism," the belief that by rejecting positivism to focus on the practical, immediate, and local, one automatically acts ethically. This opens the way for research to be used in the service of empire, a concept that is discussed in more detail in Chapter Two.

This chapter begins with some examples of the results of pragmatism in the areas of the environment, war/imperialism, education, and labor. This is by no means an exhaustive accounting, just enough to point out the ineffectiveness of the pragmatic approach. Next, connections between postmodernism/pragmatism and rightist thought will be examined, followed by features of pragmatism/postmodernism including reformism/incrementalism, calls for leftists to scale back their expectations, and radical relativism.

What Pragmatism Has Wrought

Environment

It is a common truism that reforms don't work, yet time and again, we attempt reforms while accepting the constraints of the existing sit-

uation, perhaps venturing into the occasional critique of current policies and practices if we are feeling particularly frisky. Yet, usually,
policies and practices are viewed as unsatisfactory because elements
of them aren't efficient *enough*, or because some stakeholders were not
involved in the initial planning, not because they are wrong per se.
The need for evidence-based research is often invoked, and it is a necessary element for obtaining grant funding, thereby inscribing false
pragmatism as the de facto approach. Thorp and Goldstein (2010)
present a hypothetical yet all-too-recognizable description of how
mainstream research is used to inform practice—in this case, inquiry
to solve environmental problems—and is worth quoting at length
here:

> An entrepreneurial faculty member decides to tackle global warming. To do
> so, she has to bring together colleagues—chemists, biologists, and physi-
> cists—who have the technical expertise to produce new energy sources. She
> must also have the participation of those who have the ability to understand
> environmental impacts: marine scientists, climate specialists, and computer
> modelers. People who recognize the policy implications—political scientists,
> policy studies faculty, sociologists, and even philosophers—are also needed.
>
> Rather than simply assemble the team, the entrepreneurial faculty member
> proposes to the provost the creation of a new School of Climate Change. He
> protests that the administrative costs of the program will be high because a
> new dean and development staff as well as lab and office space are required.
> But our enterprising young faculty member gets a big oil company to pro-
> vide a $50 million gift, creating the new School of Climate Change. The
> provost relents because there's now enough money to support the new pro-
> ject and attendant costs for administrators and faculty members. The presi-
> dent agrees because a high-visibility project has been created on his watch,
> and the development staff gets to count the big gift in its campaign total. A
> high-profile dean for the new school is recruited with great fanfare, but the
> appointment triggers the need for more administrative infrastructure than
> the big gift provides. Years later, the $2.5 million in revenue from the en-
> dowment gift has generated a new vice provost and scores of new nonaca-
> demic employees. Meanwhile, the earth is still getting warmer. (para. 5–8)

What is striking about this representative account is how many
wheels are spun, stakeholders consulted, upper-level managers hired,

donations raised, and corporations pleased, yet in the end, global warming remains unaddressed.

Nanda (2002) points out that postmodern reform movements such as eco-feminism do not challenge capitalism and imperialism, and in many cases only strengthen nationalist responses, as is the case with farmers' movements in India. There, "pre-existing, religion- and culture-sanctified patriarchal bargains are literally soaking up the liberatory aspects of the shift from private to public patriarchy made possible by the Green Revolution" (p. 398). Because movements such as Karnatka Rajya Raitha Sangh (KRRS) and Bharatiya Kisan Union (BKU) are easily co-opted by academics who reject modernism in favor of a romantic embracing of anything opposed to the Enlightenment/Western values, a type of dangerous populism can emerge, ushering in nationalism and privatized responses to environmental problems.

Much of the environmental solutions remain "embedded...in a capitalist context" or are presented in the form of "alternative communities...where insightful radical critique mixes with petty and medium-scale entrepreneurship" (Lewontin & Levins, 2007, p. 93). So far, the environmental policies that have been implemented have represented a severe scaling back of expectations, as with the Kyoto Protocol, carbon capture and trade schemes, tinkering with trade legislation, reconsidering nuclear power, and the like (Williams, 2012a).Wall's (2010) materialist critique of these mainstream environmental solutions identifies them as part of climate change denial in that none of these proposed reforms ever seeks to unseat capitalism, which is incompatible with environmental survival, a view shared by Allman (2007) and Wood (2002).

Imperialism

Honig-Parnass (2010) critiques the post-Zionist movement and use of multiculturalism in her analysis of nationalism. In the analysis of post-Zionism, the role of Israel as a settler state is set aside, along with the connections between Israel and the United States:

For instance, some of them tend to equate the oppression of the Palestinians with that of the Mizrahim, perceiving both as the victims of the Ashkenazi (European Jewish) Zionist state. They thus ignore the central feature of Zionism which implies the full exclusion of the Palestinians from the exclusivist Jewish state, while the class-based oppression of Mizrahi Jews does not stem from the colonial character of the state of Israel, whose main dividing line is that between Jews and Palestinians. (p. 27)

Merely applying multicultural framing to international contexts does not reform what are imperial practices.

Similarly, we cannot expect that equality extended only to isolated groups will reform the status quo. Cultural feminism is inadequate for examining the acts of torture at Abu Ghraib, many which were conducted and documented by women. As Ehrenreich (2008) points out:

You can't even argue, in the case of Abu Ghraib, that the problem was that there just weren't enough women in the military hierarchy to stop the abuses. The prison was directed by a woman. The top US intelligence officer in Iraq, who was also responsible for reviewing the status of detainees before their release, was a woman. And the U.S. official alternately responsible for managing the occupation of Iraq was Condoleezza Rice. Like Rumsfeld, she ignored repeated reports of abuse and torture until the undeniable photographic evidence emerged.... [G]ender equality cannot, all by itself, bring about a just and peaceful world. (p. 195)

Indeed, Bageant (2007) applies class analysis to the notorious figure of Lynndie England, who was holding the leash in some of the photos at Abu Ghraib, connecting her to a larger economic context of who fights the wars (most come from towns with populations of less than 40,000 people). Seeking to make imperialism kinder by focusing on equality only for specific groups is a dead-end strategy.

Calls for nationalizing resources, part of the platforms of leftist political movements in South and Central America, are not a sufficient solution, as Lewis (2012) explains:

Nationalization is not the same as expropriation, in which property is simply seized from the capitalist class, which is then cut off from profits and managerial authority alike. Under nationalization, old bosses and private command structures largely remain in place, whereas expropriations put

> workers in the driver's seat.... Nationalization can be a revolutionary step,
> but its sphere of effects is administrative. Expropriations are more revolu-
> tionary, for they imply the direct exercise of workers' class power and self-
> determination. (p. 33)

Nationalization in many ways fosters the maintenance of the ruling class by softening its impact and making it appear that things have changed. We also have the lesser-evilism of the military's Human Terrain Systems (HTS), supporting the use of embedded researchers on the rationale that their presence saves lives by tapping into knowledge of local cultures and customs so that guns and bombs aren't as necessary (Gonzalez, 2009; Price, 2011). HTS does not, how-ever, challenge the concept of occupation—in fact, it is one of the key ways in which occupation functions. Additional discussion of HTS is presented in Chapter Two.

Education

Restricting research aims to documenting better ways for schools to make annual yearly progress (AYP) does not forestall further stand-ardization and narrowing of the curriculum. For example, state standards for schools commonly include social constructivist concepts such as inquiry-based learning, higher-order thinking, critical think-ing, and problem solving, but schools are expected to assess those skills through the use of high-stakes testing (Freeman, Mathison, & Wilcox, 2012). The pragmatic and limited use of these concepts has reinforced the view that these tests, which supposedly measure stu-dent acquisition of critical thinking, are "good tests" in the eyes of teachers, thereby strengthening, not challenging, standardized testing as a form of assessment.

Improving children's opportunities is often the rationale behind programs that emphasize learning English rather than maintaining multiple languages. Fairclough (2010) critiques mainstream policy and research concerning language acquisition on four counts. First, calls for improving English acquisition assume that schools and schools alone can remove social class differences, with English as a gateway to economic success. Second, even when a home language is recognized, it is de facto assigned secondary status, because English is the gateway to economic success. Third, English is recognized as being used in "appropriate" situations, meaning that the uses of home language and dialects are for the less important, more marginal contexts. Finally, many language reform programs treat anti-immigrant racism as a matter of personally held sentiments and stereotypes, not part of a structural and historical part of racism in general.

Instead of insisting that access to education preschool through postsecondary is a human right, the argument is pragmatically framed as one of "access to social mobility" (Swidler, 2012, p. 16). This scaled-back notion involves everyone having a right of access to college, rather than guaranteed free, universal higher education for those with the interest and ability. Likewise, those who support the access line of thinking stop short of challenging prevailing wage structures and undocumented and underpaid labor; instead, they focus their attention on "deserving" students (calls for more merit scholarships) and continuous credentialing, such as through the DREAM (Development, Relief, and Education for Alien Minors) Act (2009). In the meantime, student debt climbs higher and higher (Collinge, 2009; Kamenetz, 2006; Lapon, 2012) and undocumented groups are increasingly scapegoated (Navarro, 2009; Paulos, 2012).

Labor

Fawcett and Gupta's (2010) review of the Discovery Channel's Planet Green series *Blood, Sweat, and Takeaways* alludes to the hazards of a pragmatic worldview. In the series, affluent British young adults' travels to Thailand and Indonesia are documented in a reality television format as they work with local populations and experience the horrible conditions that the majority of the world has to face. At the end of the series, the participants renounce their hedonistic ways and express sympathy for the people they have visited. While on the surface, the series does open the eyes of privileged Westerners, at the same time, the focus is primarily on personal, not structural, reform. The focus of the series is on personal narratives as the participants begin to shift their perspectives. Therefore, the drama hinges on individualism, not social change, because the message is that the only thing you can change is yourself:

> The lack of choice and agency is a refrain throughout the series.... [I]nstead, we are taught to accept life as it is, disciplining labor and behavior on either side of the commodity chain, with humility and grace. By engaging with the natural workings of the market, they learn there is no alternative to it. (p. 71)

Rather than recognizing a need for revolution for these Third World workers, the affluent youth channel their transformations into selecting fair trade foods. One of the participants concluded that, "you think the conditions are bad now, if all U.K. consumers revolt, just imagine what their conditions would be then" (p. 71). So, even mass product boycotts are too radical a solution.

Pragmatic reform also comes packaged in the wrapping of "development" as a solution. Kempadoo (2002) refers to those who support the rights of sex workers, but only in the terms of the market:

> Some prostitutes' rights advocates assume that Western development, capitalist modernization, and industrialization will enable women in developing countries to exercise choice and attain "freedom."...Western women's experience is thus made synonymous with assumptions about the inherent superiority of industrialized capitalist development and Third World women are placed in categories of pre-technological "backwardness," "inferiority," dependency, and ignorance. (p. 212)

Similarly, farming is conceptualized by NGOs as "men's work," displacing women and only increasing levels of malnutrition and starvation (Hawkesworth, 2002).

The impact of pragmatism was also felt in the defeat of the movement to recall Wisconsin governor Scott Walker. After Walker was elected in 2010 as part of the Tea Party ascent/Obama backlash, he immediately implemented severe attacks on public sector unions in the form of legislation against the ability to collectively bargain. The wave of activism against Walker in the wake of Egypt's uprising was intense and inspiring, yet the Democrats quickly discouraged tactics such as the occupation of the capitol building in Madison, and instead channeled activism into the more sensible recall movement.

After a successful signature campaign to seal the deal on the recall election, momentum began to stall after the primary election to select Walker's opponent yielded an almost equally anti-union candidate, Tom Barrett (who had lost against Walker the first time around). Pragmatism once again failed as voters were instructed to go the any-one-but-Walker route, as Cole and Gasper (2012) recount:

> The contrast between the enthusiasm for the signature campaign against Walker on the one hand, and the weaker poll numbers for any Democrat who goes up against him in a general election, is telling. It highlights the failure of lesser-evilism—the idea that workers should vote for one of the two parties of big business even though both parties refuse to champion their own demands and concerns. (p. 8)

Instead of winning gains or even relief from the ongoing assault on workers, the unions' strategy of partnering with business in the form of concessions rather than openly confronting corporations has left its membership's ability to bargain weaker, not stronger (Albo, Gindin, & Panitch, 2010).

Pragmatism/Postmodernism as Fostering Rightist Ideology

Fisher (2009) describes how both immobilizers (those who argue that there is no alternative to capitalism) and liberal communists (those who seek to minimize capitalism through altruism or multicultural perspectives) introduce a conservative and reactionary element into the existing political situation under the guise of democratic goals. Both groups effectively truncate any form of mass resistance. In many ways, pragmatism represents Fisher's description of the immobilizers, while postmodernists are the liberal wing of capitalism. These groups foster conservative responses to pressing social needs through a co-opting of revolutionary discourse to reinscribe oppression, encouraging fatalism/cynicism and basing the foundation for resistance on rejecting Enlightenment principles of solidarity, dignity, and freedom. This, in turn, only buttresses reactionary and right-wing ideologies.

Belenky, Clinchy, Goldberger, and Tarule's (1997) research on college women's acquisition of knowledge found that one of the earlier stages of thinking that women pass through involves a very procedural view of inquiry:

> Their thinking is encapsulated within systems. They can criticize a system, but only in the system's terms, only according to the system's standards. Women at this position may be liberals or conservatives, but they cannot be radicals. If, for example, they are feminists, they want equal opportunities for women within the capitalistic structure; they do not question the premises of the structure. (p. 127, loc. 1909–1912)

In many ways, this description applies to pragmatists and many postmodernists who seem incapable of directly confronting capitalism as a whole. By refusing to go the distance, these researchers are not equipped to solve problems, let alone analyze them. What remains behind—discourses such as liberal humanism—are inadequate for taking on today's pressing social problems. As Eagleton (1983) points out, the traditional humanistic figure of the unique individual is readily transformed into what capital needs: someone who has the "freedom" to choose, as long as they have the means to do so. Capitalism will use liberal humanism, diversity, democracy, and pluralism to further its ends by being very selective in the application of these concepts.

Capitalism has the ability to transform and adapt to existing situations (Fairclough, 2010). Robin (2011) outlines how conservative movements have historically been adept at co-opting revolutionary language to advance reactionary ideas. For Robin, the reworking of leftist discourse in the support of right-wing ideology is part of the process of reinvigorating counterrevolutionary movements. The left often assumes that today's right wing buys into the notion of a static, unchanging society, when in fact the opposite is the case: "The conservative's encounter with revolution teaches them that the revolutionaries were right after all: inequality is a human creation. And if it can be uncreated by men and women, it can be recreated by men and women" (p. 53, loc. 797–802). As an example, Robin describes how spokespeople of the intelligent design movement reworked creationism into a more appealing quasi-scientific cause du jour. One of the proponents Robin mentions recalls how he learned much from postmodernism about how to frame discourse surrounding science and religion. In a similar manner, backlash groups against feminism such as Phyllis Schlafley's Eagle Forum use the discourse of human rights to justify the inequality of women, even though Schlafley is herself a financially successful woman who is the opposite of the proper housewife. For example, she is educated, does speaking tours, is a successful author, and definitely works outside of the home. In this way, "conservatism adapts and adopts, often unconsciously, the language of democratic reform to the cause of hierarchy" (p. 52, loc. 786–789). Concerning education, one only has to think about how civil rights discourse has been co-opted by school reformers in the name of reducing the achievement gap (Crawford, 2007a, 2007b).

Torres and Reyes (2011) liken postmodern multivocality to the enchantment of the mermaid in mythology, who appears to be pleasing, but ends up leading followers to nihilism and a state of paralysis when the illusions turn out to be a diversion. When problems become too immediate or severe to ignore, pragmatism and postmodernism will assert that what we are seeing is either totally unexpected or just a repeat of the same old thing:

> The claim that nothing new is happening is a common device for opposing social and political action, either on the grounds that no action is possible because the present situation is an unchangeable constant of nature, or that no new action is required because things are not materially different than they have always been. (Lewontin & Levins, 2007, p. 45)

Both of these options foster cynicism and fatalism because neither one uses materialist analysis to look at the specificity of context or attempt to dialectically trace historical developments of a problem, methods of which are outlined in Chapter Three. As Giroux (2010) explains, the mass media, which often promulgates cynicism/fatalism, offers "only individual failure against a world beset with social problems, [and] privatizes politics just as they depoliticize any viable notion of agency" (p. 47). Slee (2006) finds that cynicism reduces choice to the anticollective solution of market-think.

Kandiyoti (2002) finds that in the wake of the collapse of older forms of social organization such as traditional patriarchy, people begin to search for the instigator of the collapse, or to determine why what used to "work" is no longer working. Change is thus seen to have "gone too far." Anti-Enlightenment philosophies such as postmodernism and poststructuralism oppose concepts such as emancipation because they are tied to notions of rationality, which is viewed as a Western construct and inherently antithetical to diversity (Nanda, 2002; Torres & Reyes, 2011). Politics become divorced from culture, which is "used to silence activist messages, by barring progressive groups from participating in community events and constructing a sanitized version of culture that suits elite interests and power" (Shah, 2002, p. 121). Instead of political analysis, a focus on "taking action" is privileged. Denzin's (2009) examination of the Cheney Doctrine finds that action alone isn't always emancipatory:

> Cheney's doctrine shortchanges the pragmatic maxim. He discounts the need for an analysis, interpretation of consequences, and the search for evidence. He wants action, and, in order to justify action, he will manufacture the evidence he needs. He locates the meanings of the response in the staged news event, in its dramaturgical construction. (p. 43)

We see here that pragmatism is no match for Cheney's fascism—it can easily be set aside in favor of inventing weapons of mass destruction as the justification for the invasion and occupation of Iraq.

Characteristics of Pragmatism

Reformism/Incrementalism

Mainstream political thought views institutions as reflecting what is generally seen in society. Therefore, "the present order is perceived as at least reasonably good, and no major structural changes are needed" (Tammilehto, 2010, p. 197). Incrementalism represents the concept that many smaller changes will automatically result in a big change, but we might have to wait, say, 200 years or so for that to happen, so patience is in order. For Tammilehto, a key problem consists of progress being framed as "the flow of reforms [being] somehow faster than the flow of new problems" (p. 198).

Lewontin and Levins (2007) attribute the American interest in reformism to a general distaste for theory, along with framing problems too narrowly so as not to be "impractical." They explain how, in the field of medicine, this has created a harmful form of reductionism, where cure and prevention studies break factors down to the smallest parts, ignoring larger social contexts such as poverty that contribute to widespread disease. The same has happened with the development of pesticides and herbicides—in addition to increasing crop yields and decreasing hunger their use has created more problems such as chemical-resistant weeds or disruption of the food chain. Davis (2002) finds that while politicians and the public call for reforms in the prison industry, few have analyzed the historical role of incarceration as a form of punishment. As more prison reforms are implemented, the prison population rises and the public becomes more accustomed to the security state.

Thomas (2012) summarizes the media's approach to framing the school reform debate as happening between two types of reformers, "No Excuses" and "Social Context." As portrayed in the mass media, the No Excuses reformers view poverty as a transient condition that can be overcome by individual will and effort, whereas the Social Context reformers seek to ameliorate existing conditions of poverty. Ironically, it is the No Excuses reformers who position themselves as victims, powerless against the Social Context reformers, when all along, they possess much power:

> The "No Excuses" Reformers have the political and public power in the education reform debate primarily because they have political and financial power over teachers, scholars, and researchers. "No Excuses" Reformers also receive disproportionate access to the media and are rarely challenged by that media since their narratives sound true. (para. 17)

Even though Thomas rightly critiques the No Excuses reform movement as unresponsive to a growing pathology of inequality, at the same time, he positions Social Context reformers as the only force willing to confront economic inequality (not capitalism itself, of course), ignoring the Marxist perspective against reforms altogether.

Torres and Reyes (2011) investigate how family literacy programs are established and put into practice. Most use a highly pragmatic/utilitarian view of learning and are implemented by those with the least experience in education. Or, if those developing the program occupy teaching or administrative positions, they tend to hold the view that minority families need to be changed somehow, and that the families' efforts should be turned toward the task of improving the child's functioning in the school setting, rather than changing the construct of school itself, or analyzing how schooling institutions reinforce inequality.

In this manner, reform only further entrenches the status quo, as we have seen in recent educational policy:

> And so the reformers come along. And they promise that by releasing further data reports, by raising the stakes of high-stakes standardized tests, by privatization, by authorizing more charter schools, and importantly, by breaking the power of the teachers' unions, that by doing all of these things under the rubric of "greater accountability," we will promote racial justice. (Jones, 2012, p. 11)

Indeed, educators who voted for Obama knowing his support for NCLB were presented with a far worse set of policies after his election: Race to the Top. Whereas NCLB merely codified standardized tests as the assessment of choice, Race to the Top links test scores to teacher and administrator job security. As Jones (2012) points out, it is easy to understand the support for Race to the Top from the conservative big guns such as the Koch brothers, the Walton family, or corporate foundations, but it is the alliance between these entities *and* the liberals that makes the situation all the more dire.

"Be Realistic"

A typical response to Marxism is that although it is a nice idea, it isn't realistic (Eagleton, 2011). What is often meant by the exhortation to "be realistic" is to scale back one's hopeful expectations about how things can change to a more "appropriate" level of nihilism that is acceptable to capital: "Capitalist realism presents itself as a shield protecting us from the perils imposed by belief itself. The attitude of ironic distance proper to postmodern capitalism is supposed to immunize us against the seductions of fanaticism" (Fisher, 2009, p. 5). Indeed, often accompanying calls to be more realistic are the well-worn references to the failures of Stalinist Communism and how all revolutionary movements become just as bad as the groups they overthrew (Eagleton, 2011). To "be realistic" means to work within the system and accept setbacks as unfortunate but necessary processes to go through in reaching one's goals. Part of the call to be realistic includes not being political, employing positive thinking ("don't be so negative"), and scaling back one's expectations.

When there are calls to not be political in one's research, to not resist capitalism, neoliberal neutrality is privileged and enforced. For example, research terminology used to describe teachers and students (responsible learner, lifelong learner, etc.) increasingly resemble corporate talk (Holst, 2010). Often these terms are just taken for granted. Women and minorities are also told that if they participate in activist movements, they are too idealistic or unrealistic, or they are associating with undesirable groups. The recent case of Loretta Capehart, a tenured professor at Northeastern Illinois University who was targeted by the administration for her union and community work, clearly illustrates the punishment that academics can face for political activism. Hawkesworth (2002) notes that by punishing activists or discouraging solidarity and political activism, confrontations are taken from the public sphere and shifted to individualized, private spaces where people have less bargaining power:

> What was once understood as a political struggle of citizens about the boundaries of justice can now be constructed as a dispute over private resources. In changing the framing assumptions from a discourse of citizenship and justice to a discourse of competition for scarce resources or material provision to meet private need, women's goals are re-signified as "private." (p. 307)

In the case of celebrity-soaked concerts such as Live Aid or the high-profile antidebt work of U2's Bono, the message becomes that it is unrealistic to engage politically because things won't change anyway. Instead, people are encouraged to be charitable by donating to various causes that are more short term, more "doable" (Fisher, 2009). Or activism is relegated to narrow, defensive responses in the form of isolated goals, such as union calls for protecting "middle-class" jobs (but not challenging poverty and unemployment as a whole), which has allowed neoliberal to become further entrenched (Albo, Gindin, & Panitch, 2010).

The positive thinking movement is another current within the calls to be realistic:

> Positive thinking has made itself useful as an apology for the crueler aspects of the market economy. If optimism is the key to material success, and if you can achieve an optimistic outlook through the discipline of positive thinking, then there is no excuse for failure. The flipside of positivity is a harsh insistence on personal responsibility: if your business fails or your job is eliminated, it must be because you didn't try hard enough, didn't believe firmly enough in the inevitability of your success. As the economy has brought more layoffs and financial turbulence to the middle class, the promoters of positive thinking has increasingly emphasized this negative judgment: to be disappointed, resentful, or downcast is to be a victim and a whiner. (Ehrenreich, 2009, pp. 8–9)

Lewontin and Levins (2007) point out that it is usually the attitude of those registering legitimate grievances, not the source of the grievance, that is focused upon, leading "some people to say that it is how people perceive their situation in society and therefore the people must be taught to cope with where they are" (p. 308). A problem can't be that one is poor or unemployed; it's that they aren't trying to shape their own reality enough to suit the powers that be. Of course, the problem with capitalist realism is that its terms are constantly changing and can pull the rug out from under you at any given moment (Fisher, 2009). Any previous agreements can be reneged upon, as was the case with factory owners who abandoned their historical commitment to communities by moving overseas, or communities that attempted to bribe corporations by lowering tax rates (LeRoy, 2005).

Researchers who assume that they can keep ahead of these uncertainties by promulgating research that embraces them are placing a foolish bet on a system that is rigged to begin with.

Scaling back expectations is another aspect of being realistic, but this is not applied universally. Albo, Gindin, and Panitch (2010) point out that Wall Street has not scaled back at all. They think big while we continue to be "practical." Wrapped up in calls to scale back one's expectations is the acceptance of market discourse and the idea that capitalism must not be challenged under any circumstances (Tammilehto, 2010). This has led to the logic of debt and austerity as the only possible alternatives—what is referred to as the "new normal"—embodied in the market logic of McNamee and Diamond (2004). Scaling back also applies to reducing research to just method, and allowing methods to shape content (Lewontin & Levins, 2007; Torres & Reyes, 2011).

Daily Kos blogger xynz (2010) takes on the calls from centrist elements of the Democratic Party to scale back expectations by pointing out that if the political process is itself based on irrational notions, then trying to change the system from within is a failed strategy:

> The "Pragmatists" think that a long term strategy, of "smart betting" on the best odds, will lead to victory. But in a rigged game, no matter what your strategy is, the big money always wins in the end. We don't need better game strategies, we need a whole *new game*. (para. 19–20)

While certainly it might be important to engage in political struggle over more localized concerns, if those struggles are not tied to theory and a larger project for overall social change, the status quo is strengthened (Albo, Gindin, & Panitch, 2010). Instead, we need an independent class vision:

> Independent, that is, from employers and the competitive logic of capitalism, and confident in the collective potential of workers—union and nonunion, employed and unemployed—to build a society supportive of equality, solidarity, and the deepest democratization of every dimension of society, especially of the economy itself. Limiting the analysis to specific issues and ignoring the wider context—that is, the development of global capitalism as

a social system—leads to incomplete solutions and incomplete solutions can in fact make things worse. (p. 87)

Radical Relativism and Antirationality

According to Moisio, Fitzsimmons, and Suoranta (2010), important gains made by activists in the mid-twentieth century were "turned into postmodern politics of difference, and its critical and revolutionary praxis into postmodern speaking of tongues, and to a retreat into local narratives" (p. 172). This retreat is so severe that leading postmodern scholars such as Butler (1992) claim that to even try to group and categorize scholars as postmodern is to commit a "violent reduction" of the field that is, in a sense, too big and diverse to grasp (Leavy, 2007a). Gibson's (2009) description of academia in the wake of this transformation-to-narrative connects postmodernism—capitalism as represented by the academy—with its inability to confront major ideologies such as war:

> Postmodernism, religion with an angry cloak, raised every narrow identity, every neurosis, every standpoint of what was really a tiny capital, to a central issue beyond critique, worthy of worship. Finally and predictably, it became ego over solidarity. Academic postmodernists became priests of a whine from the ivory tower, at base a whine about the vanishing of professorial protections and privileges. Postmodernism atomized academia even further than its usual state—minds crouched in little individual warrens hoping for a hint of notice, and it influenced the left, forming a kind of reincarnated right-wing Menshevism. But the very real promise of perpetual war is clearly upending the lofty dream of "changing the discourse," and, I hope, will have the hidden benefit of killing postmodernism which tried to disconnect past, present, and future; deservedly giving this Versace-clothed corpse a secret burial where it can never be found again—maybe in one of those mystical "spaces" or "interventions" it enjoyed so much. (para. 13)

Leavy (2007a) notes that postmodernism, in addition to turning away from the use of meta-narratives as devices to conceptualize and explain reality, also "rejects the positivist conception of knowledge building based on objectivity, neutrality, causality, patterning, and the scientific method" (p. 88). Instead of those means of obtaining knowledge, reflectivity and study of more elusive constructs such as "power" are preferred. The relativism of examining the copy-of-a-copy simulacrum that is sacred to postmodernism not only "replicates the logic of late capitalism; it reinforces and intensifies it" (Jameson, 1991, para. 18). As Wood (2002) maintains, to base political strategies on mystical thinking such as relativism or a turn to premodern religious constructs is, at best, self-defeating. By insisting on endless difference and the notion of organizing principles as oppressive meta-narratives, we end up with no solidarity, as Torres and Reyes (2011) explain: "Absolute contingency or relativism weakens the urgency of organizing for social change, fragments organizations, and holds back the political vision of liberation and emancipation by considering them as impossible and elusive" (pp. 2–3). Because we are not able to reach some form of consensus due to everyone having their own story and special situations, we are not able to press for social changes. The reliance on a purity of contingency hegemonically reinforces the existing situation.

A major problem with relativism is that it forestalls critique in that it becomes difficult to make and compare judgments about different concepts (Allman, 2007; Nanda, 2002). If all truths can be negotiated, then religious explanations are as equally valid as scientific ones, for example. Apple (2010) challenges the notion oft-repeated in research that reality is socially constructed. He argues that this claim has become so general that it has lost its analytical strength. One should ask: If reality is just a social construction, then why do some constructions endure while others fade away? The reliance on the social construction of reality assumes that people will construct positive and liberatory realities with little to no intervention, when history clearly demonstrates that this is not the case.

Belenky et al. (1997) found that when female college students entered a phase of hyperrelativism, they relied on "gut instincts" to guide their thinking. One of the participants rejected theory as hollow intellectualism, instead turning to her inner self for reflection and guidance. Proof, then, becomes for these students a highly sensory and elusive matter, and they spend their time corroborating ideas they encounter in class or in readings with evidence until their gut tells them they must be right:

> One depressed college sophomore told us about her discovery that there were multiple truths and multiple realities. She had concluded that, since no one could know anything for sure and each person was locked in her own world, there was no way and no reason for people to try to reach each other or communicate. (p. 84, loc. 1324–1325)

Yet, we eventually have to conclude that there are some ideas that are totally wrong, such as slavery, and no amount of including "both sides of the story" can get around that wrongness. For example, Lewontin and Levins (2007) argue that scientists need to use the postulate of partisanship to guide their research, which states that "all theories are wrong if they promote, justify, or tolerate injustice" (p. 160). This creates an overarching immediacy to research that takes precedence over narrative: "Ethicists may debate, over dinner, the rational reasons for feeding the hungry, but for people in poverty, food is not a philosophical problem" (p. 165). Even though he isn't the first person who comes to mind when one thinks of radical critique, Al Gore's (2011) summary of the importance of rationality is quite prescient, especially when facing environmental destruction:

> All things are not equally true. It is time to face reality. We ignored reality in the marketplace and nearly destroyed the world economic system. We are likewise ignoring reality in the environment, and the consequences could be several orders of magnitude worse. Determining what is real can be a challenge in our culture, but in order to make wise choices in the presence of such grave risks, we must use common sense and the rule of reason in coming to an agreement on what is true. (p. 113)

Gore's statement illustrates how bad things have gotten when calls for basic, old-fashioned rationality are viewed as bold and "edgy."

Conclusion

Lewontin and Levins (2007) conclude the following concerning mainstream approaches to research and policy: "The basic reason the programs fail is not incompetence, ignorance, or stupidity, but because they are constrained by the interests of the powerful" (p. 317). What is clear is that a different sort of research is needed, of a collective nature, with absolute, ethical criteria of social justice, and no compromises or soft selling so as not to offend imperialist interests. Hennessy (2002) calls for a dialectical dis-identification with existing practices:

> Dis-identification involves working on existing ways of identifying what we embrace and live by. This "work" opens up the identities we take for granted to the historical conditions that make them possible. It involves uprooting these identities from stories of history and suffering—the fertile ground for resentment to grow—and transplanting them into a different conceptual frame, one that allows us to see how this suffering is the product of social relations that outlaw a whole array of human needs. Dis-identification entails replacing the narrow resentment of identity politics with the power and passion of the broad collective agency from which capital itself derives. (p. 86)

While such research carries much personal and professional risk and isolation, if academics—one of the more privileged sectors of the working class, who have some degree of professional autonomy compared to other workers—cannot carry out this research, then it is difficult to imagine academic resistance happening at all. Academics can play a central role in developing the theory needed to challenge capital, but they have to begin to extricate themselves from pragmatism and postmodernism. They are also going to have to start working together with other like-minded people both inside and outside higher education.

Academics also have to resist the urge to focus their research on smaller, more doable questions in the hopes that by conducting that type of study first, they will be allowed do the work they really want to do. That trap leads to one's valuable scholarly time being tied up with grant-funded projects and administrative assessment activities such as gathering data for department reviews, leaving many academics too drained to concentrate on the work they would prefer to do: "We are fiddling with evaluation metrics while the university burns. We are hiding behind the very traditions that are under attack and we are largely opting out of service in a war whose outcome, if we lose it, will eventually imprison us" (Goodall, 2012, p. 239).

It is important to remind ourselves that being "practical" with our research has contributed to the developments of a warming planet; austerity measures/cuts in social services; layoffs; healthcare with an even larger corporate role than before; narrow, regimented curricula driven by tests; increased racism/sexism; and endless war to obtain the resources to fund all of the above. Even though a tendency within postmodern/pragmatic circles is to resist binaries, there is no escaping that what we are facing has come down to an either/or choice, as Hedges (2011a) presents: "Either we begin to practice a fierce moral autonomy and rise up in multiple acts of physical defiance that have no discernible short-term benefit, or we accept the inevitability of corporate slavery. The choice is that grim. The age of the practical is over" (para. 3).

Chapter Two

Research in the Service of Empire

Overview

> Empires communicate in two languages. One language is expressed in imperatives. It is the language of command and force... it demands. It makes no attempt to justify the flagrant theft of natural resources and wealth or the use of indiscriminate violence.... [T]he other language of empire is softer. It employs a vocabulary of ideals and lofty goals and insists that the power of empire is noble and benevolent. The language of beneficence is used to speak to those outside the centers of death and pillage, those who have not yet been totally broken, those who still must be seduced to hand over power to predators. (Hedges, 2011b, para. 1)

In many respects, institutional research has long been part of this "softer" language of empire. It is used to justify and buttress policies ranging from school closures to remote bombings of villages. Government-funded research studies are quickly reduced to sound bites and hit the media in a barrage of propaganda, as with the widely reported "successes" of educational policies such as No Child Left Behind (NCLB) and the military's Human Terrain System (HTS). In the case of NCLB, a "research-based" payola agreement was made by the Bush administration in 2004 with Armstrong Williams, a spokesperson hired for $240,000 to build support for the law among African American families by appearing on news programs as a commentator (Toppo, 2005). Regarding the HTS program, army colonel Martin Schweitzer became a frequent guest on major news networks, touting a 60% reduction in human casualties by using embedded anthropologists. When this statistic was challenged by Price (2011), Schweitzer eventually admitted that he made up the number to fit what he thought was actually happening with the program. However, the 60% figure was repeated in the media and congressional testimony, keeping the propaganda alive and building support for an unpopular occupation.

Official research in the service of empire asserts itself through the voice of neopositivist authority, immediately excluding alternative perspectives, which often happen to be those of marginalized groups who are the first victims of capitalism. This was the case with so-called "evidence-based" comparative studies examining New Orleans district test scores at well-funded charter schools (with admission criteria) and underfunded public schools in the wake of Hurricane Katrina (Quigley, 2007). The results endorsed the supposed superiority of privatized, exclusionary charter schools, with absolutely no acknowledgement of the unequal social contexts that generated the test scores. This sort of approved research sustains itself through funding networks, effectively narrowly channeling priorities in a slowly tightening noose of an economy once committed to at least minimal support for the sustenance of its workforce, university employees included. Now, even that minimal obligation is eroding as capitalism has gone global in its endless quest for cheaper labor, and unemployment is no longer viewed as an urgent liability (Fisher, 2009).

Today's institutional research takes place under the rubric of neoliberalism, which represents an alliance between conservative and liberal devotees of free-market ideology in the shaping of today's social contexts (Apple, 2010; Torres & Reyes, 2011). Key impacts of neoliberalism are outlined by McLaren and Jaramillo (2010):

> stagnating wages, economic surplus at the top, redistribution of income and wealth toward the upper classes, limited profitable investment of world opportunities within production as a result of overcapacity in key industries worldwide, the shift toward financial speculation and the financial invasion of the global economy. (p. 55)

Those who carry out neoliberal research initiatives have not only national/state support, but also support from powerful and well-funded corporate factions that are deeply entrenched in all levels of government through the remarkably resilient ideology of globalism (Fairclough, 2010; Hedges, 2011a). Even with the obvious philosophical failures of neoliberalism revealed in the wake of the financial collapse in 2008, market ideology has only regrouped to deepen its assault on the global working class.

Considering the dire situation we find ourselves in, to continue to ignore the role of university-sponsored research in promoting the neoliberal project is foolish at best, and a tacit endorsement of neoliberalism at worst. Part of this ignorance is due to our lack of institutional memory of how universities have promoted (and continue to promote) the Central Intelligence Agency (CIA) and other paramilitary organizations on campus, as well as our failure to come to grips with the CIA's global activities (Price, 2011). Perhaps the ultimate tragedy of institutional research in the service of empire is that "the greatest amount of harm is done by people with higher degrees" (Lautensach & Lautensach, 2010, p. 207). Despite claims of moral and ethical ideals within their professional organizations, postsecondary-level educators are often key players in carrying out research in the service of empire. That the best educated people could cause the most damage is nothing new — Price (2011) reminds us that the best-known anthropologist is not Margaret Mead, but Joseph Mengele.

This chapter begins with an examination of three dual-sided (i.e., with two sides of the same coin) philosophical orientations of collaborator-intellectuals devoted to research in the service of empire: neopositivism/academic capitalism, colonialism/counterinsurgency, and biological determinism/resiliency. Next, the role of pseudo-science and religion in supporting the researcher-collaborator are presented. Finally, a few historical and current examples of research in the service of empire are reviewed, including in the areas of the military, environment, and public health/education.

Philosophical Orientations of the Insider Intellectual

Researchers who work for empire are collaborator-scholars. According to Dabashi (2011), the insider intellectual as a specific subset of collaborator-researcher has a long history as a representative of colonialized mentality. An insider intellectual has the same racial, gender, ethnic, or sexuality background as the population they are studying, but they are paving the way for imperialist policies. Deloria (1988) relates that during the mass displacement of Native Americans, the government searched for "successful Indians" to serve as examples for more resistant tribes. For Dashabi (2011), Malcom X's conceptualization of the "house negro" is quite prescient, as the slave who came to identify with his/her master often worked against others in the same situation. Deloria (1988) likens these insiders to "the old timers who would tour the continent with Buffalo Bill and act pseudo-warlike" (p. 209). Even the university scholarship of leftist researchers has been used to disrupt resistance movements, as Dunbar-Ortiz (2001) describes in her account of the 1960s. Today's "native informers" have the primary goal of stopping dissent by spreading emerging neoconservative doctrines such as the 1990s' "clash of civilizations" (Huntington, 1993; Lewis, 1990) as a way to target Arabs and Muslims, for example (Kumar, 2011). This creates an ideological paving for imperialist actions in the Middle East, and manufactures consent.

The insider intellectual or collaborator-intellectual has an array of philosophical orientations from which to choose. These include a reassertion of positivist and "evidence-based" research, doctrines of colonialism and a refusal to allow for native resistance, and psychology- or biology-based paradigms. These are described below in turn.

Neopositivism/Academic Capitalism

Although it shares many characteristics with positivism, neopositivism (or scientism) distinguishes itself by turning away from philosophy and toward claims that the only knowledge worth reporting is that of specialized scientific fields that can yield numerical data and general results that can be replicated (Belenky, Clinchy, Goldberger, & Tarule, 1997; Denzin, 2009; Jaroszyński, 2007). This is done within the context of the growth of conservative movements and their impact on fields such as education and social work (Denzin, 2009). What facilitates the spread of knowledge economies is the assertion of the neopositivist research paradigm, which was introduced in force to educational and policy research during the 1990s and as part of the Reading Excellence Act (1999), leading to No Child Left Behind

(2001). Major foundations (arms of corporations) such as the Annenberg Institute for School Reform housed at Brown University use neo-positivist data in their issues reporting as a strategy of building support for their causes, which are endorsed through this legislation (Torres & Reyes, 2011).

Emerging from the field of financial auditing (literally referred to as "accountability"), the evidence- or scientifically based research movement presents itself as if the research paradigm wars were already settled and a narrow application of quantitative methodologies were the de facto victor (Denzin, 2009; Torres & Reyes, 2011). The American Association of Colleges and Universities explicitly lists "quantitative literacy" as an essential intellectual skill, but qualitative literacy is not mentioned at all (American Association of Colleges and Universities, 2002, 2004, 2007). The American Educational Research Association (AERA) opted for publishing two separate documents addressing standards for reporting empirical and humanities-oriented research. In order to be published in any AERA journal, one has to conform to these reporting standards (American Educational Research Association, 2006, 2009). Denzin (2009) traces the growth of mixed methods research as a compromise over concerns about qualitative research needing to be validated, often resulting in quantitative methods serving as the anchor with qualitative ones as mere accessories.

Research agendas are shaped through controlling mechanisms of funding and the neoliberal university's reliance on competitive productivity on the part of faculty, many of whom are members of a growing number with part-time or contingent status (Bousquet, 2008; Brenneis, 1999; Denzin, 2009; Nelson, 1997; Torres & Reyes, 2011). Brenneis (1999) outlines how at some universities, securing a grant proposal takes the place of a publication in a refereed journal when making decisions about tenure. This leads to faculty being "ready and willing to sell ourselves to whatever and whoever may give us the promise of the stability and improvement of livelihood" (Moisio, Fitz-simmons, & Suoranta, 2010, p. 190). As the university faces deeper state cuts, it relies on private grants and faculty to obtain those grants:

"As the plug is pulled on state funding, an entrepreneurial spirit is emerging at the individual and group level that is freighted toward market-based research and strategies driven by competitive funding and a corporate research culture" (Houston & Martin, 2010, p. 5). If the National Institutes of Health and the National Science Foundation view primarily quantitative methodologies as legitimate, that is where the funding will go. Questions that cannot be adequately addressed through neopositivist means are essentially "outlawed" (Belenky et al., 1997, p. 96, loc. 1475). A focus on less risky research is the result.

Another function of neopositivism as a conservative discourse is its ability to obscure issues through a fetishizing of numbers, charts, and graphs (Kushner, 2012; Lewontin & Levins, 2007; Price, 2011). This fetishizing is described by Daly (1985) and Belenky et al. (1997) as a form of "methodolatry," where the generalizable is privileged over research in more variable contexts such as classroom environments or family home settings. Further, neutrality is invoked as a way to mask political intentions of neopositivist research and to avoid responsibility by placing strategy and pragmatism as top goals while marginalizing critical research paradigms that go further to address inequities (Belenky et al., 1997; Torres & Reyes, 2011). Gupta (2010) describes how neutrality functions in the dissemination of genetic research:

> The conference presented genetic engineering and its governance as the province of neutral scientific experts who were dealing with technical questions. They downplayed the industrial agricultural and military uses... with organizers excluding awkward questions of biological warfare and human genetic engineering that molecular biologists obviously have no more claim to pronounce on in other people. (p. 35)

As part of academic capitalism, the knowledge-based economy is essentially a figment of the capitalist imagination primarily financed by college students and their families as cuts to higher education deepen:

The policies that are involved in this ideology combine antagonistic ideas of investing in people and their knowledges on one hand, and cost reductions on the other. As Western economies usually compete with cheaper states with lower wages and limited social provisions, it is cost-efficiency rather than growing investment that, in fact, becomes the chief aim of reforms in the public sector. (Szkudlarek, 2010, p. 356)

Academic capitalism insists on wise use of resources (in the public sector, not the energy sector), return on investments, research-based solutions to problems identified as important by the business community, and practical training à la the Partnership for 21st Century Skills (2012) project. Fisher (2009) outlines in *Capitalist Realism* how neoliberal institutions declare their opposition to bureaucracy and government regulations while at the same time adding layer upon layer of management positions, data consultants, review processes, and auditing schemes—the National Council for Accreditation of Teacher Education (NCATE) comes to mind. As Grosvenor (2012) explains, "in a culture of permanent and unceasing performance measurement, symbols of achievement come to be valued over actual achievement" (p. 43). This was the case with NCATE, which formerly demonstrated its commitment to social justice by including supportive language that was later removed due to pressure from conservative groups opposed to multiculturalism (Holst, 2010).

Many academics labor under the illusion that they have freedom and autonomy to determine important social policies. Lewontin and Levins (2007) point out that having a doctorate in nuclear engineering or possessing plans for a nuclear power plant does not reduce one's utility bill—we are all part of a totalizing system of capital. Through academic capitalism, research is just one of many factors involved in the process of shaping educational policy (Lingard, 2010). Academic capitalism is often invoked to "help legitimize patronizing discourse that blames the victims, under the guise of scientifically based research" to build public support for privatization and the defunding of schools (Torres & Reyes, 2011, p. 41). Miske (2010) asserts that the pressures of profit overdetermine policy directions—even if a CEO did choose legitimate, "research-based" results over profit, she would find herself replaced by someone willing to "go the distance." Rather than science having the power to shape academic capitalist discourse, it's the other way around, as Lewontin and Levins (2007) explain:

> We must recognize that the needs of capitalism for profit and social control over labor set a general agenda for science; the recruitment and organization of scientists creates a scientific community that accepts that agenda; and the ideology of science generates the intellectual environment within which the prevailing direction seems to be self-evidently the only way to proceed. (p. 328)

Colonialism/Counterinsurgency

Anthropology has always been and remains a key discipline engaged in the production of knowledge in order to control indigenous populations through colonial policies (Deloria, 1988; Gonzalez, 2009; Starzmann, 2012). Deloria (1988) views colonialism as developing alongside capitalism, and the Reformation's development of the national identity and the individual as self-seeking. Far from being a historical relic, the colonial mentality is alive and well today. For example, Grande (2010) likens the displacement of victims of Hurricane Katrina from New Orleans along with their classification as "refugees" (despite their being U.S. citizens) to Andrew Jackson's removal of the Cherokee people (who were here first) in order to obtain their land. Calling the post-Katrina debacle "nothing but a twenty-first-century re-mix of colonization," Grande views everything from the FEMA camps to the immense bureaucracy for dispersing relief funds to real estate development speculation as "a logical and intended consequence of colonization" (p. 86). In the case of pre-Katrina New Orleans, the city was already experiencing a 40% illiteracy rate, with close to one-fifth of Louisianans without health insurance (Giroux, 2010).

Two major features of colonial discourse that run through supportive research are paternalism and need for control, both key tenets of conservative social thought. Robin (2011) views conservatism as "the theoretical voice of this animus against the agency of the subordinate classes" (p. 7, loc. 145). For Robin, the conservative will use the language of liberty and freedom for the ruling classes and a language of "constraint" for the lower classes, including indigenous populations. Equality is disliked not because it is a threat to freedom, as the right often claims, but because it extends freedom to lower positioned groups. One does not have to identify as a reactionary scholar to espouse this disdain, as Denzin (2009) outlines:

> Neoliberals and neoconservatives deny the culture any legitimacy. They blame its members for the problems that the members of the culture experience. Liberals encourage assimilation to the values of the dominant culture while radical, emancipatory theorists claim that they have the formula for the emancipation of oppressed and marginalized people. These positions presume that persons inside an indigenous culture are incapable of solving their own problems. (p. 279)

Indeed, factories relocating to developing nations deliberately seek out younger women because they are portrayed as having a knack and ability to take on unskilled labor with a smile (Kempadoo, 2002; Mohanty, 2002). These racial and gender stereotypes "infantilize Third World women and initiate a nativist discourse of 'tedium' and 'tolerance' as characteristics of non-Western, primarily agricultural, premodern cultures" (Mohanty, 2002, p. 167).

Today's paternalism is disseminated by layers of 'assistance groups' ranging from missionaries to nongovernmental organizations and often includes insider intellectuals from the indigenous populations themselves. What is most galling is that members of this assistance network are outraged when the population is insufficiently grateful, as Deloria (1988) explains:

> Whites always expect Indians to be grateful according to the Whites' ideas of gratitude. Or else they expect in gratitude to be expressed and institutionalized behavior, as other members of society have been taught to do. When Indians do not respond with these accustomed ways, because the way is irrelevant to Indian modes of expression, the Indian response is attributed to the innate savagery of the Indian. (p. 99)

Deloria's description is remarkable in how it reflects current coverage of the occupation of Iraq and Afghanistan, particularly Congressman

John J. Duncan Jr.'s (2012) characterization of the Afghan people as "ungrateful." The expectation of gratitude only reinforces the legitimacy of colonization, continuing the cycle.

Colonial ideology is always leveraged to obtain some resource from indigenous groups, often by portraying these groups as in need of assistance—even though they are in that state due to the actions of the colonizers (Deloria, 1988). In the case of Haiti, nongovernmental organizations (NGOs) teamed up with economics professors such as Paul Collier from Oxford University, whose "solutions" include opening the country up to low-wage garment factories, creating a de facto reinstitution of slavery. Collier's plans were endorsed by U.S. politicians such as Bill Clinton, whose legacy in Haiti is now legendary (Reitman, 2011). In these majority world countries, economic solutions proposed to alleviate poverty usually include some sort of luxury real estate development as part of the deal. It isn't difficult to guess which of the projects receive the most funds and priority. "Nation building" is fancy talk for economic predation on the poor and working class in these countries. The promise of jobs, no matter how low-wage and poverty-inducing, leads people to flock to urban areas, further exacerbating the material problems of disease, malnutrition, and death, as Reitman describes Cité Soleil's transformation into one of Haiti's most dangerous slums. Business-friendly development has never brought prosperity to the mass of people; it only further enriches the capitalist class on a global level.

The hasty retreat of the government from the public sector has left a void for colonial doctrine to enter, as it thrives on legitimating privatization. Giroux (2010) described the aftermath of Hurricane Katrina as ushering in a new era, "one in which entire populations are now considered disposable, an unnecessary burden on state coffers, and consigned to fend for themselves" (p. 32). Post-Katrina, and post-Iraq for that matter, the public sector turned into what Giroux terms "a punishing institution" determined to displace and get rid of undesirable groups by filtering them into refugee camps, prisons, and urban centers with deteriorating infrastructure. Within the scope of capitalism, Katrina victims and Iraqis are already dead.

Counterinsurgency, related to colonialism, often is put into place as part of militaristic preemptive strategies to control resistance among populations. For example, Thomas Jefferson acted preemptively by allotting land to some Native Americans in order to build a preference for capitalist methods of farming over hunting, in the hopes that indigenous peoples would relinquish their land held in common (Price, 2011). Later, the Bureau of Indian Affairs began as a War Department agency (Deloria, 1988). Anthropologists such as James Mooney (1896/1991) were hired to assist in these efforts, though Mooney strongly identified with native peoples, much to the chagrin of the U.S. government. Today, numerous anthropologists and sociologists are hired by the U.S. military to work in more contentious zones. As Price (2011) puts it, "what the military wants from anthropology is to offer basic courses in local manners so that they can get on with the job of conquest" (p. 130).

According to Price (2011), the ideology of counterinsurgency has three themes, which come across in military publications: Culture is primarily structural, with no social context; these structural features determine future actions and can be identified and controlled; and this conception of culture facilitates colonial oversight. In the case of the military, the human terrain project "means not only identifying or manufacturing social differences, but a willingness to manipulate them as well, to attack indigenous practices of coexistence and mutual respect" (p. 26). Collaborator academics have carefully crafted frameworks around these three counterinsurgent themes, often avoiding the thorny problems of politics by limiting the range of their public statements. For example, Starzmann (2012) relates how the American Anthropological Association expressed more concern for the safety of antiquities than the lives of people during the Egyptian uprising in Tahrir Square.

As an ideology, counterinsurgency also includes a propaganda arm that it uses in two ways—against indigenous groups, and to build support for wars and economic globalization at home, especially among more skittish liberals who are reaching for any positive spin on imperialism to relieve their discomfort (Grande, 2010; Jamail, 2010). Ferguson (2003) explains these dynamics:

> Those advocating war always define it in terms of the highest applicable values, whether that involves the need to retaliate against witchcraft, defend the one true religion, or promote democracy. That is the way to sway the undecided and build emotional commitment. And always, it is the other side that somehow brought war on. (para. 33)

Similarly, Dashabi (2011) outlines how imperialist actions in the Middle East are often justified on the grounds of improving women's rights. Arab males are stereotyped as violent and sexist, while Arab females are rendered voiceless as Western nations step in "for their own good." Starzmann (2012) describes this portrayal of the invasion of Afghanistan as "one where white men went off supposedly to save brown women from brown men" (p. 39). What actually occurs is that the long-term involvement of the United States destabilizes these countries, often bringing on the backlash of fundamentalist religion which means further constraints on women. At the same time, women often are forced to rely on visible means to ensure outward protection, such as intensified veiling practices (Kandiyoti, 2002). The veiling is a small price to pay compared to the solutions that the Americans have to offer.

In the case of Obama's administration, early plans for focusing on counterinsurgency have been set aside in favor of reviving the counterterrorism narrative, thereby necessitating the threatening figure of the "Islamic terrorist" in the media and public consciousness. As Kumar (2011) explains, "to succeed in the mainstream, the anti-Muslim crusaders need the further opening created by the Democrats' liberal Islamophobia" (para. 64). Several anti-Arab writers cloak themselves in the mantle of policy research, including Frank Gaffney (2005), Steven Emerson (2006), Geert Wilders (2012), David Horowitz (2004), Pamela Geller (2011), and Walid Phares (2010). Of these, Phares is viewed as the most respectable because he has a doctorate in international relations and has appeared before congressional committees (Kumar, 2011). Phares also embodies a formidable combination: He is both Islamophobic and of Middle Eastern origin. Kumar explains the reach of these policy writers:

> Most obviously, the events of 9/11 and the launching of the "war on terror" legitimized these views and created a larger audience for the warriors. For the Bush administration, the war on terror would serve as an ideological shield to further its vision of brute imperialism in the post–Cold War world. Islamophobia flows from the logic of imperialism. (para. 34)

Price (2011) concludes that "by the time a military relies on counterinsurgency for foreign victories, it has already lost" (p. 179). Much of the counterinsurgency research done is staunchly defended by its creators as assisting the populations under study (Gonzalez, 2009; Price, 2011). However, if the collaborator researchers really meant well or wanted something better for indigenous populations, they would leave and/or support the cessation of the occupation of these countries altogether (Jamail, 2010).

Biological Determinism/Resiliency

A third, less common, though distinct philosophical set of assumptions includes evolutionary biology, biological determinism, and its closely related cousin, resiliency research. As Lewontin and Levins (2007) write, "There is no adversity whose use has not been sweetened by an appeal to natural selection" (p. 222). Evolutionary biologists and determinists are interested in locating scientific rationales for social practices such as war, sexuality, and intelligence, often relying on sweeping Hobbesian assumptions about human nature as innately aggressive, selfish, and in need of guidance by various authorities. At the same time, these writers often advocate noninterference by governments in the form of financial assistance, pointing to biology as a semipermanent feature that cannot be significantly altered, so austerity is the answer. Resiliency researchers are a different animal in that they often advocate a social justice perspective in asserting that people are enormously flexible in adapting to dire circumstances. However, their interest remains not in confronting atrocities, but in finding a "silver lining"—we can still have our wars and underfunded schools knowing that people will, in the end, pull through. Efforts are directed at locating resilient characteristics and building on those "strengths."

Certainly the history of the field of education reflects early twentieth-century eugenics (consider, for example, the origins of standardized testing), and this history is well documented (Black, 2012; Chitty, 2009; Currell, 2006; Gasper, 2004; Winfield, 2007). However, lest anyone think that eugenics is safely contained as a historical relic, there are "softer" examples today, often presented in the media as "groundbreaking." They include *The Bell Curve* by Herrnstein and Murray (1996), *Coming Apart: The State of White America, 1960–2010* by Murray (2012), *Freakonomics* by Levitt and Dubner (2009), and *The Death of the West* by Buchanan (2002). In general, the tone of these writings has an "it's out of our hands" kind of matter-of-factness, but occasionally the disdain for the poor and working class breaks through, as in Murray's (2005) reflection post–Hurricane Katrina:

> *We have rediscovered the underclass.* Newspapers and television understandably prefer to feature low-income people who are trying hard—the middle-aged man working two jobs, the mother worrying about how to get her children into school in a strange city. These people are rightly the objects of an outpouring of help from around the country, but their troubles are relatively easy to resolve. Tell the man where a job is, and he will take it. Tell the mother where a school is, and she will get her children into it. Other images show us the face of the hard problem: those of the looters and thugs, and those of inert women doing nothing to help themselves or their children. They are the underclass. We in the better parts of town haven't had to deal with the underclass for many years, having successfully erected screens that keep them from troubling us. We no longer have to send our children to school with their children. (para. 2)

In a similar vein, noted geneticist James Watson explained his theory that races have different levels of intelligence, as Milmo (2007) summarized:

> He was "inherently gloomy about the prospect of Africa" because "all our social policies are based on the fact that their intelligence is the same as ours—whereas all the testing says not really." He said there was a natural

desire that all human beings should be equal but "people who have to deal with black employees find this not true." (para. 4)

Certainly Watson is no stranger to odd applications of evolutionary biology, espousing such beliefs in public interviews, speeches, and appearances: People exposed to more sunlight have a stronger libido (the old hot-blooded, dark-skinned stereotype); thin people are more unhappy and therefore more ambitious than heavier people (who are presumably lazy, though more sexual, due to having higher levels of leptin); stupidity is a genetically based problem that could be genetically phased out (Kargbo, 2007); the world would be better if all girls could be made pretty (Bhattacharya, 2003); and today's teachers are dumber than in years past (Borrell, 2009).

Biological determinist constructions of race slide easily into conservative restoration notions of the family, crime, and pathology. This was demonstrated when William Bennett, former Secretary of Education, "applied" the lessons of Levitt and Dubner (2009) to hypothesize that crime rates would go down if more black babies were aborted (Media Matters, 2005). While Bennett did backpedal right after the statement to explain that doing such a thing would be "morally reprehensible," he continued to emphasize that the crime rate would indeed go down. What was interesting about Bennett's quote is that people were more upset at the suggestion of aborting black babies than the bald implication that African Americans are the biological source of crime in the United States—that was barely commented upon. This demonstrates the problem with popular and scholarly application of evolutionary biology—when it is safely ensconced in a science that does not address social context, and science-as-authority is not to be questioned, it is inevitably applied in capitalist/imperialist directions.

It is interesting to note, however, that more materialist conclusions drawn from science (such as the benefits of collective intelligence/cooperation, archaeological evidence of divergent economic and gendered relations, and the like) are questioned by these same authors and their followers as being "political." As Gasper (2004) points out,

> The attempt to explain important features of society in evolutionary or genetic terms—biological determinism—has two goals. First, it tries to convince us that the social order is a consequence of unchanging human biology, so that inequality and injustice cannot be eliminated. Second, in the case of problems that are impossible to ignore, it tells us to look for the solution at the level of the individual and not at the level of social institutions. The problems lie not in the structure of society, but in some of the individuals who make up society. The solution is thus to change—or even eliminate—the individuals, not to challenge existing social structures. (para. 5)

Gasper systematically critiques the tenets of Jensen (1998) and Pinker (2003) (among others), who assert that intelligence differences between ethnic groups are biological, and that war is a natural facet of human nature, respectively. Gasper points to contradictory scholarship by Ferguson (2003), who demonstrates that war has been part of humanity only for the past 10,000 years (not since the advent of humans, as Pinker maintains), and Putnam's (1973) work, which showcases the benefits of collective intelligence in her dialectical reading of the Attica prison uprising.

Resiliency research as a subset of the educational and social work professions is harder to pin down ideologically, as its tenets are masked by social justice language and confront stereotypes of deficit thinking that has a long legacy, since Moynihan's (1965) report on African American family poverty. For example, in a Google search for "resiliency research," the first site to come up is Resiliency in Action, a website and publication company specializing in this type of scholarship. On the home page's overview of resiliency research, Bernard (n.d.) presents a rationale of why it is important to focus on individual strengths rather than weaknesses:

> The capacity for transformation gives the prevention, education, and youth development fields not only a clear sense of direction—informing us about "what works!"—but also mandates we move beyond our obsession with risk identification, a statistically weaker practice that has harmfully labeled and stigmatized youth, their families, and their communities as at-risk and high-risk, a practice that perpetuates stereotyping and racism. Most importantly, the knowledge that everyone has innate resilience grounds practice in optimism and possibility, essential components in building motivation. Not only does this prevent the burn-out of practitioners work-

ing with seriously troubled youth but it provides one of the major protective factors—positive expectations—that when internalized by youth motivate and enable them to overcome risks and adversity. (para. 6)

A recent shift in this field has been from looking at innate characteristics to identifying "protective factors" such as family and community strengths (Flynn, Dudding, & Barber, 2006). Some of the topics resilience researchers explore include children in war zones and war veterans (Kimhi & Eshel, 2009; Martz, 2010; Peddle, 2007); children from high-poverty contexts (Douglass, 1996); families with drug and alcohol addictions (Castro, Garfinkle, Narajno, Rollins, Brook, & Brook, 2007; Moe, Johnson, & Wade, 2007); and victims of child abuse (Bogar & Hulse-Killacky, 2006; Wilcox, Richards, & O'Keefe, 2004). The common element in all of these studies is zeroing in on the adaptive and "bouncing back" capabilities of the children and adults in dire situations.

The focus on "positive expectations" as a protective factor brings to mind Ehrenreich's (2009) historical overview and critique of the various strains of the positive thinking movement in the United States. Ehrenreich stresses that perhaps we ought not to be so quick to look for a "bright side" when it comes to poverty, homelessness, war, and hunger. As Moisio, Fitzsimmons, and Suoranta (2010) note, "When a human being is reduced to the commodity form, her usefulness always comes into question and hence, the uncertainty of life and risk.... [C]orporate capitalism treats us as a mass by promising to us the fulfillment of our individuality" (p. 192). Resiliency research appears to be putting a positive, pragmatic spin on a bad situation, leaving the business of empire intact.

Roles of Religion and Pseudo-Science

A discussion concerning research in the service of empire would be inadequate without a brief examination of the functions served by religion and pseudo-science. Even though these stand out as sharply nonsecular topics in the secular world of research, they linger at the margins, further shaping capitalist discourse. Religion and pseudo-science intersect in interesting ways, especially in combination with the philosophies outlined above. For example, religion plays a key role in counterinsurgency discourse, as part of Islamophobia and the advantageous alliance of right-wing Christians and Zionists to support continued domination in the Middle East. Pseudo-science is used in the conceptualization of what constitutes evidence-based data as part of the standardized testing movement. Both religion and pseudo-science join forces within biological determinism, when, for example, anthropological data is shaped to fit preexisting cultural stereotypes of gender roles and propensity toward violence on the part of humans.

According to Deloria (1988), "The early colonists did not flee religious persecution so much as they wished to perpetuate religious persecution under circumstances more favorable to them. They wanted to be the persecutors" (p. 177). Though religion in the service of empire predates pseudo-science by several centuries, its tactical implementations are similar, and its utility is vast:

> Religion is for all kinds of reasons an extremely effective form of ideological control....Religion, moreover, is capable of operating on every level.... [I]t provides an excellent social cement, encompassing the highest peasant, enlightened middle-class liberal and theological intellectual in a single organization. Its ideological power lies in its capacity to materialize beliefs and practices... its ultimate truths... are conveniently close to rational demonstration, and thus absolute in their claims.... [R]eligion... is a pacifying influence. (Eagleton, 1983, p. 23)

Deloria (1988) carefully outlines how religion was used to support every stage of Native American genocide, such as the churches' support for the Dawes Act (1887), which sought to assimilate indigenous people by isolating them onto plots of land in exchange for citizenship. In order to obtain this land and citizenship, individual families had to "adopt civilized habits"—in other words, live apart from their tribes. Missionaries viewed the Dawes Act as a boon for christianizing Native Americans, while the government relied on the churches as a form of social control. It was very important for the church to wrest individuals from their tribal networks in order to accomplish this, as they did with Native American boarding schools (Smith, 2006).

Religion also functions as an oppositional force to science in general, as Lewontin and Levins (2007) describe:

> It is troubled by the challenge that scientific knowledge poses to traditional religious beliefs and social rules and rulers, does not approve of the independent judgment of ideas and values, does not demand evidence where authority has already been pronounced, and is thus disturbed mostly by the radical side of science.... [R]ather, they propose to return to faith, to the more obvious kinds of authority, and to anti-intellectual certainties.... [I]t altogether denies the importance of serious complex thinking in favor of the spontaneous smarts of uneducated certainties. (p. 92)

Entwined within this call for a return to religious values is an imperative to restore traditional forms of authority and commonsense thinking. Despite the obvious contradictions between science and religion, the two can support each other quite well under capitalism. For example, McLaren and Jaramillo (2010) point out the parallel between evangelical declarations that the victims of Hurricane Katrina deserved punishment from God for the sinful nature of the city and the abandonment of Katrina's victims by the state as a form of punishment for failing to prepare adequately for the storm, at least in the eyes of the media.

The use of pseudo-science has become a common tactic in research and policy reporting, relying on the power of mass media dissemination to shape public perceptions about issues such as global warming (Herrick & Jamieson, 2001). It can be utilized in many ways—most commonly, to limit regulations/legal compensation and to oppose environmental research on global climate change. The most common way those opposed to any form of regulation of corporations assert pseudo-science is through the "junk science movement," which creates uncertainty and builds on the public's lack of refined scientific knowledge. As Michaels and Monforton (2005) explain, junk science is similar to the construct of "political correctness" in that it becomes a charge leveled against pretty much any research perspective that challenges the status quo:

> Advocates for this perspective allege that many of the scientific studies and even scientific methods used in the regulatory and legal arenas are funda-

mentally flawed, contradictory or incomplete, making it wrong or prema-
ture to regulate the exposure in question or to compensate the worker or
community resident allegedly made sick by the exposure. The junk science
movement, which attempts to ridicule research that threatens powerful interests, was spawned by the same industries that have been manufacturing
uncertainty for decades. (p. 43)

Lest anyone question the ability of this movement to shape public
attitudes, consider the case of global climate change: In 2010, 72% of
people supported government action to alleviate climate change, but
in 2012, only 62% of people support such actions (Jordon, 2012).
Those who conducted the poll attributed the drop in support not to
economic issues, but to the introduction of uncertainty about climate
change in the media. Gore (2011) concludes the following about the
anticlimate change movement:

They are financing pseudoscientists whose job is to manufacture doubt
about what is true and what is false; buying elected officials wholesale with
bribes that the politicians themselves have made "legal" and can now be
made in secret; spending hundreds of millions of dollars each year on misleading advertisements in the mass media; hiring four anticlimate lobbyists
for every member of the U.S. Senate and House of Representatives. (p. 78)

As Michaels and Monforton (2005) relate, quoting a tobacco executive, "doubt is our product since it is the best means of competing
with the body of facts that exists in the minds of the general public. It
is also the best means of generating a controversy" (p. 40).

Herrick and Jamieson (2001) present five practices found in ques-
tionable scientific research: researchers not having the right credentials; an insufficient or absent peer-review process; weak publications;
undeveloped reviews of literature, or no way to adequately trace concepts; and fraudulent manipulation of data. In reviewing established
scientific articles that had been targeted by the junk science movement, Herrick and Jamieson found that fewer than 10% of them were
compromised by one or more of these five practices. They also found
that close to 85% of reviewed publications written by those making
accusations of junk science advanced an antiregulatory message, and
none had a pro-regulation stance (p. 14). However, the media contin-

ues to present a "both sides" false equivalency by constantly "balancing" the research of a climate scientist by including a junk science accuser on the same panel.

The opposition to regulation and legal compensation for victims of corporate malfeasance is a large part of the pseudo-science movement. Corporate budgets are devoted to keeping paid consultants on hand in the areas of toxicology, epidemiology, and biostatistics—part of a preemptive science-for-hire approach—in case a product is challenged by consumers, or a regulation is proposed by the government (Michaels & Monforton, 2005). Pseudo-science inhabits a complex network of research foundations, often set up by corporate entities, as the *New England Journal of Medicine* discovered in 2006 when lung cancer research was funded by a tobacco company (Schwartz, Curfman, Morrissey, & Drazen, 2008). At the same time, there are currently more disclosure requirements for research published in biomedical journals than for studies submitted to government agencies, which don't have the same ability to ask about the funding sources. Worse yet, many of these antiregulatory PR scientists move easily from jobs in the private sector to the public:

> Taking time off from the private firm to engage in public service has been called the institutional schizophrenia that links these Wall Street figures as double agents to the state. While acting in one sphere to squeeze through every regulatory loophole, they act in the other to introduce new regulations adds a tool for the efficient management of the social order in the public interest. (Albo, Gindin, & Panitch, 2010, p. 61)

The merging of private and public sectors to control the already minimal degree of protections the public has against the rapacity of capitalism demonstrates the strength and flexibility of a system that can easily locate researchers willing to offer support for financial gain.

The Data Quality Act (2001) facilitated the use of mercenary scientists as corporate PR agents by allowing companies to delay the release of research that could be in the public interest. Corporations are allowed to file endless complaints if they feel that the data presented in studies supporting regulations could be dubious in any way. As Michaels and Monforton (2005) explain, opponents of regulations use the Data Quality Act to argue that "The human data are not representative, the animal data are not relevant, or the exposure data are incomplete or not reliable. These assertions are often accompanied by the declaration that more research is needed before a protective action is justified" (p. 41). By using this most stringent 100%-certainty-of-data yardstick, corporations can hold most major regulations at bay or delay compensation for injuries by tying up cases in the courts.

The sudden interest in scientific rigor has occurred in the following areas: establishing what counts as food deprivation ("hunger" is not scientifically accurate terminology; "food insecurity" is better); access to the HPV vaccine to emergency over-the-counter birth control (we need to be 100% certain that no underage girls will be taken advantage of by older men through the use of these products); calls for regulations due to pollution or environmental damage (we need to be 100% certain that other causes aren't contributing to the high cancer rates); and widening access to abortion (we need to be 100% certain that not one woman will become suicidal or develop breast cancer due to having an abortion). On the flip side, the need for 100% certainty never seems to be invoked for establishing failure rates of precision "smart" bombs, for grading charter school performance, or for demonstrating proof of the existence of a deity when trying to implement religious policy that is supposedly necessary for all. There, some wiggle room is allowed.

Examples of Collaborator Research

A few examples presented below highlight the various ways that collaborator research is used in the areas of the military, environment, and public health/education. This is by no means an exhaustive list, which would be too extensive to include in one volume, let alone one chapter!

Military

One of the sectors where research is readily employed in the service of empire is the military industrial complex, because war and anthropology go virtually hand in hand. The university has played a key role in promoting the uses of anthropological research in the military, especially since World War I. Origins of today's Human Terrain System concept can be traced to the government's use of infiltrators to spy on the Black Panthers and other resistance groups during the Vietnam War, with unknown numbers of university faculty participating in covert CIA-sponsored research endeavors (Denzin, 2009; Dunbar-Ortiz, 2001; Gonzalez, 2009; Price, 2011). Other programs from this era include the Phoenix Program conducted by the CIA in Vietnam, and RAND's contracting with the CIA and the U.S. military to monitor resistance movements in Central and South America during the mid-1960s, resulting in massive civilian deaths. Much of this militaristic collaborator research elicits minimal outrage because people are not aware of this history or they have forgotten it, as Price (2011) asserts with a wry sense of humor:

> With the generational loss of memory of the roles these agencies played in the domestic and international suppression of my minority power movements, one wonders if the FBI will try and sponsor a Fred Hampton intelligence scholarship designed to recruit students from historically black colleges and universities. (p. 75)

The Human Terrain System (HTS) was created in 2005 as part of the "leaner" army of post-Rumsfeld "warrior intellectuals" supported by General David Petraeus, who remains committed to the program (Lobjakas, 2012). Five-person teams (including many university professors employed and trained by BAE, a private contractor) are embedded with U.S. troops in order to gather qualitative data concerning local cultures (Gonzalez, 2009; Jamail, 2010). Because they are employees of BAE, these researchers are not subject to military conduct laws and are exempt from institutional review board (IRB) regulations. Human Terrain researchers are often dressed in military fatigues, even at national conferences (Starzmann, 2012). Some conduct interviews in Iraq with local citizens while wearing side arms, really testing the limits of informed consent (Gonzalez, 2009). Journalists stand ready to report the goings on of HTS and other adventures, feeding the propaganda machine (McLaren & Jaramillo, 2010).

In 2006 the *Counterinsurgency Field Manual* was published and released with much media fanfare. The text contains a poorly written but interesting postmodern hodgepodge of the theories of key anthropologists such as Max Weber, Victor Turner, and Daniel Bates. Price (2011) presents several examples of passages that were plagiarized from these and other authors. When challenged about the plagiarism and presented with the offending quotes as evidence, *Manual* spokesperson Lieutenant Colonel John Nagl asserted that when quoting texts in the service of military doctrine, one didn't have to follow established rules of attribution, an extreme application of the notion of not questioning government leaders "when we are at war."

Not just faculty, but also university students are recruited into military research programs. One of the most prominent is the CIA-sponsored Pat Roberts Intelligence Scholars Program (PRISP), which has funded graduate studies in the areas of social science, foreign language, and science since 2005 (Nelson, 2012; Price, 2011). The students who participate in PRISP are forbidden to disclose their research funding source. If they should decide to terminate their involvement with the program, they have to pay back the funding at extortion-level interest rates. A related program, the Intelligence Community Center of Academic Excellence (IC CAE), targets high school students to encourage them to become involved with intelligence agencies and homeland security. In 2010 the IC CAE came under fire for directly applying its mission to tactics after James O'Keefe and three others were arrested when trying to wiretap Senator Mary Landrieu's office in New Orleans. One of the people held for arrest was Stan Dai, who was a former assistant director of Trinity Washington University's IC CAE program (Price, 2011). He was apprehended with a listening device in his car.

While funding for HTS remains in question until the program can demonstrate its effectiveness and address its problems surrounding research ethics, the government has moved on to other projects. Because it has been challenging to find anthropologists willing to participate in military programs, the U.S. Air Force University and the Naval Academy have begun to create their own majors in anthropology (De Vise, 2010). Gonzalez (2009) outlines additional programs such as a month long training session in which settlements of Iraqis (paid $4,000 each) were created at Fort Irwin, California, so that HTS participants could practice their data-gathering skills, and the development of large computerized databases using on-the-ground data to predict upcoming insurgent hotspots (including domestic U.S. protests), which will transform HTS "into a new technological fantasy world being created by the Pentagon, military contractors, and university-based research laboratories—a military-industrial-academic complex for the twenty-first century" (p. 81). At the same time, these projects accomplish the important social goal of getting people accustomed to loss of privacy and increasing surveillance.

Both Price (2011) and Gonzalez (2009) found that many of the people who participated in HTS did so in order to try to alleviate the harsher effects of occupation, claiming, for example, that HTS saved lives (i.e., that understanding cultural terrain would build acceptance of a U.S. presence by those being occupied, thus reducing the need to use force). Price (2011) concluded that the anthropologists he interviewed who participated in HTS faced two choices: They could either try to convince themselves that counterinsurgency was a "better" way, or they could end up identifying with the groups they were studying and ultimately exit the program. Those HTS participants who remain in the program seem to believe that they can change the military from within, to shape it into a less rigid institution (as if traditionalism is the military's major problem). Gonzalez (2009) illustrates the futility of this approach by relating the experiences of the English anthropologist Gregory Bateson (1904–1980), who worked with the military preparing propaganda and intelligence reports. Rather than his work ending imperialist actions, it was used to support the post–World War II British Empire's occupation in India. Bateson would come to regret his involvement in the military, but by then it was too late.

Environmental Policy

Research plays a large role in privileging corporate needs above human needs when it comes to the creation of environmental policies. In the face of irrefutable evidence of climate change, instead of mustering support for large-scale public projects that would reduce the use of fossil fuels, efforts are poured into developing "market-based" solutions for the crisis (Albo, Gindlin, & Panitch, 2010). Here, the logic of capitalism is left intact, albeit liberalized somewhat by its focus on small start-ups looking to develop solar and wind energy, or on the implementation carbon credit schemes. The media also kicks in by abstracting the enormity of the environmental crisis to statistics about average temperatures and limiting coverage to isolated op-ed segments about recycling and buying organic food (Lahde, 2010).

Gupta (2010) considers such tactics geoengineering, where the climate is manipulated on a large scale by people, as a further extension of climate change denial. Most of these capitalist-based environmental solutions (such as using fossil fuels to create the infrastructure for these "solutions") take enormous resources to implement and inevitably involve the creation of more problems:

> Even if we can efficiently capture carbon dioxide, what to do with it? To store all carbon dioxide currently emitted worldwide would require building a pipeline, transport, plumbing, and storage infrastructure that can handle eight times the volume of the entire oil economy. So why not just put all that effort into transitioning to alternative low carbon energy? (p. 34)

Gupta mentions several scientists who are on board with geoengineering, revealing an intricate network of researchers and private sector industries. They include John Latham of Intellectual Ventures; Stephen Slater, emeritus professor of engineering design at the University of Edinburgh, also part of Intellectual Ventures; David Keith, professor of physics at the University of Calgary specializing in carbon capture (who also receives funding from the Gates Foundation); Klaus Lackner, a professor and carbon capture specialist funded by Land's End; and Gregory Benford, physicist at the University of California. Gupta also outlines how the Reason Foundation, publisher of *Reason* magazine, is funded by oil companies and the Scaife and Koch Foundations.

Environmental research also impacts infrastructure, as recent research into the levee failure during Hurricane Katrina illustrates (Lahde, 2010). According to Lahde, such research highlighted the need for increased infrastructure development, especially in the poorer neighborhoods of New Orleans where the levees were the weakest when the storm hit. In many cases, the increase in the impact of climate change has created a mini land rush as the business sector seizes assets in real estate land grabs; the sector also has moved to create start-ups that look for market-based alternative energy solutions (Albo, Gindin, & Panitch, 2010; McLaren & Jaramillo, 2010). This profiting from disaster is laid out in Klein's (2007) *The Shock Doctrine*, in which she details how industries are built around disaster recovery, a situation that will escalate as the environmental situation worsens. Climate change also has a negative impact on food production, but solutions involve continuing to rely on industrial paradigms such as high-yield, petroleum-based fertilizers and "franken-seeds" whose patents are privately owned (Miske, 2010). This creates a cycle of increased dependency on outside companies at enormous expense for indigenous and smaller-sized family farms, which often employ innovative agricultural solutions on a more sustainable scale. As with other areas of research and policy, relying on the market for solutions is a dead end.

Public Health and Education

Universities have been heavily involved in the production of corporate-sponsored research aimed at the public sector since the passage of the Bayh-Dole Act (1980), which allowed higher education institutions (as well as the nonprofit and small business sectors) to hold intellectual property rights for publicly funded research. The university essentially acts as a de facto channel as public money is transferred to the private sector, closing down widespread access to research results (Torres & Reyes, 2011). Patent law might seem an obscure issue when held up against other pressing problems confronting universities, yet its application could become an ethical nightmare for genetic research. Although natural products cannot be patented, isolated genes are classified as not natural, even though they come from humans (Kankanala, 2007). Further, many high-profile geneticists are shareholders of the manufacturers of equipment used in such research, and have established biotechnology firms with outside funding (Lewontin & Levins, 2007).

Corporations also fund psychological research that can be used in advertising. Brody (2010) examines cognition studies of the differences between children and adults in how they process advertising, and finds that "before the ages of seven and eight, children are unable to understand the persuasive intent of commercials, key for being able to resist them" (p. 13). Psychological research also was used in the establishment and monitoring of Native American boarding schools, which were viewed as living laboratories for studying how children could assimilate into white society (Grande, 2010).

Oglesby (2002) describes how the research used to maximize productivity on Guatemalan sugar plantations reaches science fiction proportions:

> Industrial psychologists recruit and train the cane cutters, who are exclusively male and mostly young. Only men are permitted to live in the migrant camps. Food is prepared in industrial kitchens by male cooks, many of whom learned to cook while serving in the army. The new diets are supposed to provide 3,700 calories daily, and they include a careful balance of proteins and carbohydrates to ensure that workers don't lose weight during the harvest. Cane cutters get oral rehydration drinks and health exams. They are weighed periodically, and their muscles are measured. Their bodies and productivity levels are monitored, and all of this information gets recorded in year-by-year databases. (p. 205)

If this sounds exotic, consider "The Staying at Work Report" (National Business Group on Health & Towers Watson, 2010), the result of research on U.S. companies examining links between health and worker productivity. This report endorses a form of micromanagement of employee eating habits, exercise, and medical information on the part of employers.

In terms of public health regulations, Michaels and Monforton (2005) document how the asbestos, lead, tobacco, and aspirin industries delayed the release of information and public labeling for years. One tactic was to focus attention on the people who were the victims of these industries:

> They shifted the blame from the lead itself and the manufacturing process, and claimed that the workers had sloppy habits and were more careless... again by shifting blame, this time to the poisoned children who were sub normal to begin with. (p. 41)

Because many of the people who are the most harmed by corporations are already the most vulnerable, compromised by poverty and poor living conditions, companies are able to manufacture uncertainty on the part of the public by removing such socially contextual information. This was the case when the eroding teeth of Appalachians was attributed to "Mountain Dew mouth" (made famous by a 2009 Diane Sawyer ABC segment covering a mobile dental clinic) from babies being fed soda in baby bottles, rather than to the water pollution caused by mountain-top removal mining, which drove families to seek less expensive and safer alternatives than baby formula, which requires water (Celina, 2009). Bad parenting and stereotypes of hillbillies are identified as the culprits, steering attention away from an industry that threatens the environment of poor and working-class people and keeps them economically subjugated to boot.

When research is influenced by private and not public interests, it is highly compromised. Dartmouth College president Jim Yong Kim, who also has a background as a medical doctor and anthropologist, established the National College Health Improvement Project to investigate the drinking behaviors of college students, which had become a public health concern. Kim was also instrumental in founding Partners in Health, an NGO that operates internationally. Despite the project's amassing of data on binge drinking and its connection with the fraternity system, Kim is not likely to challenge this system, which he has openly supported in the past. Even as the president of Dartmouth, among a handful of people who hold leverage against fraternities, Kim claims that "I barely have any power.... I'm a convener" (Reitman, 2012, p. 51). Not long after he took office, Kim met with Dartmouth alums and reassured them he had no intention of overhauling the fraternities: "One of the things you learn as an anthropologist... you don't come in and change the culture" (p. 51). It is interesting that Kim reverses centuries of the interventionist tradition that has been part of anthropology since its inception, as a means of preserving the status quo. Just when anthropologists could use their knowledge to intervene on behalf of people opposed to power structures, they often decide to take a "hands off" approach.

Finally, the most famous example of collaborator research applied to education is the justification for phonics made in the report of the National Reading Panel (NRP), "Teaching Children to Read" (National Reading Panel, 2000), and related publications. One of the best sources for tracing the development of the NRP and phonics is Strauss's (2005) *The Linguistics, Neurology, and Politics of Phonics: Silent "E" Speaks Out*. Strauss, a linguist and neurologist, points out the corporate conflicts of interest among the report's authors and spokespeople, such as Reid Lyon, who had ties to the Bush administration and private publishers. He also debunks the NRP's use of the term *scientifically based research* by highlighting not only various conflicts of interest (such as authors of the meta-analysis of phonics research including their own studies in the review), but also how the NRP does not clearly outline specific ways to monitor risk, such as the harm caused by a misuse of phonics methods. It is important to note that NRP recommendations target the lowest-performing schools. Torres and Reyes (2011) conclude, "The decision of selecting and imposing the teaching of literacy based on the skill-based approach with high saturation of phonics only serves the political and economic interests of parties involved and resulted in the institutionalization of pedagogy's for the poor" (p. 117).

Conclusion

Currently, we face a formidable set of conditions that shape how research is conducted across the globe in the service of empire, as Lautensach and Lautensach (2010) outline:

> The fact that a large number of well-educated people continue to make decisions that are blatantly counterproductive in the present situation indicates that somehow, all that education has failed. This failure of higher education manifests itself in two ways. Education results in the transmission of harmful or counterproductive values, beliefs and attitudes... education also fails to widely elicit alternative, more productive learning outcomes, mainly ecological concepts in the values, beliefs and attitudes that would provide the basis for sustainable living. (p. 207)

Rather than the public schools being the ones to fail, higher education has failed on behalf of the majority of people. When the most damage is being done by those with the highest levels of education, we should be concerned. Those who have advanced degrees are often the only ones with access to formal research channels, funding, and publication. Yet, this group seems to side with power time and again. With a media firmly in the hands of the corporate sector, even the most ethical research can be utilized to support policies that harm the majority of the population. It should be clear by now that the existing system of research cannot be changed from within—the lessons of the military's use of anthropology should be enough evidence to settle that question.

We have to begin to confront the monolith of research in the service of empire and face the uncomfortable fact that we are all part of the system. We can either continue to participate willingly or attempt to resist where we can, even if that resistance means being excluded from the benefits that other researchers might receive. Our complicity has to be examined without excuses.

Chapter Three

What Makes Marxist Research "Marxist"

Overview: What We Face Today Within Capitalism

There is a common line of thought running through history within leftist analysis that capitalism is in decline, or that it is dying (Shutt, 2005; Ticktin, 2009; Varga, 1924). This belief might be due in part to confusing the majority of the world's lack of success *under* capitalism with the success of capitalism *itself*, which has been pretty good, albeit for a small portion of the population. Or, it could be due to attributing the notion of an automatic transformation from capitalism to socialism to Marx, when that is a gross misreading (Allman, 2007). Indeed, Marx (1845/1932, 1848/1969) noted that nothing is automatic or given within history. Any transformation wasn't automatically positive or negative, but a combination of both.

While neoliberalism might have lost its allure of late, there are other potentially harmful ideologies that can step in and take its place, such as fascism. The mistaken assumption of an injured capitalism needs to be challenged for several reasons. The first is that existing conditions require immediate remedies rather than just hope that capitalism will wear out its welcome on its own. After the economic crisis in 2008, the implemented solutions such as the bank bailouts made capitalism bigger and bolder in calling for even more social cuts, layoffs, and tax breaks (Albo, Gindin, & Panitch, 2010; Fisher, 2009; Ho, 2009). As Stronach and Clarke (2012) point out, the mismatch between capitalist ideology and recent results did not create a cognitive crisis in the population; instead, the direction of the market was cast as part of human fate, strengthening the continuation of capitalism. According to Albo and colleagues:

> The financial crisis has seemingly changed everything in North America and yet nothing has changed. The crisis has not led various elements that compose the capitalist classes by state, region, sector, size to turn upon each other, with contesting policy agendas that reflect divisions subordinate classes

might exploit. This intra-class unity has been crucial to the capacity of capitalist states to contain the crisis. (Albo, Gindin, & Panitch, 2010, p. 23)

To think that capitalism will die out under its own weight or that the enormity of the economic crisis itself will motivate people to overthrow the existing system is dangerous. It is akin to evangelicals hoping for the apocalypse so that Jesus will return. As Wood (2002) reminds us, "we might as well say that given the dangers of capitalism, no rational person should support it; but this, needless to say, is not how things work" (p. 285).

What we are finding today is that the traditional bargain that industrial capitalism kept with workers—a relatively livable wage and permanent employment (mostly due to the protection and militancy of union organizing)—has been broken. At the same time, workers have found themselves vulnerable to this assault by the upper class and have not been able so far to stop it (Brenner, 2002). According to Giroux (2010):

As safety nets and social services are being hollowed out and communities crumble and give way to individualized, one-man archipelagoes, it is increasingly difficult to address as a collectivity, to act in concert, to meet the basic needs of citizens and maintain the social investments needed to provide life-sustaining services. (p. 29)

Now more than ever, we need dialectical materialist research in solidarity with workers across the globe who are under assault by the 1%. After all, though they might not like to think so, academics are essentially members of the working class who also have a vested interest in a more humane world.

Clearly, the older concept of maintaining a company's long-term vision is gone, as "employees, located outside the corporation's central purpose, are readily liquidated in the pursuit of stock price appreciation" (Ho, 2009, p. 3). Fisher (2009) pinpoints the dividing line between the old, factory style of capitalism and today's version—October 6, 1979, identified by economists as the date when the Federal Reserve set the interest rate to jump by 20 points and ushered in the supply-side approach to economics. According to Brenner (2002),

during the 1980s, companies moved away from the strategy of ex-
tracting productivity from workers to laying them off completely. Indeed, at large gatherings global capitalists have speculated about sce-
scenarios where only 20% of the world's population would need to be
employed—just enough to keep the economy going, with the other
80% placed in volunteer labor or pacified with entertainment (Martin
& Schuhmann, 1997). This is the permanent underclass that Hedges
(2011a) speaks about as the United States moves toward the corporate
consolidation of power as part of fascism.

The purpose of this chapter is to present a different research paradigm, that of dialectical materialism, as an alternative to the mainstream methods discussed in Chapters One and Two. A brief
overview of the dialectical method will be presented, followed by discussion of six characteristics of Marxist research, or what makes
Marxist research "Marxist." Throughout the chapter, I emphasize that
these characteristics are the only ones that can sufficiently challenge
capitalism through research connected to praxis, in terms of both analytical power and the ability to work toward change.

Dialectics

Allman (2007) and Lewontin and Levins (2007) note that dialectical
materialism is not technically a step-by-step method, but rather a critical orientation that is inherently political in tackling how social problems are approached. Marx himself did not spend much time
addressing specifically how society would be set up postcapitalism,
thus making materialism subject to the sustained challenge, "It's a
great idea, but how are we supposed to do it?" For Marx (1845/1932),
the task was to first comprehend the human condition through historical inquiry. The process of dialectics often involves posing a series of
broad questions: "Why are things the way they are instead of a little
bit different? Why are things the way they are instead of very different? What are the relationships between the stabilizing and destabiliz-
ing processes?" (Lewontin & Levins, 2007, p. 150). Dialectical problem
framing has to be manageable enough to locate the material forces
that are maintaining the existing situation, yet too much reductionism

often shuts out materialist analysis because interconnected social factors are disguised in favor of detail. The danger with scaling back research questions too much is that it tends to create misleading solu-solutions that do not challenge the status quo. By solving the smaller problems, it is assumed that the bigger ones are addressed, which is often not the case. So dialectical framing often begins with larger-than-life questions that might seem unusual to those accustomed to narrowing down topics.

The starting point of dialectical materialism is that human needs are essential, and are the foundation of history. As Hennessy (2002) describes, "needs are corporeal because they involve keeping the body alive, but they are not natural, because meeting them always takes place though social relationships" (p. 84). Dialectical materialists consider these social needs to be essential because humans rely on interactions in order to reach their potential (Howell & Prevenier, 2001). For example, humans must eat to survive, but the growing or hunting of food to meet this biological need is a social process. The sex drive may be biological and tied to the need to reproduce the species, but sexuality involves complex gender and class relations in the finding of mates, as well as navigation of state-sanctioned practices (such as marriage). This places dialectics as antithetical to ideologies of absolute individualism and autonomy, the notion that each human is his/her own self-contained entity who acts according to the dictates of free will. For dialectical materialists, there are severe limits to human autonomy so long as humans remain under a capitalist system: "In this sense, society is something beyond us and something in ourselves" (Howell & Prevenier, 2001, p. 92).

Dialectics places an emphasis on social context—processes and networks of human activity through history—with a focus on material production through labor (Fairclough, 2010). Lewontin and Levins (2007) view Marx's (1867/2010) *Capital* as one of the first major works to employ dialectics in examining through critique an entire economic system rather than reducing it to its isolated parts or even relying on systems theory, which they view as insufficient for understanding reality. Howell and Prevenier (2001) see Marx's theory of causality as foundational to the field of modern history, especially regarding the impact of economics on social changes. By looking at larger systemic causes, problems are taken as a whole rather than reduced to isolated parts or subsystems. Common sense, idealism, and mysticism are also challenged as means by which capitalist ideology reproduces itself (Marx, 1845/1932, 1873/1932). As Fairclough (2010) explains, "rhetoric is persuasion by any available means, dialectics is persuasion to the power of argument" (p. 502).

Characteristics of Marxist Research

Anticapitalism/Anti-Imperialism

First and foremost, classical Marxist research in the dialectical materialist tradition is research against capitalism. It does not seek to make capitalism kinder or more workable, or to reform it in any way. It isn't really interested in giving "equal time" to "all sides of the story." By the same token, Marxist research is anti-imperialist and does not support the right of nations to invade or occupy each other through acts of war, though it does support the right of people to resist imperialist rule. A streak of nationalism often lurks behind research that is reluctant to take a position against war and capitalism: "For liberal educated America, you cannot say the United States did anything wrong. Maybe some individuals did, but they can't do anything wrong by definition. The U.S. can make mistakes, but they can't be criminals. That's a deep element of intellectual culture across the spectrum" (Miske, 2010, p. 20). Capitalism itself is incompatible with emancipatory goals such as world peace and environmental security, because as a system, capitalism is unable to confront its destructive results, even if individuals within the system were willing to do so (Allman, 2007; Sheehan, Dunleavy, Cohen, & Mitchell, 2010; Wood, 2002).

According to Fisher (2009), capitalism is so overpowering that even anticapitalist messages can end up buttressing it. For example, we are fond of the proverb "the love of money is the root of all evil," but we end up assigning almighty attributes to money at the same time. Our denying a love of money in the form of greed only allows us to continue to put faith in it, because we have dealt with the negative aspect of money. Therefore, simply disavowing capitalism by labeling it "predatory capitalism" or "disaster capitalism" without an accompanying clear-headed analysis through resistance is insufficient. This is due, in part, to the contradictory nature of capitalism: On the one hand it promotes progress and development, while on the other hand it is responsible for much of the misery on the planet:

> Capitalism results in a cruel irony. It serves the progressive historical purpose of raising human productive capacities to previously unimaginable levels, one that could meet, at the very least, the basic needs of all human beings and thereby overcome scarcity. However, since the use value of every commodity is internally related to its exchange value, the human needs of a vast and growing number of the world's population are never met. (Allman, 2007, p. 16)

Indeed, Marx (1845/1932) himself asserted that capitalism was a necessary stage in the move toward human emancipation, in order for production to reach enough of a level that basic necessities could be obtained without undue labor. The problem is that equitable distribution has not followed suit.

Cole (2009) points out that when Marxism is critiqued by other philosophies, it's generally held that numerous fields of research disagree with the Marxist view, as if the power of numbers is enough to invalidate dialectical materialism. His response: "Well, of course it would be disputed by mainstream philosophers, pluralist political scientists, neoclassical economists and functionalist sociologists, all of which, unlike Marxists, are, at one level or another, apologists for capitalism" (p. 35). Marxist research is therefore research that takes a side against prevailing conditions (Denzin, 2009). Needless to say, it is very difficult to locate scholars willing to directly take an anticapitalist stance unconditionally, because one major problem with most research communities is that they do not sufficiently challenge the status quo, or they attempt to make the status quo more livable (Eagleton, 1983). As a result, it is common for Marxist researchers to find themselves marginalized, labeled as "biased," or viewed as ideologically rigid (Houston & Martin, 2010).

For dialectical materialist researchers, it becomes very important to determine where people stand, particularly in the often shifting alliances of academia: "Political strategies have to be rethought and inventory taken of who can be counted on as a real ally in the struggle and who is likely to vacillate at crucial points or even change sides as the requisite amount of corporate, financial, or political pressure is brought to bear" (Williams, 2012a, p. 65). Marxist researchers often find themselves having to confront other leftist research paradigms, such as postmodernism or neo-Marxism (Banfield, 2011; Rikowski, 2006). For example, Hennessy (2002) contrasts the more recent incarnation of cultural materialism with previous uses of historical materialism, which is the foundation of socialist feminism. She argues for reclaiming the term *Marxist feminism* and resisting tactics such as red-baiting (e.g., tying all Marxian philosophy to Stalinism in an attempt to refute its ability to "work") and assertions that there is no alternative to the status quo. For Holmstrom (2002a), "feminism that speaks of women's oppression and its injustices but fails to address capitalism will be of little help in ending women's oppression" (p. 2).

Characteristics of anticapitalist/anti-imperialist pedagogy can include what Torres and Reyes (2011) describe as research as praxis (RAP). RAP means taking on the difficult work of siding with those who are oppressed while at the same time employing the principle of radical critique to ensure that existing practices aren't just reproducing the status quo (Denzin, 2009; McLaren & Jaramillo, 2010). In terms of educational research, dialectical materialism can be a form of resistance to pedagogical rule by practices such as standardized testing, regimented curriculum, militarization of schooling, racial segregation, and the like. As Torres and Reyes (2011) point out, "most research on educational issues is just a holographic view of the same apparent problem, with no attempt to challenge the system to address the disparity of quality education for poor and minority children" (p. 43). For Torres and Reyes, the problem that education faces isn't one of low-quality research, it is a lack of equality within the educational system overall. Marx (1848/1969) himself did not have much confidence in reforming the institution of education as a means for emancipation, yet "every social relation formed in the struggle against capcapitalism needs to be an educative relation" (Moisio, Fitzsimmons, & Suoranta, 2010, p. 174).

Ultimately, the challenge becomes one of trying to confront capitalism while living within it as a system (Allman, 2007). Malott (2011) outlines what this entails:

> We must not hesitate to embrace the possibility of living a different paradigm, with fundamentally different values, non-capitalist worldview, and relationships not based on the coercion and exploitation of capital over labor; it requires that we develop the ability to imagine life beyond capital.... To get to a meaningful life after capital we must therefore not fear fundamentally transforming who we are; that is revolution, and that is the challenge of Marx. (p. 13)

Albo, Gindin, and Panitch (2010) ask, "can the left structure its responses so they strengthen popular capacities to think ambitiously and to act independently of the logic of capitalism?" (p. 106). This is a major problem that dialectical materialists investigate, and it starts with opposing capitalism, not trying to negotiate with it.

Rejection of Hyperrelativism

A second characteristic of Marxist research is that while it recognizes that individuals and situations have unique aspects that can make it challenging to group them by characteristics for analysis, it rejects radical relativism as an antitheoretical path to impeding the ability of researchers to comprehend the world in order to change it. As Holmstrom (2002b) explains, "Marx stresses that human freedom is exercised only within certain constraints—set by social, historical, and economic conditions as well as biological facts" (p. 362). Indeed, one of Marx's (1852) most famous quotes mounts an ultimate challenge against both radical relevancy and the notion that people have total autonomy and free will:

> Men make their own history, but they do not make it as they please; they do not make it under self-selected circumstances, but under circumstances existing already, given and transmitted from the past. The tradition of all dead generations weighs like a nightmare on the brains of the living. (para. 2)

Rather than an algorithm that can be universally applied to various situations, dialectical materialists start with the assumption that change is universal, with many factors existing to prompt such changes (Lewontin & Levins, 2007). The dialectical method involves grasping how those in power use ideology to make oppression appear natural and assured. Research as praxis enables people to create sound counterhegemonies while avoiding the endless detour of relativism (Torres & Reyes, 2011).

Eagleton (1983) finds that the resistance to theory found in relativist scholarship often reflects both hostility toward others' theories and an inability to recognize one's own theoretical identity: "[I]deology is always a way of describing other people's interests rather than one's own" (p. 211). Instead, Marxist research views theory-building as necessary, not just an arbitrary activity based on human whim; in other words, we can't really discard theory:

> The search for an appropriate theory is itself a theoretical movement because it is laden with considerations regarding judgment and intelligibility, history, and contacts, as well as who speaks. In effect, what has transpired in mainstream scholarship is a separation between theory and research, between conceptual complexity and a methodological absence. (Leonardo, 2010, p. 157)

If we are not able to conceptualize the ability of people to resist capitalism (and to conceptualize capitalism itself along a historic continuum), it becomes difficult to act effectively, especially when many of the most prominent social movements are not allied with progressive ideas (Apple, 2010).

One of the female college students discussed in Belenky et al. (1997) described her encounter with larger theory and how it can alter one's conception of the world by freeing individuals from the epistemological traps of relativism:

> I feel that everyone has something unique to say, but some people know how to develop it. Some people go even further—they can go outside the given frame of reference. Most people have something to say inside given frames of reference. But then you take someone like Freud or Darwin—they are able to jump outside of the given to create a whole new frame of reference. That doesn't happen too often. They stay with it. They create their whole life around it. They change everything for everyone. (p. 133, loc. 1973–1976)

This illustrates how when experience alone is used as a basis of evidence, it can end up reinforcing the status quo because we then can only talk about, rather than act on, oppression or inequality, because of our reluctance to generalize (Leonardo, 2010). Theory allows us to get past the spiral of relativism by taking action. Without the ability to both reject hyperrelativism and carefully apply theory, "we may get good answers to the wrong questions" (Lewontin & Levins, 2007, p. 163).

Direct Address of Class

The third characteristic of Marxist research is that it places class at the center of inquiry, rather than regarding it as one of several equally weighted factors such as race, gender, sexuality, or ability to conceptualize the world. Besides directly addressing class, it urges caution when attempting to make sweeping, transhistorical interpretations of human history; therefore, specificity of social context is key to the dialectical method. Particular conditions act together to create distinct periods of human history. In order to change the world rather than just describe it, we have to understand the dynamics of class and the historical conditions that shape our reality. At the same time, we can't assume that humans are just the same anywhere you go, or that history repeats itself simply because very specific sets of events are occurring at any given period. What we know about failed revolutionary movements as well as successful moments of mass resistance should be enough to warrant careful class analysis where "the ultimate aim of conflictual collective action and social struggle is control over historicity" (Litmanen, 2010, p. 234).

Marx presented three concepts of capitalist social relations: the introduction of private property and resulting class strife, transformation of labor into commodity, and alienation of labor (Fairclough, 2010). Allman (2007) outlines how Marx developed the concept of capitalist social relations as historically situated, "an inimitable and revolutionary theory of consciousness that permitted no dichotomy, or binary separation, between consciousness and reality" (p. 32). For example, those who lived under feudalism had a different manner of social relations, a different consciousness, than those who now live under capitalism. The economic context shapes not only conditions of living, but also how relationships are formed. Leacock's (1986) anthropological work demonstrates how the more egalitarian gendered division of labor in North American tribes was altered after the arrival of European missionaries, for example. For Allman (2007), the recognition that what we know about reality is historically situated also means that history isn't finished—the possibility for change remains.

Marx (1867/2010) was highly suspicious of transhistorical interpretations of human history and tradition, assumptions that whatever occurred in the past is automatically fixed and generalizable to any other given time period. His description of the dialectic method as a way to disrupt stable readings of history and human nature follows:

> In its rational form it is a scandal and abomination to bourgeoisdom and its doctrinaire professors, because it includes in its comprehension and affirmative recognition of the existing state of things, at the same time also, the recognition of the negation of that state, of its inevitable breaking up; because it regards every historically developed social form as in fluid movement, and therefore takes into account its transient nature not less than its momentary existence because it lets nothing impose upon it, and is in its essence critical and revolutionary. (p. 16)

As Allman (2007) explains, "the laws of Marx explicate identification of factors which govern the movement and development of capital. They are for Marxist science a historically specific capitalism and will be of only historical interest once capitalism is abolished" (pp. 6–7). What we view as "true" under capitalism will no longer be the case once capitalism ends. In order for the historical conditions under capitalism to change, we have to create an anticapitalist political vision, with the understanding that existing social conditions are not enduring, but can be altered (Brenner, 2002).

Howell and Prevenier (2001) note that although comparing different events can be a useful technique for historical analysis, it is at best an imperfect art. Surface similarities often cover over important differences that, if not identified, run the risk of transhistorical fallacy. For example, it is common to see comparisons made between the Great Depression and the economic recession of 2008, or between the invasion and occupation of Afghanistan and the Vietnam War. Yet, all of these situations are dramatically distinct, each with specific historical conditions. During the Great Depression, a strong manufacturing base was operational within the United States and was quickly utilized at the start of World War II (Albo, Gindin, & Panitch, 2010). Today, the United States relies mostly on exports. Vietnam was a nation-state with economic and military infrastructure; Afghanistan less so at the time of the U.S. invasion (Miller, 2010). In many respects, the U.S. Afghanistan involvement is better compared with the Soviet Afghanistan adventure than with Vietnam.

Understanding the specificity of social context is critical in dialectical research. Without a complete understanding of the many factors that comprise events and conditions, we are often left with obscured information that only furthers the power of capital. Marxist research means getting at the root of the problem, which is the opposite of mainstream, "post-political" or cultural research that does not acknowledge class:

> It is indeed considered methodologically rigorous and analytically sound to fashion oneself as the post-political anthropologist who merely collects and protects traits of a shared human past…. [U]nder the pretense of being completely apolitical, the post-political anthropologist or academic in the wider sense simply commits to politics that do not "dwell on the issues" and will never ask the question, "who has power and why?" (Starzmann, 2012, p. 40)

Deloria (1988) describes how in the 1970s Native American poverty was treated as a transhistorical reality, where the root of the problem—imperialism—was totally overlooked. Instead, it was cultural factors, deficit models of the family, alcoholism, and other aspects of poverty that were seen as the cause of the problem, not the aftereffects of centuries of colonialism and white supremacy.

Applying dialectical materialist analysis to the study of revolutions and resistance can be one way to begin to shape change. Howell and Prevenier (2001) emphasize the importance of context in the analysis of social revolts and what can move people to action: "The historian who does not place the Luddite revolts of the early nineteenth century in a longer history of social protest against unrestrained economic growth can understand very little about how it was that people like these workers could have been moved to collective violence" (pp. 84–85). Indeed, it was (and still is) quite common to see activist social movements conceptualized as mentally ill or crazed, rather than as acting in distinct, historically driven ways (Litmanen, 2010). Touraine's (1977, 1981) research was among the first of post–World War II scholarship to view social movements as constructive—rather than destructive—entities that were capable of creating change in the interest of the working class. His work is much more fruitful for Marxist scholars than that of Hoffer (1951), who tended to use centrist-extremist theory (Berlet & Lyons, 2000) to cast both leftist and fascist movements as equally prone to totalitarianism. For Hoffer, any kind of strong commitment to a set of principles meant that a social movement couldn't be trusted, and this makes him a reliable go-to citation for today's liberal-left gatekeepers who are simultaneously concerned about the extremism of today's Republican Party and militant activism in general (bernardpliers, 2012; Blumenthal, 2009; Kornbluth, 2011).

Research as Not Just Description, but Also Praxis

The fourth characteristic of Marxist research is that its purpose is not just to describe or understand the world, but to change it. Lewis (2012) quotes from a letter drafted by people's movements in Bolivia against neoliberal "compromisers": "the process is not propaganda, it is not a speech, it is not about marketing: the process is to change the lives of the people" (pp. 28–29). A problem with just describing the world or even recognizing its flaws but going no further is that it leaves the status quo intact (Harman, 2010). *Praxis* is a term often used by dialectical materialists to capture this dimension of theory merged with practice that happens when people organize for change and realize that they are compelled to act (Holst, 2012; Torres & Reyes, 2011). This should be distinguished from uncritical praxis, which only reproduces the status quo (Allman, 2007). Engels (1880) viewed revolutionary praxis as the only way to resolve the contradictions of living under capitalism:

> The proletariat seizes the public power, and by means of this transforms the socialized means of production, slipping from the hands of the bourgeoisie, into public property. By this act, the proletariat frees the means of production from the character of capital they have thus far borne, and gives their socialized character complete freedom to work itself out. Socialized production upon a predetermined plan becomes henceforth possible. The development of production makes the existence of different classes of society thenceforth an anachronism. In proportion as anarchy in social production vanishes, the political authority of the State dies out.... To accomplish this act of universal emancipation is the historical mission of the modern proletariat. To thoroughly comprehend the historical conditions and this the very nature of this act, to impart to the now oppressed proletarian class a full knowledge of the conditions and of the meaning of the momentous act it is called upon to accomplish, this is the task of the theoretical expression of the proletarian movement, scientific Socialism. (part 3, para. 1)

A major challenge for those who seek to enact praxis is that what we view as changeable is itself shaped by capitalist social relations (Allman, 2007; Lewontin & Levins, 2007). Deconstruction of existing ideologies needs to occur in order to begin praxis, which is an entirely different starting point than that used in mainstream research, where the boundaries of a problem are viewed as a given, with inquiry acting within those boundaries (Lingard, 2010). However, stopping at the deconstruction/critique phase is the same thing as working within the boundaries of a problem, as Deloria (1988) describes: "abstract theories create abstract action" (p. 86). Moisio, Fitzsimmons, and Suoranta (2010) urge that we need to go beyond reinterpreting interpretations in order to use praxis to create new visions for education and other social institutions. Litmanen (2010) envisions social movements engaged in praxis as needing two kinds of researcher-members: those who take on organizational tasks such as preparing the group for confrontations, getting the message out, and conducting meetings, and those who scientifically record events taking place in the group. This would allow for constant reflection as the group moves forward in order to achieve its goals.

Holst (2010) used critical discourse analysis to research texts of key social movements for justice, including individual authors and platform writings from the abolition to civil rights eras. He identified six dispositions along the lines of Che Guevara's pedagogical concepts: internationalism/anti-imperialism; intrinsic motivation of love and empathy; discipline/perseverance; honesty and self-criticality; flexibility in thinking and audacity; and a willingness to sacrifice, a rejection of privilege, and an orientation toward service. Grande (2010) describes red pedagogy as a form of praxis where education is used as decolonization and to build collective agency on a global level in order to achieve solidarity between peoples. Change-oriented praxis movements employ all of these necessary characteristics. As Behrent (2012) concludes:

> There is no greater school than a revolution. It is therefore not surprising that some of the most innovative, radical, and successful literacy campaigns are those that are born out of revolutions—when on a mass scale, people fight for a better society. In revolutionary periods, ideas matter as never before, and literacy needs no motivation as it becomes a truly liberatory endeavor. (p. 52)

Interdependency of Factors Under Class

A fifth characteristic of Marxist research is that it explores the interdependency of social factors such as race, gender, and sexuality as they operate under class: "In the United States, histories of slavery, indentured servitude, contract labor, self-employment, and wagework are also simultaneously histories of gender, race, and heterosexuality, nested within the context of the development of capitalism"

(Mohanty, 2002, p. 161). A common misconception about Marx is that he wrote about only capitalism and class relations and nothing more. Instead, Marx (1847/1955) viewed racism in the 1800s as a key means by which capitalists not only extracted labor from slaves, but also used the presence of slaves to leverage low wages in the north. Marx (1867/2010) also distinguished between women's productive and nonproductive labor, not as a means of describing domestic work as "less important" than wage work, but to illustrate how capitalism depends on what Hennessy (2002) calls "an outlawed set of needs" (p. 85) existing outside the margins of paid labor and often disguised by being attributed to women's nature. Contemporary Marxist scholars address everything from ethnicity (Cole, 2009) to gender (Smith, 2005) to sexuality (D'Emilio, 1983, 2003; Zavarzadeh, Ebert, & Morton, 2001) as a means of exploring how capitalism uses these factors to its advantage.

Wood (2002) explains that while human categorizations of race and gender can be used in the most brutal of ways, capitalism can tolerate some degree of movement toward rights for women and ethnic minorities. Capitalism has a wide degree of flexibility in using various social prejudices, as well as getting rid of ones that might stand in the way of profit. For example, many major corporations today have strong antiracist and antisexual harassment policies, and require yearly training workshops for employees on multiculturalism, not because they are inherently generous in spirit, but because they view racism and sexism as bad for business. Racism and sexism are often framed as being antithetical to the values of the educated bracket of the managerial upper middle class. Additionally, sectors of ethnic groups can also achieve financial success, and this success is often leveraged against lower-income members of that ethnic group (Deloria, 1988). As Wood (2002) concludes: "If capital derives advantages from racism or sexism, it is not because of any structural tendency in capitalism toward racial equality or gender oppression, but on the contrary, because they disguise the structural realities of the capitalist system and because they divide the working class" (p. 279).

Feminist standpoint theory can be used in a dialectical way to shed light on the concept of interdependency of various factors such as race, class, gender, and sexuality. Brooks (2007) describes how women, being members of an oppressed group, possess a "double consciousness" about their own experiences and the ideology of dominant groups at the same time. The same may not be the case for men, who are often able to overlook necessary but unpaid feminized practices that come out of the social reproduction of labor, such as child care and housework. Socialist feminists carry standpoint theory further to claim that the *working class* as a whole is oppressed under capitalism (Smith, 2005). It's just that capitalism at this particular historical juncture happens to function ideologically through gender, race, and sexuality, inscribing the nuclear family as the ideal foundational form for privatizing reproductive labor (Coontz, 1997, 2000; Smith, 2005).

Interdependency can also refer to how the environment shapes human behavior and knowledge, and humans, in turn, also act on their environment. Lewontin and Levins (2007) note that while we have acquired more knowledge about how human and nonhuman organisms shape their environment by acting upon it (rather than by passively being impacted by it), there is still more to learn. Hennessy (2002) notes how "affective capacities are tied to cognition and to the traces of social contexts that register in them" (p. 84). Because humans require shelter, food, and health to reach their potentials, they ultimately rely on networks that result from social cooperation. The theories that humans develop to explain the world derive from this interdependency (Eagleton, 1983). Unfortunately, capitalism and for-profit science have commodified human interdependency, particularly through colonialism and the seizing of indigenous resources and knowledge (Denzin, 2009).

Interdisciplinarity as a form of interdependency is an important feature of dialectical research, which draws upon history, sociology, archaeology, feminism, medicine, psychology, law, and other fields to inform inquiry as to cause and effect (Howell & Prevenier, 2001). For Apple (2010), education has to be viewed as a political endeavor, which requires that we start to frame problems in relational ways: "Understanding education requires that we situate it in the unequal relations of power in the larger society and in the realities of dominance and subordination—and the conflicts—that are generated by these relations" (p. 152). To develop an effective praxis, Marxist scholars need to treat the individual/collective and the general/outlier not as binary or isolated categories, but as parts of the same system of reality, whether one is a qualitative or quantitative researcher (Lewontin & Levins, 2007).

Necessity of Collectivity in Analysis and Solutions

A sixth characteristic of Marxist research is that collectivity is emphasized over individuality when it comes to creating solutions through praxis. Lewis (2012) describes the collectivity resulting from praxis for the self-emancipation of the working class as "the space within which thought and action, ideas and reality, come together in an electrifying unity to produce general social effects" (p. 32). Dialectical materialist research, in its interest in collectivity, also uses analytical constructs such as false consciousness, and examines how ideology functions to sustain oppression. This is not to say that people can be painted with a broad brush, or that uniqueness isn't valued. It is just that framing research around individual will, resiliency, motivation, or similar traditional psychological constructs leads to a dead end when it comes to social change. As Lahde (2010) asserts, "forces of nature…never act in a vacuum, but in a world that has been formed by history of human action with all its problems objectified into infrastructures" (p. 74). Certain neoliberal ideologies center around individualism, which is a form of naïve hope: progress, endless growth, optimism mixed with complacency, and consumerism (Lautensach & Lautensach, 2010; Torres & Reyes, 2011).

Currently, individual factors are used to explain nearly every social phenomenon. Take, for example, mental illness: Any possibility that mental illness could be brought on by social factors is rejected in favor of treating individual biological traits. The saliency of individual explanations is beneficial to capitalism, because it creates markets (e.g., for the pharmaceutical companies) while alleviating calls for potentially collective solutions (e.g., national health care) (Fisher, 2009). The remedy is treating isolated cases in a privatized manner. However, individualism as an explanation only goes so far for elites. If negative publicity hits a corporation in such a manner that the "bad apple" argument will no longer hold, suddenly the larger, abstract structure will be identified as the culprit, and therefore no one can be held accountable—individuals disappear into the system that is too big to fail. Instead of seeing that society is a mere collection of isolated problems, we need to see these problems as pointing to one enormous cause: capitalism.

There are dialectical psychologists and cognitive scientists who have questioned traditional applications of mental processes. These include Neill (1949, 1960) and Reich (1946, 1971), who traced the roots of fascism to authoritarian family structures that emphasize harsh corporal punishment and gender stereotyping. Adorno's (1969) landmark study of the authoritarian personality is another example of dialectical use of Freudian theory to examine how the family provides a foundation for totalitarian thought. Behrent's (2012) analysis of Vygotsky places him as one of the more radical cognitive scientists who used Marxist theory to develop his own concept of how people learn. What sets these scholars apart is their connection of the inner world to larger societal context, bringing even greater explanatory power to the field of mental health, which unfortunately remains mired in the individual as cause/solution. Litmanen (2010) concludes that we need sociology, rather than individualism, in order to confront the current situation:

> The sociologists must create a social situation where an entire group is forced to interact with their real opponents.... The aim of the sociologist is to reveal claims, conflicts, and debates which are often overshadowed by the authority of social norms and by repression, which is imposed for the sake of institutions or those who hold positions of power. (p. 241)

Mohanty's (2002) study of female pieceworkers in India reveals the limitations of individualism. Because they are isolated within their homes, the workers do not perceive that they need to organize collectively, nor do they see themselves as oppressed, even though they face a double shift of daily labor, doing housework and assembling products:

> While some of the contradictions between their work and their roles as housewives and mothers were evident to them, they did not have access to an analysis of these contradictions which could lead them to a) seeing the complete picture in terms of their exploitation; b) strategizing and organizing to reform their maternal situations; or c) recognizing their common interests as women workers across caste/class lines. (p. 165)

Likewise, Sheehan et al. (2010) found that their teacher education candidates were reluctant to address harsher aspects of history, often claiming that such content was too violent for children and that parents would complain. This "disabling of culpability" (p. 109) is deeply entrenched within university culture, and is connected to the analytically inhibiting characteristics of focusing on individual causes/solutions.

Collective solutions are a challenge to achieve because there are many ideological strategies used by capital to keep people divided, such as false consciousness. False consciousness creates a zero-sum game where people begin to perceive that if a group is able to achieve some degree of rights, then their own rights must as a result be diminished (Allison, 2002). Carspecken (1996) explains how this is enacted:

> Most people gain a sense of worth through cultural systems that pit them against other groups of humans. This is why many people enjoying a privileged position in society feel threatened by the plight of the poor. They do not want to know too many of the details. They want to explain social inequality by blaming the victims or in any other way that leaves their accustomed identities intact. They are afraid of being wounded. (p. 171)

The willingness of people to participate in their own oppression, what Allman (2007) terms "uncritical/reproductive praxis," has been a major subject of inquiry for dialectical researchers since Marx. One example of reproductive praxis is using the media to frame the problems of the poor as a result of bad character, which provides a convenient justification for those on the margins of the middle class to join with elites to deny the poor government assistance, even though those same individuals on the margin might require such assistance in the future (Brenner, 2002; Miske, 2010). Similarly, with problems that seem too large (e.g., the legacy of slavery/racism or environment/climate change), responses are often along the lines of absolving one's self of responsibility because one can't see the social context of the problem or even a way out (Lautensach & Lautensach, 2010; Torres & Reyes, 2011). Starzmann (2012) notes that even within academia, "we are not only aware of our ideologically warped beliefs, but we consciously accept that these constructs constitute reality" (p. 40).

Robin (2011) describes interpellation of individuals through right-wing populism as a means of appealing to large groups without in any way disturbing elite power structures; indeed, it supports such structures. He examines the case of the South leading up to the Civil War, where poor whites were relied upon to buttress the slave owners. Technically, non-slave-holding whites had no common cause with slave owners, yet through rallying support for slavery, "a poor white man could style himself a member of the nobility and thus be relied upon to take the necessary measures in its defense" (p. 56, loc. 860–861). Racial domination was the bait provided to the white working class, as Marx and Engels noted:

> The number of actual slaveholders in the South of the Union does not amount to more than 300,000, a narrow oligarchy that is confronted with many millions of so-called poor whites, whose numbers have been constantly growing through concentration of landed property and whose condition is only to be compared with that of the Roman plebeians in the period of Rome's extreme decline. Only by acquisition of new territories...is it possible to square the interests of these "poor whites" with those of the slaveholders, to give their restless thirst for action a harmless direction and to tame them with the prospect of one day becoming slaveholders themselves. (2009, pp. 40–41)

False consciousness, therefore, is one of many ideologies that serve to keep the working class separated under capitalism and prevent the solidarity required for revolutionary praxis. Fairclough (2010) provides an apt definition of ideology:

> An ideology is a system of ideas, values and beliefs oriented to explaining a given political order, legitimizing existing hierarchies, and power relations and preserving group identities. Ideology explains both the horizontal structure of a society and its vertical structure, producing ideas which legitimize the latter, explaining in particular why one group is dominant and another is dominated.... [D]omination and compliance require the belief of the dominated in the legitimacy of the dominant. (p. 257)

Eagleton (1983) views ideology as a concealed system that connects what we say and do to the power structure at large, even penetrating to the level of feeling. What makes an ideology appear true is its ability to isolate aspects of consciousness and make them appear unconnected (Allman, 2007). When reflection is denigrated and "gut feelings" are privileged within the mass media, ideologies are all the more quickly absorbed as common sense (Torres & Reyes, 2011). For Fairclough (2010), the legitimacy of an ideology depends on its ability to appear to address three key needs: stimulation, security, and justice.

Conclusion

Rejecting capitalist ideology and exposing commonsense myths are part of collective praxis (Fairclough, 2010). Allman (2007) asserts that with the end of capitalism, "infinite humanization would be a major objective, fully supported such that individuals would be able to develop all of the potentials of which they were capable" (p. 62). Currently, the only research paradigm capable of overcoming capitalism and the rightward drifting of politics in the United States is dialectical materialism, or Marxism (Brenner, 2002). We are seeing a rapid acceleration of rightist policies alongside environmental collapse and economic assaults on the working class that make such solutions seem impossible.

Yet, it is a mistake to assume that the conditions most of the world experiences are inevitable, or that somehow the working class is beyond revolutionary thought, as authors such as Houtman, Achterberg, and Derks (2008) and Frank (2005) suggest. These authors, along with proponents of the cultural focus of whiteness theory (where white workers' racism erases their class position) that Lynd (2009) critiques, view racism as a culturally embedded feature of this group. In fact, the meme of the reactionary white working class is a capitalist class fantasy stoking middle-class resentment created and sustained by those seeking to divide workers of different races. The stereotype endures precisely *because* of the lack of a unified leftist alternative, not because the white working class is inherently reactionary (Turl, 2008).

What we know about revolutionary praxis is that it can often emerge at unexpected junctures or in unpredictable locations. It may be hard to trace or document while it is developing, but it is there:

> The official doctrines and companies are full of noble principles, the emptiness of which is obvious for many insiders. The subjective surplus is partly channeled to unofficial activities, partly it exists only as dreams and as potentiality for a future society. Thus, even under the polished face of the most diligent worker and citizen there may be surprise waiting. (Tammilehto, 2010, p. 201)

As researchers, we need to be equipped not only to record, but also to participate in the surprise.

Chapter Four

Dialectical Empiricist Research

Overview

This chapter presents a summary of the scholarship of dialectical materialist researchers who work in the fields of biology, medicine, statistics, public health, and education. These writers operate from an empirical standpoint that also embraces critical realism as a worldview, setting them apart from traditional positivist researchers who often stop at describing the world as it appears: "Critical theory is unabashedly political. That is, unlike noncritical quantitative, and even many qualitative views, critical theory is sustained by an interest in emancipation from all forms of oppression, as well as by a commitment to freedom, happiness, and a rational ordering of society" (Baez, 2007, p. 19). Collectively, these researchers are often labeled interchangeably as quantitative criticalists, critical empiricists, dialectical biologists, dialectical statisticians, or feminist empiricists. What they have in common is extending the traditional tenets of positivism beyond neutrality to recognize that political forces create what often appear to be "natural" phenomena, and that these same political forces also shape the discipline of science itself (Howell & Prevenier, 2001). Lewontin and Levins (1985) frame the materialist empirical imperative thus: "Things are similar: this makes science possible. Things are different: this makes science necessary" (p. 141).

Positivism, beginning with Descartes, Comte, and Bacon in the emerging Enlightenment, sought to create mechanistic models of the world, which was believed to be knowable and measurable. This epistemology had specific characteristics, including a notion of reality as existing outside of one's conception of it and a belief that aspects of reality could be examined in isolation to form conclusions about the natural world (Leckenby, 2007; Lewontin & Levins, 2007). However, some interpretations of positivism can be carried over to dialectical thinking, such as Comte's view that the cultural is determined by economic factors, and that the world is knowable and therefore changeable (Howell & Prevenier, 2001). What matters is who positivism is working for—the capitalists, or the working class? Lesser (2005) relates how the nineteenth-century statistician Eugene Buret once stated, "It no longer suffices to know how things are constituted: we need to seek how things should be constituted so that this world of ours may present less suffering and destitution" (p. 2269).

How Marxism became disassociated from quantitative and empirical research is a mystery. Qualitative methodologists might be surprised to learn that there is a long history of validating the practice of scientific research within Marxism. As Little (1986) explains,

> Even a cursory reading of Marx's writings makes it clear that his claim to having conducted a scientific analysis of the capitalist mode of production is central to his system as a whole. His theory of historical materialism requires that empirical investigation replace social philosophy as a basis for social criticism; his critique of the utopian socialists turns on their lack of a scientific analysis of existing institutions. (p. 4)

A few of the many earlier works addressing connections between dialectics and science include writings by Pannekoek (1912), Lenin (1908, 1922), Engels (1883), and Marx (1881), who even wrote about mathematical theory! Despite this legacy, there are qualitative researchers who are skeptical about positivist research used in the service of social justice, Torres and Reyes (2011) among them.

This skepticism may be due in part to the current reassertion of empiricism, which declares that Scientifically Based Research, and particularly the double-blind clinical trial, is the only viable form of inquiry (Denzin, 2009; Torres & Reyes, 2011). Mende (2005) distinguishes between *empirical* and *empiricist*, where empirical inquiry can provide useful methods for gathering data, whereas empiricism often becomes a form of scientism, or research cultism: "The textbooks of Research Methodology either implicitly adopt the empiricist doctrine, by excluding all research methods other than the empirical methods, or explicitly adopt the empiricist doctrine, by suggesting that empiricism is necessary for an academic discipline to achieve scientific status" (p. 197). Mende goes on to describe how this form of narrow scientific thinking, rather than being uniformly embraced from the get-go, has been the subject of critique since Bacon in the 1600s. Mende calls for empirical methods to be considered as one of many possible forms of inquiry, depending on how it fits with the problem to be studied, and to be open to related fields such as the history and philosophy of science.

In this chapter I present the case that Marxist research should include those dialectical materialists who work in the sciences and positivist/empirical fields. This form of research can be quite valuable for building praxis, as traditional forms of research often receive a fairer hearing compared to more qualitative forms. Many of the insights that these authors provide can be helpful to qualitative and quantitative researchers forming their own interpretive frames. The chapter opens with an overview of the philosophical orientation of critical realism, including feminist empiricism. A summary of some of the past and current research in a critical vein is presented below, starting with the dialectical scientists and followed by those who write in public health and education fields.

Critical Realism

Critical realists operate on the same basic assumption as realists—that there exists a "real" world, including the social domain, and this existence is fact even if we lack of knowledge of it. Without a set of common epistemological starting points, it would be impossible to even conduct research: "[O]ne group of theorists and researchers would continually produce work that the second group of theorists would then examine for flaws and refutations," and so on (Stage, 2007, p. 8). As Fairclough (2010) explains, "critical realists assume a stratified ontology, which sees process/events and structures as different strata of social reality with different properties. A distinction is drawn between the real, the actual, and empirical" (p. 355). The "real" refers to structures and causality, while the "actual" involves events and processes. The "empirical" is "part of the real and the actual is experienced by social actors" (p. 355). Yet, what is actual isn't necessarily reflective of reality—the study of this complex interaction is what Fairclough and others (Lewontin & Levins, 2007; Litmanen, 2010; Stage, 2007) mean by "critical realism."

Lewontin and Levins (2007) outline components of dialectical materialist science that involve critical realism. First, knowledge comes not just from experience, but also from reflection on that experience. Second, experience alone is not enough—we need to be self-conscious about the differences in the historical conditions that emerge between old and new discoveries. Third, all epistemological positions have a point of view, which is necessary to make sense of a world with too large an array of sensory information to handle without some sort of framework. Fourth, science has positive and negative aspects. While it can promote emancipation and progress, it can also be influenced by power structures. Fifth, what we think of as contemporary science is, in essence, capitalist science. For Lewontin and Levins, rather than viewing all scientific processes as inevitably hierarchical and isolated, we should recognize that systems have reciprocity and shifting positions.

Those who espouse a critical realist worldview often deliberately choose challenging and provocative research questions (Stage, 2007). St. John (2007) describes how he frames policy research not with preestablished arguments that privilege elite policy writers, but by putting different arguments to the test. Lewontin and Levins (2007) are especially interested in results that contradict expected outcomes—sometimes, "wrong" conclusions can seem correct to us, and we should investigate why that is: "We use our scholarship to push the boundaries of what we know by questioning mainstream notions of higher education through the examination of policies, the reframing of theories and measures, and the reexamination of traditional questions for nontraditional populations" (Stage, 2007, p. 5). Stage also notes that when data are examined on a large scale and methods of analysis take context into consideration, patterns of injustice are often revealed where before they were hidden.

Holmstrom (2002b) identifies Marx as embodying a critical realist position for both the natural and human sciences: "Marx believed that the distinction between accidental and lawful generalizations applied to social phenomena and that certain social entities had natures, saying repeatedly that science was necessary to uncover the hidden laws of motion of capitalist society" (p. 362). Humans then, operate within particular constraints, which are established by historical and economic developments. For Allman (2007), dialectical researchers have to be constantly on the move, relentlessly testing knowledge for its ability to assist with praxis. Holmstrom (2002b) explains that while there isn't a specific entity called "human nature" according to Marx, there are different forms of humanity that have been shaped under feudalism, capitalism, and communism. For critical realists, methods such as statistics can help to reveal the often hidden dimensions of life under capitalism, which has a historical context (Howell & Prevenier, 2001).

Both Ehrenreich (2009) and Nanda (2002) critique radical relativism from a critical realist standpoint. Ehrenreich (2009) lays much of the blame for irrationality at the feet of positive thinking, which creates a hyperrelativist vision of reality by telling people that they and only they as individuals can change things by simply altering the way they think about reality:

> To base a belief or worldview on science or what passes for science is to reach out to the nonbelievers and the uninitiated, to say that they too can come to the same conclusions if they make the same systematic observations and inferences. The alternative is to base one's worldview on revelation or mystical insight, and these are things that cannot be reliably shared with others. In other words, there is something deeply sociable about science; it rests entirely on observations that can be shared with and repeated by others. (pp. 71–72)

Nanda (2002) sees much danger in valorizing antipositivism to the point where things such as local custom and religious beliefs are placed beyond critique just because they reject Western empiricism. She argues that this particular assertion of the local "verges on culturalism which regards the conceptual and imaginary representations of existing cultures in modernizing societies to be the ultimate and irreducible force in development" (p. 399). Critics of objectivity and rationality often assume that the testimony of oppressed groups is enough to counter the Western bias of empiricism, when many local practices are themselves sustaining exploitation.

One offshoot of critical realism is feminist empiricism, which includes quantitative methodology applied to scholarship concerning problems facing women. Rather than viewing statistics as incompatible with feminist philosophy, several empiricists embrace it as contributing to the emancipation of women (Brooks & Hesse-Biber, 2007; Kinzie, 2007; Leckenby, 2007; Miner-Rubino & Jayaratne, 2007). Miner-Rubino and Jayaratne (2007) describe their experiences with using empirical methods, which they encountered in their feminist graduate studies:

> I was floored when I became aware that researchers could provide hard data to document what I was observing. As I became more proficient in statistics, I further understood the powerful story numbers could tell about women's lives—not simply the proportion of women affected by this or that, but the consequences of those experiences. (p. 294)

For example, Miner-Rubino and Jayaratne's research centers on gender-based workplace harassment. Not only do they report how often such behavior occurs, they also show the aftereffects of harassment, including stress, absenteeism, and physical/mental health problems. This illustrates the focus on context that feminist empiricists view as essential to good research (Leckenby, 2007).

Brooks and Hesse-Biber (2007) explain that while feminist empiricists value objectivity, they also recognize the limitations of such an orientation and readily critique concepts such as neutrality, especially when they are used to maintain patriarchy and the status quo. Additionally, not all quantitative feminist researchers share exactly the same philosophical orientation, just as not all qualitative researchers, and not all feminists, share exactly the same perspectives (Miner-Rubino & Jayaratne, 2007). Feminist empiricists often work across a variety of disciplines such as public policy, science, medicine, education, law, and other fields, giving their work an interdisciplinary flair (Leckenby, 2007). By combining a feminist ethos with positivism, these researchers seek to meet the call to objectivity as much as possible, as Leckenby (2007) describes:

> With other empiricists, feminist empiricists are located firmly in the positivistic belief that the social and natural world at large is accessible and understandable. As positivists, feminist empiricists want to develop knowledge that is objective and truthful; they believe strongly that such knowledge is obtainable. (p. 28)

The importance of objectivity for Leckenby and other feminist empiricists stems from the fact that in the past, women were left out of the research process, stereotyped, or saw their needs marginalized. Therefore, it is traditional science—not feminist empiricism—that has not been truly "objective." The ability to dialectically interact with data while maintaining the ethics of objectivity provides a powerful means of bringing feminist perspectives to the forefront (Miner-Rubino & Jayaratne, 2007).

The use of quantitative research methods by feminist empiricists can often provide an important inroad into public discourse and advance social change for the better (Leckenby, 2007). Miner-Rubino and Jayaratne (2007) provide the example of a 1960s statistic comparing women's wages to men's wages. This became a permanent talking point in the media that was accessible and really hit home with people—much as "we are the 99%" has done for the Occupy movement:

> Quantitative survey research can provide a vehicle for feminists to introduce sexism, racism, classism, heterosexism, and other social justice issues into mainstream discourse...quantitative research may have more appeal for these groups of individuals, and thus they may be more apt to listen and consider quantitative research legitimate. (p. 302)

Much of the survey research done by feminist empiricists has been translated into important policy changes and outreach in the areas of eating disorders, rape, partner violence, and health—issues that directly impact women and families.

Dialectical Science Writing

Dialectical materialist scientists write across a diverse range of fields such as economics, mathematics/logic, agriculture, medicine, and history/philosophy of science. A starting point for their work is to set themselves apart from metaphysical speculations. Marxist scientists view reality as generated by the material world, not by superstition or intuition. Materialism is therefore incompatible with idealism, as Pickard (n.d.) explains:

> The development of scientific thought in the European countries in the 17th and 18th centuries displayed some really contradictory characteristics, which still remain typical of the approach of bourgeois theoreticians today. On the one hand there was a development towards a materialist method. Scientists looked for causes. They didn't just accept natural phenomena as god-ordained miracles, they sought some explanation for them. But at the same time these scientists did not yet possess a consistent or worked-out materialist understanding; and very often, behind the explanations for natural phenomena, they also saw, at the end of the chain, the hand of God at work.... According to this approach, the development of mankind and of society—of art, science, etc.—is dictated not by material processes but by the development of ideas, by the perfection or degeneration of human thought. And it is no accident that this general approach, whether spoken or unspoken, pervades all the philosophies of capitalism. (para. 7–9)

Therefore, materialist scientists often have to struggle against two fronts: the privatization of science, which effectively supports capitalism under neoliberalism, and the reassertion of religion, which has intensified since the conservative restoration of the 1970s.

Fitch (2012) dissects the tenets of creationism, including its newest form, intelligent design. He presents readers with seven ways of knowing, some of which can be either useful for dialectical analysis or deceptive: experience, observation, logic, authority, intuition, revelation, and faith. For example, on their own, experience and observation both can be misleading, because we can never be sure that we are interpreting our experiences in a larger social context. We can also see selectively, or misinterpret what we see. Yet, experience paired with regular observation can be reliable, as we build track records that confirm our experiences with what we are seeing in the world, or add nuances to what we see. Authority can be equally unreliable—creationists assert the literal interpretation of the Bible—yet authority can be developed over time through testable theory:

> The paradigm is to discover what contradictory predictions the two views make and how to discover data and perform experiments that will give results that determine which of the opposing views, if not both, is clearly incorrect. A scientist's explanation must function; that is, it must permit control over some observed condition of the material world. A creationist's explanation for the same observations need only be asserted. (pp. 32–33)

Skybreak (2006) mounts a militant defense of evolution against primarily religiopolitical forces who seek to confuse the public in order to impose their own world vision, which often is tightly allied with neoliberalism and the assault on the working class. What conservatives oppose about evolution has to do with its tracking of not merely individual change, but systemic change over time; this was revealed in the Center for the Renewal of Science and Culture's "Wedge Strategy" (1998), which laid out their long-range plans to dethrone materialism, which they see as the root of societal problems. For them, evolution is a direct attack on the idealistic concept of an unchanging moral universe, where things are the way they are either because they were created to be that way, or because people are being punished for transgressing the way things are supposed to be (which is usually determined by elites in the first place). The notion that humans have the ability to inquire about their world and to be open to what they might find is what is appalling to creationists:

> Nothing in our human "tool-kit" is more important than a thoroughgoing materialist scientific *method* for uncovering the actual truth of things—a method consistently applied—a method which itself is the product of evolution, and revolution, in human development, including in our modes of thinking. To forward-looking religious believers and nonbelievers alike I say: why not make a pact to go wherever scientific methods for uncovering the truth of things may take us, even if what we uncover ends up posing some serious and uncomfortable challenges to some old assumptions and cherished traditions? (Skybreak, 2006, p. 193)

Similarly, Gould exposes the political side of antimaterialist think-ing among not just religious groups, but also so-called evolutionary psychologists who cite science to justify inequality and war. In *The Mismeasure of Man* (1996), Gould takes aim at the eugenics movement (new and old versions) by exposing its selective application, using the example of tracing criminality to genetics:

> We all tend to generalize from our own areas of expertise. These doctors are psychosurgeons. But why should the violent behavior of some desperate and discouraged people point to a specific disorder of their brain while the corruption and violence of some congressmen and presidents provokes no similar theory? Human populations are highly variable for all behaviors — the simple fact that some do and some don't provides no evidence for a spe-cific pathology mapped on the brain of doers. (p. 175)

It is remarkable how similar the quotes from phrenologists sound next to excerpts from the *Bell Curve*, just with softer language. In pre-senting these examples, Gould illustrates how the misuse of science served to buttress the status quo, and how it continues to support pol-icies such as cutting public spending and privatizing education.

Slee uses game theory to deconstruct and challenge several com-monsense notions about individuality, choice, and the market in *No One Makes You Shop at Wal-Mart* (2006). Using the characters Jack and Jill who live in the fictional town Whimsley, he peppers his book with several allegorical scenarios to illustrate dialectical, sociological un-derstandings of problems. Many of the Whimsley scenario outcomes come as a surprise to readers, especially those who are prone to ac-cept the mother of all market-think, "individual choice":

> The moral of the story is simply that individual choice carries no guarantee of a happy ending. Choices are rarely made in isolation. They come quickly and intricately tangled, and their outcome is not often what we intend or hope for.... [P]eople who believe firmly in the virtues of individual choice will assert that Jack must be happier now than he used to be, because he has exercised his freedom of choice. If he didn't like Wal-Mart, he would not shop there. If he valued the lively downtown so much, he would shop there to save it. They will assert that, as a consumer, Jack is sovereign and the market always gives him what he wants. Yet in this story there is no indi-vidual choice that Jack could have made that would have improved his out-

come. Even if Jack had chosen to continue shopping downtown, his miniscule individual contribution to the revenue of the downtown stores would not stop the closing. (pp. 13–14)

Slee asserts that the illusion of consumer choice serves as a populist veneer on a system that privileges those with the most resources to do the real choosing, for the rest of us.

Slee also presents several scenarios to problematize social situations, such as the need for government regulations. He talks about "free riding" and the problem of littering, where people will discard their trash because they assume that their one tiny cup or piece of paper won't matter much in the long run. As Slee explains, "the root of free riding is that the cost of carrying the cup is private, while the cost of dropping the cup is public" (p. 39). Even though one person's "free" choice to litter might be small, it adds up because the effects are shared among us all—we aren't able to enjoy clean sidewalks. He then applies the same metaphor to the need for vaccinations and environmental regulations. Simply relying on individual habits of recycling and installing energy-efficient lightbulbs to solve environmental problems will not work; we need collective solutions to lead us out of the trap of individual choice.

Likewise, businesses are not going to act in environmentally responsible ways unless they receive a "push" in the form of regulation that everyone has to abide by. Slee uses the example of large-scale fishing, where countries are compelled by the existing system to collect as much fish as they can. No individual fishing boat can improve the outcome unless there is a large-scale effort to reduce commercial fishing and preserve fish supplies. On a much larger scale, as long as the *other* countries have to restrain themselves, but *my* country does not, then my country is likely to continue to release carbon emissions unabated, because that is in its best financial interest. In the case of public transportation, until it is made very convenient (e.g., running several bus or train routes a day in multiple locations), people are likely to remain drivers. This requires massive public infrastructure, not individual choices, such as the example Slee gives of London charging commuters £5 to drive during rush hour in the city. This simple charge provided "a more realistic portion of the cost imposed as a whole on road users.... [I]ndividual choice remains, but the balance of incentives is tilted to reflect more accurately the true costs and benefits of the decision, including the public costs" (p. 58).

Slee's discussion concerning the game of tit-for-tat beautifully illustrates the principle of reciprocity. Years ago, game theorists were challenged to come up with the most successful strategy that one could employ in various scenarios. The winner was tit-for-tat, outlined as follows: "On the first move, cooperate. On every subsequent move, play what the other player played on the previous move. If the other player cooperates, then tit-for-tat cooperates on the next move. If the other player defects, tit-for-tat defects on the next move" (p. 81). Slee explains that this strategy garnered the most overall points during the rounds of play, even though tit-for-tat can never outscore a specific opponent. By encouraging cooperation, the strategy results in the most overall points shared by the players. Unfortunately, Slee currently sees this principle at work mostly in business, where owners collaborate on price fixing. Most items, especially higher-priced necessities such as cars and appliances, are relatively similar in cost. Slee would like to see tit-for-tat extended to collective action, where the benefits can be shared as a whole by the group, rather than split among the few. He sees current calls for volunteerism and philanthropy as woefully inadequate and without historical precedent. Instead, what is needed are regulations and enforcement, so that the working class doesn't shoulder the bulk of the burden.

Lewontin and Levins (1985, 2007) are dialectical scientists who write across a range of fields including biology, public health, environmentalism, and ethics. In *The Dialectical Biologist* (1985) they outline qualities of materialist science. One chapter from this work, "The Commoditization of Science," demonstrates how contemporary science is part and parcel of capitalism, not existing in a separate realm: "Activities that previously were the direct result of human interactions—entertainment, emotional support, learning, recreation, child care, even human blood and transplantable organs or the use of the womb—have now entered the marketplace, where human relations hide behind impersonal buying and selling" (p. 199). For Lewontin and Levins, research is undertaken in much the same manner as a business contract, with investments and shareholders supporting the process. As discoveries are made, privatized patents immediately socialize the costs related to research, making results affordable only to those with the most wealth. Scientists, like other members of the working class, have become alienated from their own labor, even though they work under more privileged conditions than most.

Their most recent book, *Biology under the Influence* (2007), is an excellent collection of essays concerning a variety of pressing topics to which they apply an unabashedly materialist analysis. In the opening pages of their book, they reject both the antiscience movement (religious and corporate-based) and scientism, where what is measurable is held higher than other forms of knowledge. At the same time, they stand against postmodernism and the rejection of scientific knowledge, in that some things are indeed knowable. While many aspects of today's science are worthwhile, Lewontin and Levins find the field lacking somehow:

> None of these theories, all meant to tame diversity and change, and most important, to expunge historical contingency, envisions the alternative, that living beings are at the nexus of a very large number of weakly determining forces so that change and variation and contingency are the basic properties of biological reality. (p. 16)

What Lewontin and Levins find missing is that today's science doesn't allow for the full flexibility of organisms to advance change. For example, on the surface a chance event might appear random, but when presented with large numbers of opportunities, it could become a certainty: "Randomness means causal independence, not the lack of causation" (p. 28). They apply this thinking to the betterment of the human condition and the potential for positive change on a large scale. Lewontin and Levins also answer the common assertion that inequality is inevitable and part of biology, and that certain traits are unequally distributed at random, from birth: "But this claim leaves untouched a second question. Suppose it were true that there were such genetically determined individual and group differences. Those differences in themselves do not dictate a hierarchical society. Why not 'from each according to ability and each according to need?'" (p. 59).

Lewontin and Levins also trace the history of modern statistics to the eighteenth century, when it began as primarily a way for the state to record census-type data for the purpose of maintaining records of the population. With the formalization of the theory of probability beginning in the early nineteenth century, fusing with statistics, causal relationships between variables could be systematically explored:

> There are essentially only two techniques of statistical inference. In one, contrast analysis, individuals are sorted into two or more populations based on some a priori criteria....The alternative technique, correlational analysis, is to assemble all the individuals into a single population, to measure two or more characteristics, again chosen a priori, and then to look for trends in one or more of these characteristics as other characteristics vary. (p. 67)

The hallmark of traditional statistical research is that all methodological decisions are done ahead of time, making this approach vastly different than qualitative research, which unfolds as it happens. When it comes to using statistics in political contexts, such as policy making, different forms of reporting are used. Lewontin and Levins point out that the mean is often used to highlight how well a group is doing, whereas a more realistic portrait of something such as family income would require the median statistic.

Public Health and Education Research

Recently, historians such as those of the Annales school have become interested in systematically mining quantitative data from the past in order to overturn long-standing assumptions about human civilization and resist "official history." The Annales approach to history involves using basic units of study such as the family, a farm, or households to extrapolate data and construct a distinct "history from below tradition: it exposes mainstream histories as serving the interests of the ruling classes, and takes the perspective of the oppressed of

indigenous peoples, slaves, native rulers, and other colonial populations—as essential for understanding the truth about empire" (Jani,
2012, p. 68). For example, most early narrative accounts of regular
contraception use date from the eighteenth century. However, historical research of marriage and birth records in Europe show that con-
traceptive use first appeared in wealthier circles in the seventeenth
century, filtering down to the middle classes, with all but the agricultural classes using birth control (Howell & Prevenier, 2001). Howell
and Prevenier also discuss climate records and their connection to the
production of food, which can provide insights into how agriculture
shaped historical trajectories. Similar uses of statistics have been applied to the study of criminality, with surprising results: "In sixteenth-century England there were five to ten times the number of
murders than in the twentieth century, and the sixteenth-century figure was itself only half of the thirteenth" (p. 54). Howell and Prevenier maintain that statistical data in such cases can raise important
historical issues that may not be quantitative in nature, such as the
social context of violence, what constitutes a "murder," and so forth.

Early public health research uncovered connections between poverty and disease, often systematically tracing outbreaks to the most
overcrowded and unsanitary tenements, requiring political as well as
medical solutions (Chadwick, 1843; Taylor & Rieger, 2008). Michaels
and Monforton (2005) describe how a cholera epidemic in 1850s London was stopped by a doctor using a city map to indicate which of the
households had members with the disease. Eventually, the cholera
source was traced to a specific well pump in one of the poorest neighborhoods, which was shut down, averting further deaths. Even today,
the link between income level and proximity to pollutants remain:

> Polluting industries are more frequently located in and around poor com-
> munities and communities of color, a phenomenon known as environmental
> injustice or environmental racism…. [O]ne study found that bad housing
> and poor neighborhood conditions in African American communities in St.
> Louis, Missouri were associated with a 2.5 times increase in the odds of de-
> veloping diabetes. In Anniston, Alabama, there is clear evidence that Mon-
> santo polluted the community with PCBs. (Donohue, 2011, p. 36)

In response, some communities are taking action through the use of quantitative data tracking. Williams (2012b) documents how ordinary citizens in Fukushima have begun keeping track of radiation levels in their towns. They have even created a Citizens' Radioactivity Measuring Statement, complete with equipment needed to test food, water, and soil, and to monitor levels within one's body. Data are posted in public locations such as individual apartment buildings so that people are fully informed. Lewontin and Levins (2007) conclude that public health is an area rich for potential collaboration between physicians and laypeople:

> Public health workers should...explore ways of collaborating with nonprofessional sections of the public, making use of their numbers, detailed knowledge of their own situations, organizing ability, and creativity, rather than treating the public as objects of research, as a passive mass to be reassured or a recalcitrant mass to be cajoled or coerced into particular behaviors. (pp. 211–212)

LeBow is an M.D. who was inspired to go into public health after a stint in the Peace Corps. He soon realized that the United States' medical system wasn't too far removed from that of Third World countries for many Americans. His book *Health Care Meltdown* (2002) is one of the most readable and cogent arguments for universal health care in existence. It is an excellent example of critical empiricist writing in support of public health policy. From the opening pages, LeBow takes aim at the reform efforts of the Clinton administration, which were based on market principles, and he would likely make the same criticism of Obama's recent health insurance mandate:

> Instead of commitment to community and cooperation, the overriding ethic of health care in America has been driven (on the supply side) by self-interest and the pursuit of profit. The American people have been left out of the equation. Even worse, they have been systematically duped and then blamed for being over-utilizers by some of the same special-interest groups that misled them. Americans are told to exercise more "personal responsibility," a code word for shifting costs to the consumer. (p. 4)

As an alternative to the current system, LeBow asserts that true health care reform would involve universal coverage (regardless of gender, national status, preexisting condition, or employment status); expansion of the current Medicare system, which is tax-financed; coverage for all necessary procedures; an emphasis on prevention; and physicians trained in a public health ethos. The only involvement for private insurers would be for specialized procedures.

Chapter by chapter, LeBow takes on existing myths about socialized health care that are propagated by the corporate-owned mass media, presenting solid counterevidence in the form of statistical data to debunk them. The main overarching "alpha myth" of health care is that Americans have the best medical care in the world. Underneath this myth rests an array of falsehoods concerning health care, such as the claims that everyone already has access to care via the emergency room, that the market is the solution for efficiency, that Medicare is in financial trouble, and that socialized care will overburden the already insured. Probably the best debunking comes with the final myth, that incremental change is the only way to achieve universal health coverage. Here, LeBow explains how incrementalism is detrimental to health care:

> The vested interests may have more cynical reasons for encouraging incremental change. They appreciate that such limited tweaking of the system will basically maintain the status quo and thereby assure the present balance of power and profits. The more cynical among them also may be encouraging the incremental path because it gives the appearance of doing something while avoiding the more fundamental questions. (p. 42)

A major strength of LeBow's writing is that he sides with the oppressed, those without health care coverage, and those who are paying extortion-level costs to receive basic care. He is not interested in soothing the fears of the elite. LeBow urges that we need an everybody in, nobody out approach, all or nothing, instead of getting bogged down in resentment politics of who is or isn't eligible for coverage (a concern of those obsessed with, for example, immigrant status):

Health care cannot really be viewed in a vacuum. It interrelates with other social and economic issues, such as poverty, hunger, racism, a living wage, adequate housing, and education. In a larger context, our current dilemma with health care raises the whole issue of whether, as a community, we have some responsibility to care for each other—as opposed to "personal responsibility." (p. 240)

The tone of LeBow's writing is hopeful in that he believes that Americans are already in support of many aspects of universal coverage, and that this support is growing beyond the media and government's ability to control the public. He also asserts that a universal system must maintain patient dignity. Currently, the divisions between Medicaid and Medicare recipients result in stigmatization much the same as those on food stamp assistance receive. A national health care system would remove that stigma because everyone would receive care from the same system.

Another key aspect of public health that is open to dialectical inquiry is the connection between stress and mental health, especially in the post-Fordism era. Fisher (2009) cites the work of Marazzi (1994/2011) and concludes, "if…schizophrenia is the condition that marks the outer edge of capitalism, then bipolar disorder is the mental illness proper to the interior of capitalism" (Fisher, 2009, p. 35). Psychologist Oliver James's (2008, 2009) work on "affluenza" is also critical in tracing the rise of mental illness and stress over the past quarter-century, directly attributing the increases to conditions lived under capitalism. Chilean economist Max-Neef (1991) reconceptualized basic human needs to include subsistence, protection, affection, understanding, participation, idleness, creation, identity, and freedom. He also pinpointed pseudo-satisfiers such as the accumulation of weapons, which on the surface appears to meet the need of protection, but in reality inhibits the other needs of affection, subsistence, and participation. Max-Neef concluded that many of First World countries are impaired in their ability to meet these basic needs, while less wealthy countries do meet these needs. Rather than drawing the conservative conclusion that "money isn't necessary," Max-Neef explains that a certain degree of growth can meet needs to a point—beyond which neoliberalism creates even greater problems.

In *Bright-sided* (2009), Ehrenreich uses a combination of empirical and historical inquiry to trace the origins of the positive thinking movement from metaphysics to the self-help industry, and examines how it has impacted health. Along the lines of Marazzi (1994/2011), Ehrenreich (2009) looks at the post-Ford era and the rise in corporate downsizing and an every-man-for-himself kind of approach to career development:

> Downsizing did not, of course, increase the number of salespeople, but it did increase the number of people who were encouraged to think of themselves as salespeople. In a hazardous new corporate workplace, everyone was encouraged to engage in a continual sales effort, selling him or herself.... [T]he motivation industry could not repair this new reality. All it could do was offer to change how one thought about it, insisting the corporate restructuring was an exhilaratingly progressive change to be embraced. (pp. 114–115)

For Ehrenreich, the sales-oriented, "flexible" economy has been expanded to a strategy for saving markets. In order for capitalism to continue to expand, people have to be talked into buying things they don't want or need, thus the extreme saturation of marketing, including recent e-forms in the blogosphere.

What Ehrenreich finds the most insidious about positive thinking is that it steers attention away from true causes and maintains the status quo at all costs. Most of the motivational speakers and authors Ehrenreich encountered were against social change, and instead called for individual transformation, or, at the very least, changing one's attitude. These authors cited studies about well-being and happiness, but used data in a way that underscored resignation or making peace with the way things are. Ehrenreich concluded that "the big advantage of the American approach to positive thinking has been that people can be counted on to impose it on themselves" (p. 204).

Research into marketing aimed at children—now reaching a global level—can also be a useful area of inquiry for Marxist scholars. Children are viewed as an underutilized resource, a notion boldly expressed in McNeal's (1992) unambiguous *Kids as Customers: A Hand-book of Marketing to Children* and Smith's (1997) *Children's Food: Marketing and Innovation*. As Brody (2010) outlines, even though we have mounting evidence of the ill effects of marketing on children's health, in the United States there are few regulations on companies' use of advertising on children, whereas other countries such as Sweden have stricter controls. According to Brody, between 1999 and 2005, companies increased their spending on children's advertising from $2 billion to $15 billion (p. 12). The Swedish Consumer's Association Factsheet (2001) proposed the following as a way to limit the power of advertisers:

> A European ban on television commercials directed towards children. A common general law within the EU. Legislation in the area shall be horizontal. That is, the same rules shall apply to marketing to children regardless of the medium employed. Greater social resources devoted to increasing awareness and debate about the intense commercial pressure being put on our children today, and its forms and consequences. Increased support to public schools so they can equip pupils with sufficient stimulation and knowledge to defend themselves against all the commercial messages forced upon them daily. Active protection for a vulnerable group. (p. 2)

Because much of the research on the impact of advertising on children involves quantitative gathering of data (Linn, 2005; Schor, 2005; Strasburger, Wilson, & Jordan, 2008), this would be a rich area of research for critical empiricists who want to investigate the effects of consumerism on the most vulnerable citizens.

There are also a few educational researchers who do critical quantitative inquiry, much of it in the form of response to mainstream policy centered on standardized testing. Quantitative researchers with a critical orientation do acknowledge the problems of working with test score data, as St. John (2007) explains:

> Although I do not agree that standardized tests adequately define the nature of basic education rights, as a researcher I can use test scores as measures of achievement, especially if I use them along with equality measures, such as the rates of students passing a grade level or students graduating from high school. (p. 72)

For St. John, the key is identifying and isolating variables tied to equity and rights, which are used to formulate policy alternatives.

The late Gerald Bracey's annual Rotten Apple Awards is a who's who of high-stakes nonsense, using statistics to oppose the stars of the school "reform" movement. He also produced his yearly *Bracey Report* from his Education Disinformation Detection and Reporting Agency website. One of the key strengths of Bracey's writing is that he carried it to the mass audience, rather than confining it to formal educational journals. He was a blogger at the *Huffington Post* and a regular contributor to the nonprofit National Center for Fair and Open Testing (FairTest), as well as an invited writer for the education journal *Phi Delta Kappan*. In his publications, Bracey (2004, 2006, 2009) defends public schools as actually doing better than they are often portrayed, while at the same time pointing out the many flaws of privatization schemes such as charter schools and vouchers. His writing is accessible and of enormous assistance to those attempting to interpret educational statistics and formulate appropriate research questions, whether qualitative or quantitative.

Promising critical quantitative work in education is also emerging from the National Education Policy Center, part of the University of Colorado at Boulder's College of Education. Briggs and Domingue (2011) replicate the statistical analyses used in value-added modeling to find several holes in the approach used for evaluating teachers in Los Angeles. As they explain in the introduction to their study,

> The term "value-added"... is intended to have the same meaning as the term "causal effect," that is, to speak of estimating the value-added by a teacher is to speak of estimating the causal effect of that teacher. But once stripped of the Greek symbols and statistical jargon, what we have left is a remarkably simple model.... It is a model which, in essence, claims that once we take into account five pieces of information about a student, the student's assignment to any teacher in any grade and year can be regarded as occurring at random. If that claim is accurate, the remaining differences can be said to be the value added or subtracted by that particular teacher. (p. 4)

Of course, the value-added model leaves out the all-important factor of classroom assignment, which the model's proponents assert is random and easily accounted for. However, Briggs and Domingue point out that student placement in classrooms is anything but random — look at cases where parents push to have their children placed with specific teachers. Additionally, there are variables that in combination could impact a teacher's effectiveness, such as whether or not students receive speech/language services, the impact of student personalities when in groups, and the teacher's success with individual students.

Darling-Hammond, Holtzman, Gatlin, and Heilig's (2005) systematic empirical study of Teach for America (TFA) participants illustrated how K–12 certification is indeed correlated with better schools. Their research was conducted in response to negative media coverage of teachers that asserted that "new blood" was needed in the profession, and that traditional certification didn't matter. Darling-Hammond et al. found otherwise. Not only do wealthier schools tend to have full certification among faculty, but also their teachers are certified in the same subject areas that they teach. This is not the case with schools serving lower-income populations, where high turnover in the form of substitute teachers and new teachers holding alternative or unrelated certifications proliferate. The study concluded that:

> Over the course of a year, students taught by uncertified TFA teachers could be expected to achieve at levels that are, in grade equivalent terms, one-half month to 3 months lower than students taught by teachers with standard certification. Those taught by other teachers who are uncertified or who hold nonstandard certification generally achieve at levels 0.2 to 1.5 months behind their counterparts taught by standard certified teachers. Students in the most impacted...schools, who have a steady parade of such teachers each year, would generally lose 1 to 2 years of ground in grade equivalent terms between kindergarten and sixth grade, assuming the effects we found for fourth and fifth grades generalize to other grade levels. (pp. 20–21)

Perna (2007) discusses how traditional statistical models used in higher education research have often assumed that factors such as status attainment are powerful predictors of college enrollment patterns and student retention: This "traditional economic perspective assumes that individuals make decisions by weighing the costs against the benefits for all possible alternatives and then selecting the alternative that maximizes utility with respect to individual preferences, tastes, and experiences" (p. 56). However, as Slee's (2006) work critiquing "market choice" illustrates, a key problem facing college students is asymmetry of information. Traditional statistical approaches take as a starting point that all students have an equal amount of preparation for and socialization into higher educational settings.

Kinzie (2007) used discriminant function analysis to examine how women chose science and math career paths. In terms of choosing these fields, differences between boys and girls were already apparent by the eighth grade. Math achievement appears to be one of the key factors influencing a pathway to a science or math career, which means that policy makers should be focusing related educational efforts on children aged 11 to 13 years old. Kinzie also incorporated feminist analysis, which took her research to a more critical level. Rather than simply bemoaning the lack of women in math and science, she speculated as to why the inequities are there to begin with—in other words, what is it about math and science that makes them historically patriarchal fields? Kinzie also framed her results in terms of multiple pathways, suggesting that women don't necessarily follow a linear track to choosing math and science careers, and that there may be additional entry points that educators can capitalize upon. For example, there were differences between the "departers"—those who selected math/science in high school but not in college—and the "joiners"—those who had rejected math/science in high school but chose to major in those subjects in college.

Conclusion

As information resulting from research grows, we can expect that more quantitative scholars will begin to approach their work from criticalist perspectives. This approach creates a fresh way of infusing formerly remote and difficult to decipher methods with social critique. Carspecken (1996) points out that "quantitative methods are not threatened by critical methodology, but the ultimate meaning of such methods would take on a different significance" (p. 40). Instead of rejecting empirical research as incompatible with dialectical materialism, it should be seen as an important ally, as Lesser (2005) urges:

> After all, how can people recognize, analyze, or fight against social inequalities without the tools to identify statistical group differences or patterns? How can people talk about what is unfair without knowing how to calculate the value of a fair share and how much statistical deviation from that might be tolerated as innocuous? How can people produce or interpret depictions of quantitative information without awareness of pitfalls? (p. 2269)

Teachers who have found themselves the target of public attacks concerning their effectiveness cannot afford to shy away from mathematical analysis because it might appear too difficult, theoretical, or off-putting. The more that educators refuse to engage with quantitative language, the more policy makers will misuse that same language to support their own ends, unchallenged.

Like other Marxist scholars, critical empiricists are constantly pushing boundaries, and they often experience a degree of marginalization similar to that of qualitative researchers, who work from the same theoretical perspective. The denial in the government and mass media that greeted the publication of the peer-reviewed *Lancet* surveys (Roberts, Lafta, Garfield, Khudhairi, & Burnham, 2004; Burnham, Lafta, Doocy, & Roberts, 2006) that estimated the casualties of the U.S. invasion of Iraq at close to 1 million illustrates the potential of dialectical research to disturb the status quo. For Baez (2007), critical research in support of equality and justice should not be defined along mere methodological lines:

> Although quantitative research is not often thought of as furthering these goals, there is absolutely no reason why it should not be thought of in such a way. Indeed, one must ask why any research can be said to be otherwise. Why are any researchers relieved of responsibility for the social world that they help create? (p. 22)

Chapter Five

Dialectical Materialist Ethnographers

Overview

This chapter presents examples of dialectical materialist qualitative researchers who use classic ethnographic methods of gathering data. These are methods with rich anthropological and sociological heritages (Walford, 2008a). As with Chapter Four, the purpose of this chapter is to introduce readers to possibly unfamiliar faces (or reintroduce readers to familiar ones)—those who use Marxist principles to engage in research that sides with the oppressed rather than collaborating with the oppressor. Although some of the ethnographers discussed here do not directly identify themselves as Marxist, their work features the six qualities of Marxist research presented in Chapter Three. Contemporary ethnographers fit into five general types: native (research conducted in familiar settings); urban (work in cities); multisited/global (examining how people from different places are tied together by similar experiences); critical; and applied (Buch & Staller, 2007). Additions to this list would include arts-based (performance, visual sociology, ethnographic fiction, ethno-poetry) and virtual ethnographic spaces (chat rooms, social media, blogs) (Denzin, 2009). Often, ethnographers blend different subgenres in terms of methodology.

As a methodology, ethnography can refer to a wide range of data gathering methods (interviews, observations, artifacts, census information) that are largely qualitative in nature (Creswell, 2007; Patton, 2002). Features of ethnographic work include full participation in the research site (participants are fully aware of the researcher's role and presence); fieldwork as the primary means of data collection (participant observation and documentation through field notes, memos, and transcripts); culture as the focus, along with understanding cultural norms according to participant definitions and experiences; and publicization of research in order to translate data into a cohesive narrative account (Walford, 2008a).

According to Beach (2008), ethnographic research in the critical tradition includes eight characteristics. First, such research is steeped in criticalist theory in that data are interpreted in light of dialectical materialism. Second, though theory is important, critical ethnography isn't just about applying a particular theory to a situation. Instead, theory is used to expand understanding of how people's experiences are mediated by a range of ideologies. Third, individuals' lives are analyzed in terms of examining how to change lives. Fourth, context is essential, and it has to be understood as being in a constant state of change. Fifth, critical ethnography involves symbolic production, and isn't just a reflection of the world as it appears. Sixth, the best critical ethnographies show "the relations of indeterminacy as the autonomy of culture within larger processes of social reproduction" (p. 171). Seventh, everyday social practices are described in such a way that they are tied to larger contexts. Eighth, the goal of critical ethnography is more than recognition of common experiences; it should enable people to make sense of their own experiences through deconstruction.

As Beach (2008) explains,

> Theoretically informed critical ethnographic representations build upon a dialectic between ethnographic data and thinking about this data in evocative, imaginative, and transformational ways, in order to provide important new questions for (new) life projects and important new answers to existing life questions as a catalyst for re-examination of the (hegemonically) accepted parameters of common culture. (p. 172)

Dialectical ethnographers examine the existing status quo in order to investigate how it is naturalized and internalized in groups and individuals, as well as how it is resisted in subtle and overt ways. This chapter presents excerpts of the writings of two ethnographic historians, Studs Terkel and Angie Debo, which are followed by summaries of the scholarship of three ethnographers who make the working class the center of their inquiry: Joe Bageant, Staughton Lynd, and Karen Ho. Two educational ethnographers are presented next, Jean Anyon and Pauline Lipman, followed by the autoethnographers Adrienne Rich and Roxanne Dunbar-Ortiz. Finally, a brief discussion of alternative arts-based ethnographic scholarship is outlined. This is by no means an exhaustive list of all of the critical ethnographers past and present, but it is hoped that this chapter will serve as an introduction to the variety and integrity of the work, as sound examples of dialectical materialist inquiry in the qualitative tradition.

Historical Ethnographic Researchers

In his long life, Studs Terkel produced much in the way of authentic populist research, the best being *Working: People Talk About What They Do All Day and How They Feel About What They Do* (2004) and *Hard Times: An Oral History of the Great Depression* (2000). Encountering these texts, the reader is struck by how Terkel's method is simple yet complicated at the same time—it comes down to his being a superior conversationalist and listener with a keen sense of humor. In *Working* (2004), Terkel organizes his study of laborers by the most evocative of categories: the concrete nature of the work itself. With section titles such as "A Pecking Order" (profiling an airline stewardess, model, executive secretary, prostitute), "Cleaning Up" (garbage man, janitor, washroom attendant), and "Watching" (policeman, doorman, film critic), Terkel goes beyond job titles alone to create interesting analytical combinations based on the essence of particular forms of work, highlighting what jobs have in common though they do not originate from the same type of labor.

Each of the sections introduces a person by name, and creates an in-depth portrait of background and on-the-job insights. Every occupation one can think of is included, from housewife to bank teller; Terkel also talked with retirees to obtain retrospectives on a lifetime of work. Each and every interview excerpt is lively and full of rich description, such as this interview of a receptionist expressing a mixture of alienation and devaluation:

> The machine dictates. This crummy little machine with buttons on it—you've got to be there to answer it. You can walk away from it and pretend you don't hear it, but it pulls you. You know you're not doing anything, not doing a hell of a lot for anyone. Your job doesn't mean anything. Because

you're just a little machine. A monkey could do what I do. It's really unfair to ask someone to do that. (pp. 30–31)

In another section, Terkel talks with Roberta, a sex worker since age 15, who provides several biting insights about how not much separates women of different strata when it comes to relations with men:

> A hustler is any woman in American society. I was the kind of hustler who received money for favors granted rather than the type of hustler who signs a lifetime contract for her trick. Or the kind of hustler who carefully reads women's magazines and learns what is proper to give for each date, depending on how much money her date or trick spends on her. (p. 57)

Roberta's testimony illustrates how capitalism intersects with patriarchy and infuses language and culture. She comments that she was already trained to turn tricks even before she started sex work, because the culture around her always spoke of interactions between males and females as involving money and favors. To mentally survive her profession, it was important to keep a distance between herself and her clients—to "fake it"—as a way to maintain a shred of control and self-respect. No genuine emotions should be shown under any circumstances.

As the reader moves back and forth between the highly diverse accounts, several similarities appear. The disassociation that Roberta describes is also mentioned by several other interviewees, though they are all talking about different situations. Deception also plays an important functional role. The notion of hustling is part of various accounts, some of which even use that specific term. One finds similar content in the interviews of the receptionist and a spot welder: accounts of letting one's mind wander as a way to cope with the monotony of the day. Suspicion is part of many of the jobs, seen in the auditor who relates being feared by people, even though the kind of work he does is more concerned with large-scale fraud. Moments of compassion shine through, as grocery cashiers allow shoplifters to save face. Even though some aren't as forthright as the blue-collar workers, those with more autonomy on the job echo these commonalities of experience, as with this commercial writer/producer:

> I don't think what I do is necessary or that it performs a service. If it's a very fine product—and I've worked on some of those—I love it. It's when you get into that awful area of hope, cosmetics—you're just selling an image and a hope.... It's a crock of shit! I know it's part of my job, I do it. (p. 72)

All of the workers in Terkel's book have to grapple physically and psychologically with wage labor in some way, shape, or form, or with its aftermath during retirement. One is struck by the sense of solidarity not just between the workers profiled, but also between them and the readers as the ethnographic accounts are presented.

Terkel's journalistic prose shines through in *Hard Times* (2000) as he combines personal insight with an oral history of people from a variety of backgrounds who experienced the Great Depression. Originally published in the early 1970s, the book's re-release during the tech bubble was prescient and possibly prophetic, considering the economic crisis of 2008. As with *Working*, *Hard Times* is organized into books, or sections, with each one titled in a vernacular manner to capture the essence of analysis. Each of the sections features accounts from participants such as manual laborers, hobos, and even wealthy individuals.

The sheer uncertainty and the unjustified feelings of failure on the part of the suddenly unemployed jumps out at you. Participant accounts also help to explain the enduring mythology built up around World War II as "the good war":

> I'd rather be in the army now than outside, where I was so raggedy and didn't have no jobs. I was glad to put on a United States Army uniform and get some food. I didn't care about the rifle what scared me. In the army, I wasn't gettin' killed on a train, I wasn't gonna starve. I felt proud to salute and look around and see all the good soldiers of the United States. I was a good soldier and got five battle stars. I'd rather be in the army now than see another depression. (p. 43)

Several sections of *Hard Times* present similar participant accounts that position military service as part of Roosevelt's New Deal recovery package.

The Great Depression is also presented as contrasting narratives between generations, as in the chapter "Man and Boy." Terkel opens with an interview excerpt from Alonso, who is 20. Alonso remarks: "All I know about the Depression is what I studied about it. People suffered and had to carry out food stamps. My parents mentioned it vaguely. I could get no information from them" (p. 82). Clifford, who is 68, has a far more nuanced and descriptive view of his experiences during the Depression: "The Negro was born in depression. It didn't mean too much to him. The Great American Depression as you call it. There was no such thing. The best he could be is a janitor or shoe-shine boy. It only became official when it hit the white man" (p. 82). The reader is struck by the lack of dialectical connection in Alonso's comment, especially the sentence, "All I know about the Depression is what I studied about it," which was probably, at best, a few isolated historical dates and events. Clifford, however, deconstructs the historical meme of the Great Depression by removing many of its key narratives, particularly that of sudden poverty, to point out that African Americans were already living under deprived social conditions prior to the economic crisis.

Tensions between historical and contemporary union organizing are brought forth in the chapter "Bonnie Laboring Boy," where a printer notes the loss of solidarity and radicalism that unions of the past once had:

> The union man today knows absolutely nothing about the struggles. They don't want to upset the wonderful apple cart they have. We used to sing, in the organizing days of the CIO, "Solidarity Forever." The Communists were active in it. Hell, we'd even sing the "Internationale" on occasion. Could I get a young printer today, who drives a big Buick, who has a home in the suburbs—could I get him to sing, "Arise ye prisoners of starvation"?... Here I am, a printer who makes $200 a week. It sounds silly as I chant, "I want freedom now." I know it's theirs I'm asking for, and, in a way it's mine. But it does sound silly, as I say it. (p. 116)

The same printer goes on to explain how his father, an anticommunist, shifted his allegiance from Bob La Follette, a supporter of workman's compensation, to Father Coughlin, a fascist radio personality whom he followed for the rest of his life. This pairing of memories regarding union organizing juxtaposed with propaganda of the period adds a further dimension to comprehending the United States in the 1930s.

The scholarship of Angie Debo illustrates the struggle to achieve some degree of recognition as a woman in a relatively hostile academic world. Often working with meager funds and no personal and academic support, Debo managed to conduct ethnographic and historical field work in support of the rights of indigenous people. At an early age, Debo was influenced by Catherine Barnard, an outspoken activist against child labor and poverty whose efforts also extended to labor rights and protections for all workers. Barnard was elected to lead the Office of Charities and Corrections in Oklahoma, yet she had the smallest office, in a remote part of the building near the men's room, and she was also the lowest paid of all state officials (Leckie, 2000). Later, Debo would experience the same kind of treatment, from her search for a tenured faculty position (which never came) to struggles to maintain the integrity of her work despite censorship by publishers. Only later, with the establishment of women's studies programs on campuses, was her work rediscovered by feminist researchers and indigenous studies programs. By then, she was in her eighties.

Like Deloria (1988), Debo viewed the treatment of Native Americans as an imperialist project and felt that it should be considered the first foreign military engagements in United States history. Unlike most historians writing about Native American history, Debo incorporated ethnographic and oral history data collection with living people into her writing. She also insisted on teaching her college courses at the University of Oklahoma from the indigenous perspective:

> The course, The United States and its Original Inhabitants: An Indian Interpretation, was entirely Angie's. However, her syllabus informed students that the class would be taught from the Indian point of view. This would

apply to the geographical setting, Debo noted. For example, Lewis and Clark did not go out from St. Louis and encounter the Indians, but the Indians saw the explorers coming up from the Missouri River to them. The same, she added, will apply to intangibles; events and policies will not be traced from above, but from the inside looking out. (Leckie, 2000, p. 149)

Debo expanded her studies during an extended stay in Mexico. There she noticed powerful similarities between the Mexicans and native peoples in the United States, and noted how the U.S. government maintained low wages by using Mexican labor.

Two of Debo's works are worth discussing here. The first, *And Still the Waters Run* (1991), outlines the functioning of empire in the form of the second displacement of the Five Civilized Tribes by white settlers in 1890s Oklahoma, prior to statehood and the granting of citizenship to Native Americans. As Debo (1991) outlines, the military conquest of native lands was only part of the imperial project, with economic exploitation a sure second event. Prior to the land grab at the turn of the twentieth century, the Five Tribes were self-governing and held property communally in the aftermath of their relocation during the Trail of Tears. For Debo, the land grab was an intense and remarkable rapid event that required documentation, if for no other reason than its sheer criminality: "Obviously the rapidity of the spoliation called for crude methods, in many cases even criminal methods, and the immense value of the loot exerted a powerful influence upon contemporary opinion and standards of conduct" (p. x).

Debo ties the dislocation of Native Americans since the appearance of the first white colonists, and eventually the western settlers, to capitalist growth. Aided by missionaries, encroachment on native-held lands backed up by government treaties continued unabated. Debo details the legal struggles of the Five Tribes to remain sovereign, to no avail. Eventually, white politicians were allowed, through recently passed laws, to appoint supervisors, which they did, from an array of those friendly to land speculation. This emboldened a figure known as "the grafter," who dealt in Native American land by inserting himself into the allotment process:

Enterprising scouts went into the full-blood settlements, gathered up the Indians, loaded them on trains and brought them in, and sold them to the highest bidder among the real estate dealers, at 10, 35, or even 30 dollars a head. The purchaser then coached his Indians to choose as their surplus the land to which he claimed some sort of possessory title, and secured a lease that was a virtual gift; and the allottee returned to his distant mountain home, content to be relieved of all responsibility for his new possessions. (pp. 95–96)

Lumber companies often joined in this process, purchasing timber at rock-bottom prices and leaving Native Americans with a stripped and worthless plot of land. Grafters also become involved in going after the assets of Native American children by appointing guardians who could then gain access to their land.

The allotment process had an important ideological function, which was to relieve whites of guilt over how they treated indigenous populations. Debo relates how popular opinion centered on the Indian getting more than his fair share, and that he should be content with his allotment. However, not only did native people grieve for the loss of communally held lands and institutions, they also found that the allotment process was a rip-off:

The allotment period brought financial loss to all classes of Indian citizens. The wealthy were reduced to the common level through the loss of their excess holdings. The poorer citizens found the expenses incident to the selection of their allotments a severe strain on their slender resources. Those who were forced to move because their homes had been included in townsite or timber segregations found themselves with raw land on their hands and no means to improve it. With the settlement of the country and the more efficient development of agriculture, their free range was gone and their livestock lost or stolen. (p. 127)

Those who resisted the allotment process faced the most dire conditions—uncertainty prevailed because their homes and property could be seized at any given time.

After Oklahoma was granted statehood in 1907, land speculation intensified. Those who owned allotments were wined and dined in an effort to secure their deeds. Additional legal challenges led to further federal intervention to investigate some of the more outrageous cases of fraud. Eventually, though, Native groups soon found themselves outnumbered by whites, and the process of assimilation had begun. However, the arrival of oil drilling soon brought another wave of speculation and attempts to influence government agencies to work on the oil companies' behalf. Further impoverishment of Native peoples was the inevitable result, and this led to another cycle of government intervention during the Roosevelt administration, which is where Debo's book comes to a close.

In *Prairie City* (1998), Debo creates a historical ethnography based on several small towns in Oklahoma from the land run to the 1940s, looking deeply at white settler culture. It was one of her most controversial works because she didn't hesitate to name names, though publishers were reluctant to include them. Debo captures the arrogance of the white settlers in small Oklahoma towns who thought of themselves as self-made from the get-go:

> Never for a minute did the settlers feel that in giving them a farm the Government was bestowing a bounty upon them. They felt rather that they were conferring a benefit upon their country by establishing a new commonwealth. And as soon as they had attended to the most elemental requirements of shelter and subsistence, they entered with zest into the creation of political institutions. (p. 12)

Indeed, the settlers of prestatehood Oklahoma were assisted by numerous government interventions, from monies to establish public schools to taxpayer-funded roads and bridges, not to mention the appropriated lands of Native Americans to give them their "fresh start."

Debo chronicles the cultural practices of Prairie City, and a portrait emerges of a restless, lively, and somewhat tawdry sort of place. This was contrasted by a strong religious presence, which was probably sustained by a certain degree of lawlessness to give it meaning. The opening of the Cherokee Strip, a stretch of land near Prairie City, brought a land rush and accompanying frenzy:

> Some of the riders reported grimmer experiences. One found the body of a man lying in a hollow; his throat had been slit and his skull crushed in. Another had met a man who appeared demented, wandering around in a circle and asking helplessly, "Where can I stake a claim? I want to get a home."

> Two others had found a man groaning with a broken leg; his wrecked wag-
> on lay in a ditch, and his team had kicked itself loose and run away. (p. 48)

The homestead law put a deadline of 6 months on settlers to set up their residences. It wasn't long before a saloon was built, and it became a popular feature in the area and a center of political campaigning.

The 1890s brought several setbacks to the town, including drought, a drop in wheat prices, and low crop yields. Debo tracks the economic impact of these events on Prairie City and how those who were forced to move away made room for newcomers on the scene, including the railroads:

> A right of way agent arrived in May, a breezy Kansan full of talk and opti-
> mism. He bought most of the land without difficulty; nobody wanted the
> track to cut across his farm, but all were too eager for the road to interpose
> serious objections. All, that is, except George Hadley, who stood out alone
> against the corporate enemy. "They ain't no damned railroad goin' to cross
> my land," he shouted. "I've got a patent from the United States Gove'ment,
> and I'd like to see anybody take it away." It was necessary to serve papers
> and institute condemnation proceedings. (p. 96)

With the economic expansion and growth following the arrival of the railroad, a variety of political perspectives became available to citizens, including the Socialist Party, which was growing in popularity. Debo mentions the influence of socialist ideas, disseminated through newspapers and political speeches that emphasized the exploitation of workers at the expense of elites. At the same time, during World War I the Ku Klux Klan experienced a growth in membership in reaction to a combination of factors: job shortages, wage devaluation by leveraging racism, anti-Catholicism, German immigration, and Prohibition. The slogan "One hundred percent American" permeated Prairie City throughout the Great Depression. Prairie City was not without its creative ways of surviving the Depression by generating revenue, as Debo describes:

> The "Beer for Oklahoma League" ran fillers in the News before the people
> voted on the measure in the summer of '33. The arguments were very prac-

tical and statistical. In territorial days eight main Oklahoma counties had drunk 147,600 barrels of beer annually, with the saloons open only six days a week. That was 22 gallons per capita. Now in a seven-day week at drug stores, grocery stores, filing stations, and restaurants they would drink at least 44 gallons. Multiplying the population of Oklahoma by 44, with the tax of $2.50 a barrel, that would bring ten and a quarter million dollars in revenue to the state. (p. 225)

Though the churches were opposed to the proposal, beer won out, albeit at the still-remaining alcohol content level of 3.2%. Unfortunately, the prosperity that beer proponents promised was as disappointing as what followed after casino construction, for several reasons. First, the town took a while to warm up to drinking beer after a decade or so of Prohibition propaganda. Second, bootlegging continued until the end of Prohibition, with harder liquor being more popular than beer in some circles. Finally, the revenue only amounted to one tenth the expected monies.

Debo closes her book by carrying Prairie City through World War II and deepening uncertainty. She notes the waning impact of agriculture and the fact that several residents had already lost their homes during the Depression. The railroad and oil boom expansions were long gone, and many people, including World War II veterans, had relocated to cities to find work and postwar prosperity. Instead of seeing just the loss, Debo speculates on an alternative future for Prairie City and other similar locales: "Why not a new village of farmers, citizens of the world through schools and radio and space-consuming transportation, grouped together in friendly sociability, building directly upon the soil?...As for me, I live in a small town, where I am willing to continue, lest it grow smaller" (p. 245).

Ethnographers of the Poor and Working Class

In *Deer Hunting with Jesus* (2007), Bageant dissects the many ideologies that inform poor whites' mind sets. He carefully describes how a combination of corporate mass media and small town hierarchical fiefdoms work in concert to keep this segment of the working class in check:

Members of the business class, that legion of little Rotary Club spark plugs, are vital to the American corporate and political machine. They are where the institutionalized rip-off of working-class people by the rich corporations finds its footing at the grassroots level, where they can stymie any increase in the minimum wage or snuff out anything remotely resembling a fair tax structure. Serving on every local governmental body, this mob of Kiwanis and Rotarians has connections. It can get that hundred acres rezoned for Wal-Mart or a sewer line to that 2,000-unit housing development at taxpayer expense. (p. 45)

Bageant asserts that despite the centering of the system around larger corporate interests, smaller businesses and many low-income workers support this right-wing agenda because they desire to achieve the kind of power to be able to do the same thing someday. It is false consciousness writ large.

One of the best chapters in *Deer Hunting with Jesus* uses the process of purchasing a trailer home as a case study of the lack of affordable housing and of how people easily get into debt that they cannot escape from. Tommy Ray wants to secure a loan for a $79,000 mobile home from Mike Molden, who recounts the story to Bageant, "He's got a buck fifty for a down payment. And he comes into my office, jams his fingers in his belt loops and says: 'whatever it takes'" (p. 100). Bageant explains how Tommy approached Mike with seven credit cards as part of his "plan," thinking that would increase his credit score, but Mike saw the number of cards as "seven opportunities to screw up" (p. 105). Tommy is given a loan, but one that will never be paid off (the $79,000 magically turned into $130,000 after added fees and expenses). Bageant explains:

The trailer is worth practically zilch the day it is sold and the owner has to pay for space to park it. This is the polar opposite of equity lending. In fact, legally speaking, the mobile home owner is living in a vehicle and paying for a parking space, which is why trailers are titled like cars and have no deed. (p. 106)

Bageant compares the "benefits" of owning a trailer, renting an apartment, and buying a home, and in none of the scenarios would Tommy come out ahead. Even if Tommy had enough money to scrape together to buy a traditional house in his price range, he would be a glorified renter of a house that is depreciating in value; most likely he would be eligible for only an interest-only loan. The only difference Bageant sees between Tommy's apparently foolish decision and the purchasing decisions of McMansion buyers is that McMansion buyers can absorb the loss somewhat, whereas Tommy's strata will be economically devastated.

As he punctuates his descriptions with humor and regional dialect, Bageant's writing maintains an immense sense of compassion and empathy, rather than disdain and lecturing. He starts with where people are at, while at the same time connecting personal accounts with larger social issues:

> Still, Tommy is a guy who often cannot get 40 hours' work at a living wage and has to scramble for a nickel more an hour, then kid himself that opportunity is knocking at his door. I know these things because he is a relative of mine. And like many others in my family, he was taught by his experience in American society that he is not worthy of a traditional house or decent treatment in the labor market or a living wage. (p. 115)

Bageant delves deeper into poor white history with his *Rainbow Pie, A Redneck Memoir* (2010). The book's title refers to the promotion of city life as a form of rainbow pie, with dreams and hopes, to entice low-income country folks to relocate to urban areas for work. Bageant traces the migration into the cities of Southern whites from rural homesteads during the 1950s, using oral histories of his family members who hail from Over Home, in Morgan County, West Virginia. In constructing this history, Bageant aims to describe the moment of transformation of many poor whites into supporters of ultraconservative reactionary politicians. As he explains in the opening paragraph, "The United States has always maintained a white underclass— citizens whose role in the greater scheme of things has been to cushion national economic shocks through the disposability of their labor, with occasional time off to serve as bullet magnets in defense of the Empire" (p. 1). Bageant finds that few academics are willing to address the unique location of low-income whites, or that they—much like the low-income whites themselves—subsume poor white identity into the "middle class." This is due in part, he asserts, to theories of white privilege, or the confusion about how whites can be economically disadvantaged as a group. Yet, Bageant also spares his people no criticism as he points out how racism has kept low-income whites in a marginalized position. For example, many working-class whites supported the poll tax and literacy tests (creations of white elites) to prevent African Americans from voting. As a result of this racist support, many whites ended up disqualifying themselves from voting as low education and income levels came to bear when it came time to head to the polls.

The mass migration of low-income whites to urban areas was a tremendous endeavor. Bageant cites 1940s statistics with 44% of Americans living in rural settings; by the 1970s, that figure had dropped to 5% (p. 5). Because the rainbow pie never materialized for the majority of the 22 million out-migrants, they essentially became part of the permanent white underclass that exists today (p. 5). This runs counter to historical images of the postwar housing boom brought about by automotive culture and suburbanization that we often see in nostalgic documentaries. As one of Bageant's interviewees, Ernie, a World War II veteran, remarked after being shown an old brochure promising progress, "I wish somebody had told me; I would have waved at the prosperity as it went by" (p. 6).

Bageant explores the history of the Scotch-Irish in the United States throughout the book. Self-reliance and independence were hallmarks of the Scotch-Irish and German immigrant cultures, which Bageant saw in his mother's constant hard work at domestic chores and odd jobs. He observes:

> These politics are still part of conservative political culture in heartland America. They can be seen in the rejection of any government role in such things as nutrition programs and aid to single mothers, and the claim that community and religious organizations can do the job better than what they refer to as "government giveaway programs." Unfortunately, though, when they put this belief and their own money into practice, history shows that they tend to take care only of their own kind—white Protestants. (p. 46)

What Bageant finds ironic is that the frugality and thrift that are part of the Scotch-Irish legacy are repellent to most of the capitalist politicians today who call themselves "conservative." For example, banks were instrumental in convincing struggling sustenance farmers to sell low and move to the cities for better work and more money. These same banks were all too happy to loan money to rural out-migrants for washing machines, cars, and other "necessities" of urban life, which built a dependency through debt, breaking the cultural value of frugality once and for all.

The fundamentalist church, while contributing to the oppression of the white working class, still provides a sense of community. Rather than blaming religion, Bageant points to our system's refusal to commit to the notion of education as a human right, placing college beyond the reach of many families. This leaves them vulnerable to groups all too willing to step in and provide answers. In one of the most powerful chapters of the book, "The Sediment of Memory," Bageant opens by recounting a recent conversation with his elderly parents. He found that his memories of the family's transition from the country to the city were very different than those of his mom and dad, who merely remarked, "Them were good years... this country's been good to us" (p. 257). Bageant's reaction:

> I was stunned in disbelief. All the times he'd been screwed on car loans and mortgages, cheated at jobs, the 173,000 hours of his life he'd worked at below-minimum-wage salaries, the loss of his small trucking company, the fact that only one of his three children ever graduated from high school, that two of his three children had fathered babies out of wedlock, the emotional collapse of his wife, the piles of medical bills that smothered him most of his working life, the moving from one rental to another every time the rent went up as little as five bucks, the fact that he never had a vacation in his life, and that he had to suffer massive heart attacks to finally get some leisure time.... (p. 257)

After these conflicting memories resulted in a brief argument with his father, Bageant realized that his parents' memories were shaped by postwar mythology, and sustained by icons of religious symbolism decorating the house. He connects his parents' whitewashing of their family history to America's national project of forgetting, as a result of capitalism and nationalism.

Bageant pulls no punches in his final reflections on what it will take to turn things around. Without collective solutions steeped in historical context, even personal, heroic acts of survival are relatively meaningless:

> We may possibly yet enjoy dignity. If we do, it will only have come through unity and solidarity. Because dignity must be social reality before it can be a personal one. A secretly self-nursed sense of personal dignity in the face of insult and oppression makes for good movies, but in the real world it is like a diamond set in lead. The nonmanifested dignity of a man in jail or an elderly woman eating cat food may be spiritually noble, but it also means that the bastards have won. (pp. 222–223)

The mixture of sadness and resignation combines with a lingering fighting spirit to make Bageant's writing among the best of the contemporary working-class ethnographers.

Staughton Lynd's *Lucasville* (2009) is the account of a 1993 prison rebellion that resulted in the deaths of nine prisoners and one correctional officer, all killed by prisoners at the Ohio facility. Lynd and his wife served as legal researchers for five of the prisoners, all of whom ended up with death sentences. Under extraordinary conditions they recorded extensive interview testimony, gathered court transcripts, obtained transcripts of tapes during the uprising, and presented media reports to weave together a portrait of a legal system that is stacked against those without money and those who choose not to testify for the prosecution in exchange for lighter sentences. Readers with little knowledge of the justice system will still find this study easy to follow and approachable.

Lynd's writing will knock you off your feet. From the opening of the book, which describes the mostly white community of Lucasville that supports the super max/death penalty concept of incarceration, to the portrayal of the prison population, split 50/50 between white and black prisoners, most of whom belong to separatist organizations (resulting in racial tensions) and the book's conclusion and call for amnesty, the reader is thoroughly engaged. This is not a neutral ethnographic account. Lynd presents a convincing case that the five prisoners were not guilty of murder; in fact, there was no physical evidence other than testimony by inmates who sided with the prosecution in order to receive lighter sentences. He details several separate corroborating accounts from inmates and guards to show that there was no way that any of the five sentenced were present during the murders. The prisoner whom Lynd believed to have been guilty of killing the correctional officer had cooperated with the prosecution and was untouchable. Lynd uses the example of the aftermath of the Attica uprising and the amnesty that was granted due to prosecutorial misconduct to assert that the same should be done for those at Lucasville.

Despite the desperation portrayed in the book—the backgrounds of the Lucasville Five are quite revealing of the dynamics of race and class tied to the systemic injustices of incarceration—Lynd also demonstrates how solidarity can work under the most dire circumstances. After the uprising began and hostages were taken, electricity and water were shut off. This led to the formation of a committee to create a list of immediate and future demands along the lines of basic prisoner rights. What was remarkable was that the committee—led by the Lucasville Five—was a mixture of black and white separatists who put aside their hostilities in order to work together. Lynd blows the myth of the inherent racism of poor whites out of the water by showing the evolution of the white prisoners' attitudes on race. Many of them, on arriving at the prison and suddenly faced with a large black population and guards who did not intervene in altercations, joined the Aryan group thinking that was a solution for protection. Later, they began to realize otherwise, as one prisoner's account demonstrates:

> It's the WHITE police, administrators, and nurses who treat me like a "nigger"; treat all of us like that. It is so frustrating to live under such an intense, voiceless oppression; to be picked on just because I'm an inmate; to be pushed and harassed, physically, while I'm in full restraints, and to be antagonized nonstop. (p. 151)

One of the most harrowing parts of the book for those who do not have more than a cursory working knowledge of the criminal justice system is Lynd's description of the jury selection process. He includes transcripts of the voir dire process to illustrate how those who are opposed to the death penalty are systematically excluded, while those who express an openness to the death penalty—or even an enthusiastic support of it—are simply asked a follow-up question about being open to other forms of sentencing, and are retained if they answer in the affirmative. This results in juries with limited representation from those opposed to the death penalty, which many prosecutors who work within more reactionary communities support in order to keep the public satisfied and maintain their positions What is ultimately eye-opening is that the attitudes of the prosecution and the public seem to be that the presumption of guilt doesn't matter—the "they would have done it anyway if they could have because they are prisoners" line of thinking. Lynd concludes that the decision by the prison to clamp down even further in the aftermath of the uprising is an unstable and rash response that is only likely to result in more casualties—as Lynd was compiling the research for *Lucasville*, three prisoners committed suicide.

Ho (2009) takes a different approach, researching the privileged end of the working-class spectrum. Her remarkable ethnography of Wall Street, *Liquidated*, investigates a central question in the wake of the economic crisis that began in 2007: Why do liquidity, job insecurity, and layoffs happen when corporate profits are at an all-time high? In preparing her research proposal, Ho found that when boom/bust cycles were addressed in the media, usually they were attributed to an amorphous, mysterious "market force," with no attempt to specifically identify economic and cultural factors that create and sustain what we view as capitalism. The participants in her study—investment bankers on Wall Street—echoed "the market" with their own attitudes toward constant layoffs and bailouts. As they described their own experiences, they fused them with the language of the market, making it challenging for Ho to keep them separate. Additionally, Ho discovered that investment bankers "have themselves been

subjected to the revolving-door model of employment that they rec-
ommend for other workers" (pp. 17–18). Yet, the relatively privileged
backgrounds of the participants made their own experiences with being laid off very different than the experiences of most workers who
find themselves in the same situation—they just couldn't see it as different.

Ho gained access to participants by working for 6 months as an
investment banker before her entire department was laid off. Her
own background as a graduate student from Princeton—one of the
key recruiting pipelines to Wall Street—enabled her to easily approach gatekeepers. Her research was not covert—everyone knew
about what she was studying, and she did not experience any resistance from participants, who were forthright and unguarded. In
presenting the environment of the study, Ho describes the hierarchies
and structures, from how offices are arranged (i.e., the back office has
the less prominent employees, such as secretarial support, and the
front office is where everyone aspires to work) to promotional levels
(from analysts, who make $50,000 a year plus bonuses, to associates
making $90,000–180,000, to managing directors, a position that few
analysts will ever reach). Ho likens the structure of bank offices to a
white-collar sweatshop where even the sparse furnishings and cubi-
cles suggest a lack of permanence.

Using a discourse of "smartness," analysts are heavily recruited
right out of college, and there are ready supplies of those eager to
make it on Wall Street. They are willing to work for what is essentially minimum wage because they receive enough perks to keep them
loyal. For example, some of the banks provide analysts with meals
and transportation home via cab or limo for pulling late nights at the
office (most analysts work 100 hours per week). The promise of future
bonuses and promotions keeps them on the treadmill. Ho found that
many of the participants combine complaining and bragging about
the long hours, recounting not bathing for 3 days, skipping meals, etc.
This shapes their attitudes toward the "regular" workforce:

> It is extremely common for investment bankers to interpret their own expe-
> rience of overwork as a sign that they know how to "get things done," as

proof of their "smartness," in contradistinction to the masses of complacent, less capable workers out in "the real world" who therefore need to be restructured to more efficient use. (p. 104)

This form of false consciousness makes Wall Street analysts forget they are part of the waged working class, so much so that they see working 9 to 5 as "slacking."

The embodied meritocracy Ho found on Wall Street is often contrasted with corporate governance structures that are labeled "old fashioned." Analysts view themselves as cutting edge and revolutionary, using market populist language that Frank (2001) describes in *One Market Under God*. One of the key ways that participants frame the contradictions of Wall Street capitalism is by asserting the primacy of "shareholder value." Instead of growth and productivity being major goals, shareholders are the focus. Even though some participants are sympathetic to the impact of downsizing, they still assert shareholder value as fact, with no necessary contradictions to explore. Many of the participants speak in positive terms about the shareholder takeover movement in the 1980s and the birth of corporate raiding, though they leave out the government's involvement in facilitating that movement. They feel it was a necessary step to shake up the stagnant corporate model built around workforce development and traditional investments:

> The concept of disciplining through debt was popularized and widely accepted by the business community in the 1980s. What was rendered invisible by this discourse was that this debt was a mechanism through which corporate wealth was transferred from the multiple stakeholders of a corporation to a small number of owners. (Ho, 2009, p. 146)

In this sense, a handful of shareholders are the company and the banks work for the shareholders.

Ho found that by using market discourse, participants were not able to comprehend larger forces involved in shaping the economy, participating in their own exploitation, and perpetuating economic crises on a larger scale. Instead, participants saw the naturalized market as setting the tone, rather than as a socially created institution sustained by elites. When things go south, as they often do on Wall Street, the banking industry and its employees can rely on the marshaling of government funds to bail them out. Yet, Ho describes how the participants were not empathetic to what average workers experience as a result of what Wall Street does. Ultimately, workers on Wall Street have a mentality not that different from Las Vegas gamblers:

> My Wall Street informants and friends often described their job strategies as holding on as long as they can before the axes fall: Do as many deals and get as much experience with transactions as possible while the stock market is rising and deals are much easier to sell to corporations. (p. 288)

This attitude explains in part why capitalism, though bruised, somewhat ideologically speaking, suffered little in the wake of the 2008 housing bubble. Instead, the corporate sector and banking have used a narrow window of opportunity to double down on the working class in the form of debt talk, social cuts, foreclosures. and the like, while they have political support from neoliberal and neoconservative politicians.

Educational Ethnographers

Educational ethnography has grown beyond traditional contexts of the classroom, building, or district to include virtual, adult, and informal learning settings (Walford, 2008a). Currently, educational ethnographers reach into a variety of settings—the kindergarten classroom, the day care center, military bases, and college dorms. These settings often involve pedagogical interactions, as information is transmitted through teaching and learning. Because schools are situated within a larger context of social institutions and norms, contemporary educational ethnographies seek to go beyond the classroom into other settings. This is well illustrated by the fine longitudinal documentary *7 Up*, which has revisited the same group of children every 7 years, beginning with film segments and interviews in their elementary and middle schools.

The use of ethnography applied to educational settings was a later development, emerging from the fields of anthropology and sociology. In the United States, educational ethnographies tended to be conducted in anthropology departments, whereas in the U.K., such research was done by sociology and education departments. Another difference was a greater focus in the U.S. on ethnic minorities, with the U.K. specializing in urban settings and the impact of social class (Walford, 2008a). Eventually these topics grew to include the curriculum and pedagogy within the specific context of the classroom. Most are familiar with Willis's groundbreaking educational ethnography of the reproduction of the working class, *Learning to Labor* (1977), which explores not only the classroom setting, but the pedagogical exchanges between factory workers after the students have left school. His work has set much of the tone for today's dialectical materialist educational ethnographers.

Walford (2008a) and Woods (1986) identify ethnography as especially suited to the classroom setting due to similarities between the theory testing and refining that is done in research and the same processes that happen during learning. Woods (1986) outlines how ethnography and teaching share many common elements, including story telling as a way to present information, teachers and researchers sharing experiences with the methods of observation and interviewing, an emphasis on practical value as the information that results from the pedagogical/ethnographic encounter cannot be obtained in any other manner, and an intense form of engagement with the processes of teaching/researching.

Two educational ethnographers are discussed here, Jean Anyon and Pauline Lipman. Both have spent extensive time observing in classroom settings, and they trace the impact of educational policy on teachers and students. Like Willis (1977), their work highlights the reproductive aspects of capitalist schooling, including the shaping of future workers and the internalization of accompanying ideologies about democracy, freedom, and making it in America.

In *Race, Class, and Power in School Restructuring*, Lipman (1998) takes aim at the so-called collaboration model of teachers involved in

recent efforts at reform. Using case study methodology, Lipman focuses on what occurs in African American schools when they are put
under the microscope of corporate systems analysis and evaluation.
First, Lipman locates her research within the larger contexts of how
policy is shaped in the public's eye, and how majority-black schools,
and African Americans themselves, are often positioned as "problems" to be solved. Related to this are discourses of a lack of interest
in education on the part of parents and, unfortunately, many educators themselves:

> A related issue is the way in which public policy has constructed low-
> income and children of color as "at risk." The "at risk" label operates as if it
> were a scientifically determined trait of youth who embody a diffuse set of
> supposedly perverse personal and social characteristics. In popular use, "at
> risk" has become a signifier for race and class and a badge of deviance to be
> pinned on urban youth. (p. 13)

In fact, Lipman, a white college professor, recounts finding more resistance from white educators who were reluctant to go into detail
about their views concerning race, whereas the African American educators were more open in describing their experiences.

In a later work, *The New Political Economy of Urban Education*, Lipman (2011) connects school reform, high-stakes testing, and the twenty-first-century American city in her analysis of the impact of
neoliberalism in Chicago. Here we find the educational reform efforts
of first Arne Duncan and eventually Rahm Emanuel writ large; they
involve the dismantling of public schools as a way to make room for
gentrification. Lipman explains that the closing of a school is key in
shaping the twenty-first-century city:

> Closing schools in African American communities is facilitated by their con-
> struction in the media and public policy as dysfunctional and violent. These
> portrayals mask the nexus of racialized public policy and investment deci-
> sions that produced deindustrialization, disinvestment, unemployment, and
> degradation of public health, the built environment, and education in com-
> munities of color over the past 50 years. The predicament of urban schools
> cannot be understood outside this history. And closing schools to reopen

them as mixed-income schools branded to appeal to the middle class and whites is located in this social process. (p. 94)

Lipman cites evidence that only a handful of the children who were promised slots in the new schools were ever able to attend those schools. Most of the time, either children are turned away or information about enrolling in the new school is not broadcast, so parents do not know what is happening.

The use of school closings is part of a competitive citizenship where those with the most means obtain the most ends. Lipman also critiques the small schools movement, for its corporate foundational support and undemocratic tendencies. After beginning as a liberal and open concept of fostering education in urban communities, small schools soon shifted to business talk after the Gates Foundation became involved. A similar phenomenon has occurred with the charter school movement, which is also supported to a lesser degree by those minority communities who want more oversight in how their children are educated. Yet the neoliberal vision of charters is what is privileged, even when they are cloaked in civil rights rhetoric. Lipman lays the blame for the rise of charter schools in African American communities on the unwillingness of collective efforts by the public schools as a whole. If the public schools had been more committed to equality than to "closing the achievement gap," charters would not have had much of a head start at developing.

Lipman concludes her study with an examination of anticapitalist movements, particularly in the global south, and of the collapsed housing market in the United States, which has further squeezed schools financially. This resistance in the face of economic crisis creates an urgency expressed in the way that only ethnographic inquiry can portray. For Lipman, "The right to the city is radically democratic and fundamentally anticapitalist. It's a call for a wholly different city and society, socialism, by whatever name" (p. 161). Rather than being a peripheral institution, education has an important role to play in reclaiming urban spaces as multicultural and justice-centered ones, instead of responding to the needs of only the middle and upper classes by making way for gentrification.

Anyon's concise summary of institutionalized schooling in "Social Class and the Hidden Curriculum of Work" (1980), identifies not one, but four different public school systems within the United States: working class, middle class, affluent professional, and executive elite. Her conclusions were based on extensive ethnographic research in various schools to document how the day-to-day practices and inter-actions within classrooms reinforce the reproduction of the working class. It remains one of the best studies to introduce to students in foundations classes (if there is still such a thing in most universities these days).

In the working-class school—which nowadays could be labeled the "prison pipeline," or "Wal-Mart schools"—the emphasis is on ex-ternal discipline and regulation. Decision making and choice are lim-ited to authority figures, not the students. Children are handed worksheets and told to copy what the teacher has on the board. Cur-riculum is limited to procedural details such as punctuation or fol-lowing templates. Rote memorization and isolated facts reign supreme. Even teacher interactions with students are kept as curt and minimal as possible, and usually only when a student is being cor-rected: "the four fifth grade teachers observed in the working-class schools attempted to control classroom time and space by making de-cisions without consulting children and without explaining the basis for their decisions. The teacher's control thus often seemed capri-cious" (para. 17).

The middle-class school featured several elements similar to the working-class school, but there was more emphasis on correct presen-tation and form. The right answer is what matters. Though there are a few hands-on projects, the majority of the curriculum comes from the textbook:

> While the teachers spend a lot of time explaining and expanding on what the textbooks say, there is little attempt to analyze how or why things hap-pen, or to give thought to how pieces of a culture, or, say, a system of num-bers or elements of a language fit together or can be analyzed. What has happened in the past and what exists now may not be equitable or fair, but (shrug) that is the way things are and one does not confront such matters in school. (para. 22)

In this way, the status quo is preserved and students learn not to go further than accepting the existing situation, a major ideological practice of the middle class. Middle-class students are also allowed a modicum of freedom of movement, but within constraints.

In the affluent professional school, student work is framed in creativity and choice. These are the children who are slated to occupy managerial positions such as lawyers and doctors. Teachers acclimate these students to greater autonomy, which is a necessary component of their future work. Discipline is built from within, along with the ability to carry out one's duties without direct supervision—in other words, to internalize the mind set of the professional. Group projects are also part of the affluent classroom, which mimics the project management structure many of the children will later encounter. Management of the classroom occurs through the teacher negotiating with the students, often reminding them of their obligations.

Finally, the executive elite schools are aimed at students who are expected to be CEOs or high-level business owners, the capitalist class. Many of these schools are private, whereas the other schools are public. Curriculum occurs in the context of classroom discussions and research projects, not teacher-directed work. Students are permitted much movement and freedom to come and go as they like. In summarizing the differences between school types, Anyon concludes the following:

> The "hidden curriculum" of schoolwork is tacit preparation for relating to the process of production in a particular way. Differing curricular, pedagogical, and pupil evaluation practices emphasize different cognitive and behavioral skills in each social setting and thus contribute to the development in the children of certain potential relationships to physical and symbolic capital, to authority, and to the process of work. School experience, in the sample of schools discussed here, differed qualitatively by social class. These differences may not only contribute to the development in the children in each social class of certain types of economically significant relationships and not others but would thereby help to reproduce this system of relations in society. In the contribution to the reproduction of unequal social relations lies a theoretical meaning and social consequence of classroom practice. (para. 52)

Even though Anyon's later work (2011) has been correctly critiqued as more Weber than Marx (see Banfield, 2011; Malott, 2011), her 1980 study of how the classroom functions to shape worker identity under capitalism is spot on, and a superior example of dialectical materialist analysis applied to education.

Dialectical Autoethnographic Work

Autoethnographic research writing is yet another way that dialectical materialism can be applied to inquiry. Denzin (2009) maintains that

> Communitarian journalists and ethnographers have an obligation to show how their performative skills, interpretive methods, and their models of truth, knowledge and politics can be used to interrupt, disrupt, and intervene in the course of political events as those events are unfolding. Such interventions call for an interruption of history itself. (p. 126)

Yet Denzin also cautions that autobiographical research can easily slip into unintentionally validating what he terms "trauma culture," which we commonly see on display in talk shows and news documentaries. This culture ends up reinforcing oppressive aspects of society by sensationalizing it, keeping people in awe of the violence they are witnessing. Pelzer's best-selling shock memoir *A Child Called It* (1995) is a prime example of privileging the discourse of trauma over sound autoethnographic inquiry. Unfortunately, this text is often assigned reading in secondary schools and universities, inculcating students with an intensely privatized rather than communal form of biographical writing.

In *Red Dirt: Growing up Okie* (2006), Dunbar-Ortiz describes her childhood as a member of the white rural working class, which made it difficult for her to later fit into academic circles. The companion volume to *Red Dirt* Is *Outlaw Woman: A Memoir of the War Years* (2001), in which Dunbar-Ortiz uses Marxist autoethnography to historically document the protest movements of the 1960s through reflections on her own life as a mother and activist. She also writes about how women often were marginalized in activist movements, relating her own experiences through a socialist feminist lens.

Dunbar-Ortiz (2001) is unapologetic when discussing her poor rural background. She felt alienated when talking about the Socialist Party in Oklahoma, of which her family was a part, with other faculty who were dismissive of the possibility that there could be a revolutionary consciousness within the white working class. Even though she had long since relocated from rural Oklahoma, the place was still with her:

> During the Watts uprising, I had listened to the voice of an LAPD officer on the radio and could almost place the part of Oklahoma his family had come from. Many of the young white men—some of my own relatives—who'd been drawn to the LAPD were sons of dustbowl... migrants from Oklahoma and surrounding states who settled in South Central Los Angeles... in close proximity to huge defense plants in which their fathers worked. (p. 53)

Here Dunbar-Ortiz traces the history of the white working class and their economically forced migration to California; unfortunately many of them were channeled into the defense and prison industries. Her past had come full circle to confront her. As she began to realize that many of the police were attacking Watts residents, she became ashamed of being a part of the same Okie culture. Later, Dunbar-Ortiz recounted meeting a white person from South Africa who had the same sentiments about whites in her country. At that moment she made the connection between colonial settler states and the reality of her own history. For many low-income whites, the populist ideology of the "true native born" permeates their consciousness, where they view themselves as dually oppressed by the bankers and ethnic minorities alike.

Dunbar-Ortiz also described her growing consciousness of how women's issues often were put aside during activist meetings:

> I argued that the freedom of women would require a social revolution and the social revolution would require liberated women. The two were inseparable. That was why none of the revolutions—not the Leninist nor the Trotskyist nor the Third World liberation movements—had triumphed and created real freedom and equality.... [S]everal of the women at the first meeting believed that our modus operandi should focus on validating women's experiences, to modify definitions, and to raise the status of

> housework, childbearing, and motherhood by demanding that women be paid for these services. I disagreed and insisted that those tasks should be validated for men's participation and that the whole society must be organized to participate in them. (pp. 128–129)

The liberation of both women and men by not continuing the gender segregation of child care was advanced in order to disrupt the real enemy—the power elite, i.e., capitalists. This notion was not received well by many of the feminists with whom Dunbar-Ortiz was involved, who wanted to pursue a wages-for-housework strategy as well as to not offend participants who valued traditional notions of the family.

Dunbar-Ortiz points out that every civil rights and revolutionary movement supported an increase in paid women's work, yet that alone didn't ensure women's liberation. In fact, gender-typed work remains segregated in terms of pay and benefits to this day. In responding to the postmodern feminist idea that Marx has no relevance for women, Dunbar-Ortiz provides a nuanced view:

> I am a Marxist and a revolutionary and I don't believe that has to be contradictory to women's liberation. It is a given that women will not be liberated under capitalism. No one will. But socialism is a long way off in this country, and women in existing socialist societies are not liberated despite sweeping economic and social changes. One thing is not changed under socialism where it exists—the nuclear family and male supremacy. (p. 251)

Though it was written prior to its author's self-identification as a socialist feminist, Adrienne Rich's *Of Woman Born: Motherhood as Experience and Institution* (1986) is an excellent dialectical example of using autoethnographic methodology in combination with feminism and historical research to explore the complexity of the role of mother. In the foreword to the second edition of the text, Rich notes her concern with how the phrase "the personal is political" has been stripped of meaning, making analysis of women's lives difficult. The "personal is political" has now become "personal-for-its-own-sake" (p. x).

What makes Rich's exploration of motherhood dialectical is that she takes the personal dimension of pregnancy, childbirth, and mothering and connects these to larger historical and social contexts. For example, in the foreword she poses questions about child care and gendered labor, pointing out that day care centers are private, corporate entities that are still beyond reach of many working families. Current systems of child care serve those who already have the means of obtaining such care, putting many families between a rock and a hard place. Rich comes down firmly on the side of the working families:

> Between a patriarchal State and the patriarchal family as guardians of children, there is little to choose. But there is another possibility: the emergence of a collective movement which is antipatriarchal, which places the highest value on the development of human beings, on economic justice, on respect for racial, cultural, sexual, and ethnic diversity, on providing the material conditions for children to flower into responsible and creative women and men, and on the redirection and eventual extirpation of the propensity for violence. (p. xxxiv)

Rich presents two different definitions of motherhood, the first being the relationship that women have with children (actualized or not) and the second an institution with an accumulated set of historical assumptions. The first portion of the text includes autoethnographic data that presents stark and moving accounts from Rich's day-to-day journaling of her experiences as a mother. In one entry, she describes the difficulty of maintaining basic privacy:

> From the fifties and early sixties, I remember a cycle. It began when I picked up a book or began trying to write a letter, or even found myself on the telephone with someone toward whom my voice betrayed eagerness, a rush of sympathetic energy. The child (or children) might be absorbed in busyness, in his own dreamworld; but as soon as he felt me gliding into a world which did not include him, he would come to pull at my hand, ask for help, punch at the typewriter keys. And I would feel his wants at such a moment as fraudulent, as an attempt moreover to defraud me of living even for fifteen minutes as myself. (p. 23)

Eventually the cycle would come to an end when her husband arrived home, deflecting her role as the center of the children's needs. Rich comments that at the time she didn't realize that this cycle wasn't a natural one, but one created by the institution of mother-hood.

Rich analyzes motherhood as a sacred calling, and explains that the privatization of the family has made it difficult for mothers to ne-gotiate feelings of guilt over being failed women. While workers (male and female) outside of the home can unionize or find solidarity, mothers who are in the home often are isolated. As Rich explains, "our wildcat strikes have most often taken the form of physical or mental breakdown" (p. 53). In investigating the current situation that women find themselves in, Rich delves historically to trace the roles of fathers, mothers, and the unique aspects of relationships between mother/son and mother/daughter under patriarchy. Like Leacock (1986, 2008), Rich (1986) points out that societies before the develop-ment of social classes were nonpatriarchal. Notions of "power over" others were relatively nonexistent; instead, women were viewed as possessing transformative power, due to their ability to give birth. Over time, motherhood has been domesticated by being institutional-ized and stripped of its original power.

Rich's tracing of the medicalization of pregnancy and childbirth begins with the role of midwife. Institutionalized misogyny resulted in the midwife being marginalized and replaced by the physician, who was thought to know more about women and their anatomy. The invention of the forceps, for example, was done under the rubric of profiting from its distribution—not all women who had difficult births had access to this instrument, mainly because midwives were denied its use. By minimizing the significance of the midwife, women lost a primary means of emotional support:

> The midwife not only gave prenatal care and advice, but came to the woman at the beginning of her labor and stayed with her till after delivery. She gave not only physical assistance but psychological support. The male birth at-tendant was historically called in only to perform the functions which were forbidden to the midwife. He was a technician rather than a counselor, guide, and source of morale; he worked "on" rather than "with" the mother. (p. 150)

In the final chapter, Rich takes on the taboo topic of violence and motherhood, looking at a 1974 case in which Joanne Michulski decapitated the two youngest of her eight children, who ranged in age from 2 to 18 years old. Rather than simply expressing horror and disbelief at this crime, Rich dissects the pressures that motherhood brings in the social context of capitalist patriarchy. Instead of recognizing the institution of motherhood as unsustainable and pathological, individual women are singled out as the ultimate "bad mother." Even those who were sympathetic to Michulski, suggesting that she should have had access to counseling, overlooked the marginalizing that happens to women within the psychiatric system. Add to this limited access to abortion and reliable contraception, male resistance from husbands/fathers/relatives, the power of the church in shaping moral attitudes toward sexuality, and lack of socially supported child care, and the case was hopeless from the start. Rich concludes with a degree of compassion and empathy in solidarity with women:

> What woman, in the solitary confinement of a life at home enclosed with young children, or in the struggle to mother them while providing for them single-handedly, or in the conflict of weighing her own personhood against the dogma that says she is a mother, first, last, and always—what woman has not dreamed of "going over the edge," of simply letting go, relinquishing her sanity so that she can be taken care of for once, or simply find a way to take care of herself? (p. 280)

Arts-Based Ethnographic Forms

Arts-based inquiry provides for diverse forms of data and analysis that can also be dialectical in nature. These forms include but are not limited to autobiographical fiction, layered text, performance narratives, visual sociology, art making, and performance writing. Denzin (2009) asserts that these alternative approaches to research can help to reveal contradictions that can expose day-to-day practices that are often hidden from view. There are four functions of what Denzin and Giardina (2012) term *critical imagination*: It assists people with thinking dialectically through incorporating history and sociology, it exposes sources of oppression, it creates a critical self-consciousness through tapping into aesthetic learning, and it helps to shape a radical self-awareness that can facilitate the collective move to making a different future.

Critical arts-based research is activist. It embodies both performance and politics and it is public in nature. As Finley (2012) relates, "critical arts-based research can create the necessary momentum for a profound revolutionary educational aesthetic that is transformative and productive in terms of ecojustice" (p. 205). The arts are also one of the few means by which the fantastical can become doable, because in general, people don't usually attempt to confine the limits of what art or fiction can do, as they might in the realms of politics or education. Action research is often combined with arts-based data gathering. Riddett-Moore (Riddett-Moore & Siegesmund, 2012) describes how the arts impacted her own research as a teacher:

> My art making did not illustrate an idea. My art making became a site of my own research. I made my data. I used photographic journaling and poetic journaling to document my process of working in fabric. In turn, the created data were helpful tools in analyzing my primary research interest: the life-worlds of students and the meaning they created through experiencing my curriculum. (p. 115)

Denzin (2009) describes performance ethnography as a particularly potent way of engaging audiences. In this type of theater, co-performers read from scripts based on data collected from field work. *Mama Hated Diesels* (Myler & Wheetman, 2010) is one such ethnodrama and live documentary about long-distance truck drivers. The play, which features dialogue between country song sets, is based on the photographs of Jim Steinberg, who usually makes nature his subject. Steinberg spent over a month photographing truckers in their various settings, covering more than 8,000 miles and taking 7,738 photos that are displayed as backdrops during the performance (Moore, 2010). The play addresses labor issues such as the physical effects of truck driving (wear and tear on the body), isolation during long runs, and the impact on relationships and family. It is an excellent example of how documentary research can investigate critical issues and reach a wide audience at the same time.

Bacon (2012) describes his photography documentary project where images about immigration are posted along the border wall in Mexicali, Mexico and Calexio, California. The large photographs include images from the day-to-day lives of migrants living in the U.S. as well as pictures from their home in Mexico. "As a photographer, I've tried to create images that aren't neutral. They are, first, a reality check, showing what life is actually like, trying to do it through the eyes of the people themselves. But they are also a form of social criticism" (p. 45).

A recent art exhibit at the National Veteran's Art Museum in Chicago, *Overlooked/Looked Over*, featured paintings and installations by eight women veterans that address the issues of rape and sexual abuse in the military. Three of the eight women had been victims of rape while in the military. "In the art world, the work of female artists has been overlooked for decades. As explained by participants, in the military, being "looked over" by male soldiers can have dangerous consequences" (Redmond, 2012, para. 2). One of the pieces, *Fatigues Clothesline*, addresses military sexual trauma. The artist, Regina Vasquez, embellished fatigues by writing her thoughts on them, displaying the clothing to resemble wash drying on the line. Another artist participant, Erica Sloan, curated the show and created an installation, *Uncovering My Crime Scene*. The installation depicts a bare mattress visible behind a white door. Sloan related that she "didn't report the crime because she's a lesbian and was serving under 'don't ask, don't tell'" (para. 15).

Minnie Bruce Pratt's (2011) poetry addresses late-stage capitalism and its destructive path. Her poems describe being laid off, and her work connects the commodification of women to labor issues. The poetry of Adrienne Rich (1993) and June Jordan (2007) also tap into feminism, labor, sexuality, and violence as they confront capitalism in the form of patriarchy. For Rich (2003), the tragedy is that poetry has become divorced from day-to-day life. She calls for a revolutionary poetry:

> Any truly revolutionary art is an alchemy through which waste, greed, brutality, frozen indifference, "blind sorrow," and anger are transmuted into

some drenching recognition of the *What if?* —the possible. *What if?* —the first revolutionary question, the question the dying forces don't know how to ask. (p. 242)

As Rich explains, poetry can often remind readers that labor doesn't have to be alienating; it can be a powerful force.

Octavia Butler's remarkable novel *Kindred* (2003) takes the traditional oral historical narrative further, combining fantasy and autoethnography to describe the incredible journey of Dana, an African American woman who is transported from the mid-1970s back in time to the antebellum South to confront her ancestors, one of whom is a plantation owner. Her interactions with Rufus, her white great-great-grandfather, reveal the psychological as well as the social conditions of racism. Dana soon finds herself unprepared to deal with the realities of slavery, despite being well educated about history. Butler's style of prose manages to capture the immediacy of experience, despite writing about society in the 1820s. Commenting on *Kindred*, Crossley (2003) notes: "In foreshortening the distance between then and now, Butler focuses our attention on the continuity between past and present; the fantasy of traveling backwards in time becomes a lesson in historical realities. We may also be reminded that historical progress is never a sure thing" (p. 279).

These are just a few of the many examples of how arts-based research can embody Marxian analyses and further add to the value of qualitative research.

Conclusion

At its core, qualitative research is about looking at, and possibly experiencing, phenomena from the perspective of participants. At the same time, the critical researcher's role involves making sense of what she or he is seeing, bringing external framing to highlight what has often become unrecognizable through the process of hegemony. Both work in concert to provide readers a picture of what is going on. As Sprague (2005) reminds us, "To create knowledge that is more complete and less systematically biased toward elite views, we need to ground each view of the social world in the standpoint from which it is created, and foster dialogue among those developing the picture from different social positions" (p. 2).

Far from being monolithic, dialectical materialist inquiry can reach into various methodological approaches, offering the qualitative scholar much to choose from, showing that it isn't only postmodern research that can be compelling, interesting, or even entertaining. Whether one chooses to use traditional ethnographic methods or to explore arts-based inquiry, the single thread that runs through it all is the dialectic, the ability to fuse historical knowledge into the present, to think toward the future. This chapter aimed to provide readers with an introductory sample of the insights and writing styles of representative authors; it is recommended that readers locate the original texts to grasp more fully their ways of working.

Chapter Six

Theoretical Research in the Dialectical Tradition

Overview

This chapter presents examples of basic research, also known as theoretical research, criticalist research, or pure inquiry. Scholarship that falls into this category includes work that seeks to build on existing knowledge—in this case, dialectical materialism—by analysis and examination alone, rather than through data collection or testing theory. As with ethnography, theoretical research is interdisciplinary in nature and works across diverse fields such as politics, technology, law, medicine, history, psychology, physics, and education. In this type of research, the focus of the researcher isn't on "what works," but on examining existing conditions in light of particular theories (Patton, 2002). Much of this research in the sociological fields is critical in nature, seeking to deconstruct the status quo in order to change it.

The importance of theory is addressed in just about any traditional applied research text, yet little exists about what constitutes basic or pure inquiry in and of itself. Often, turning to what makes up critical research can be helpful, though criticalist epistemologies are also used with qualitative and quantitative data gathering methods. Kincheloe and McLaren (1994) define a criticalist as:

> a researcher or theorist who attempts to use her or his work as a form of social or cultural criticism and who accepts basic assumptions: that all thought is fundamentally mediated by power relations which are socially or historically constituted... that certain groups in society are privileged over others.... [T]he oppression which characterizes contemporary societies is most forcibly reproduced when subordinates accept their social status as natural, necessary, or inevitable.... [M]ainstream research practices are generally, although most often unwittingly, implicated in the reproduction of systems of class, race, and gender oppression. (p. 139)

Along these same lines, Apple (2009) presents seven tasks of a critical researcher: highlighting inequality and oppression, pointing out possible spaces for action, redefining traditional research in terms of where it is needed and under what circumstances, being a public intellectual willing to work on the side of people, preserving the history of radical scholarship and activism, relentlessly critiquing one's own research, and being an activist in the struggle, otherwise known as "hitting the street."

Ortner (1999) explains that "ethnography is not enough.... [I]t is theory that allows us to map the world in such a way that we can understand the relationship between various claims, rather than engaging in a competitive struggle for authority" (p. 83). In Ortner's study of how members of Generation X experienced class positionality, she not only collected interview data, but also utilized several theories to make sense of the data, as she describes: "Theory, in this case, includes rethought narratives of capitalist development in the late twentieth century, feminist arguments concerning the centrality of intimate relations to the reproduction of all relations of inequality, including class and theories of representation" (p. 84). Like Ortner, Marxist basic researchers combine several frames in looking at the centrality of social class and examine matters of race, gender, and sexuality.

Marxist Historians

Du Bois created a masterwork of dialectical materialist analysis in his historical study *Black Reconstruction in America, 1860–1880*. Up until his book was first published in 1935, no one had undertaken as detailed an analysis of the role of African Americans in the post–Civil War era. By framing the Civil War as America's second revolution fought over labor, Du Bois took historical inquiry into a new direction:

> The true significance of slavery in the United States to the whole social development of America lay in the ultimate relation of slaves to democracy. What were to be the limits of democratic control in the United States? If all labor, black as well as white, became free—were given schools and the right

to vote—what control could or should be set to the power and action of these laborers? Was the rule of the mass of Americans to be unlimited, and the right to rule extended to all men regardless of race and color, or if not, what power of dictatorship and control; and how would property and privilege be protected? This was the great and primary question which was in the minds of the men who wrote the Constitution of the United States. (1935/1998, p. 13)

Du Bois traces how slavery was intertwined with the exploitation of the white working class during emerging industrialization. Maintaining a system of plantation slavery required rounding up escapees with the assistance of poor whites serving on slave patrols, the precursor to today's police force. Many of the newly arrived white immigrants and Northern whites who opposed slavery did so only because they viewed it as a threat to their wages and aspirations to become capitalists. Activists' attempts to frame slavery and wage oppression in terms of class were often thwarted by racism, leading to later difficulties within the labor movement, such as segregation of trade unions:

> The plight of the white working class throughout the world today is directly traceable to Negro slavery in America, on which modern commerce and industry was founded, and which persisted to threaten free labor until it was partially overthrown in 1863. The resulting color caste founded and retained by capitalism was adopted, forwarded, and approved by white labor, and resulted in subordination of colored labor to white profits the world over. Thus the majority of the world's laborers, by the insistence of white labor, became the basis of a system of industry which ruined democracy and showed its perfect fruit in World War and Depression. (p. 30)

Rather than viewing Union troops as freeing the slaves, Du Bois takes the radical position that slaves were already engaging in a form of a general strike against the conditions of their labor. This strike took various forms, including running away or joining the military. The slaveocracy was already crumbling under the weight of overconsumption of plantation owners and the endless quest for more land to obtain greater crop yields. Because it took war and the onslaught of industrialization to finally compel the South to give up its system of agrarian rule, the rage of white Southerners was projected onto African Americans:

> The bites and blows of a nation fell on them. All hatred that the whites after the Civil War had for each other gradually concentrated itself on them. They caused the war—they, its victims. They were guilty of all the thefts of those who stole. They had impoverished the South, and plunged the North into endless debt. And they were funny, funny—ridiculous baboons, aping men. (p. 125)

Du Bois concluded that there was no single "type" of black person who was emancipated. There was a wide range of African American experiences in the period known as Reconstruction. Some already had advantages, such as owning businesses; others were suddenly thrust into wage labor, a secondary form of slavery.

Du Bois remarks that "When a right and just cause loses, men suffer. But men also suffer when a wrong cause loses" (p. 129). The aftermath of the Civil War created hysteria and frenzy among white Southerners who intoned about the dangers of a society with free Negros in it. Attempts to form an alliance between poor whites and freed slaves with voting at the center were quickly quashed by members of the former planter class and their low-income white supporters. Du Bois presents evidence in the form of correspondence and newspaper articles of Reconstruction-era racism and its divisive effects. He demonstrates that the lack of definitive leadership in the South in support of full integration allowed the experiments of the early Reconstruction era to become subsumed into Jim Crow laws and violence after Andrew Johnson, who himself came from a poor white background, found himself president after Lincoln's assassination. All of these events were supported by capitalists in the North and the South who were all too eager to stoke racist sentiment in order to extract even more labor from poor whites and blacks alike.

Du Bois's description of the Reconstruction era is an example of the careful retelling he employs throughout his scholarship, which works against simplistic portrayals of the era as completely overtaken by racial violence and corrupt carpetbaggers:

One cannot study Reconstruction without first frankly facing the facts of universal lying; of deliberate and unbounded attempts to prove a case and win a dispute and preserve economic mastery and political domination by besmirching the character, motives, and commonsense, of every single person who dared disagree with the dominant philosophy of the white South. (p. 347)

In this way, Du Bois hopes to rectify the crisis of representation that has plagued the period of Reconstruction, particularly among historians. In reading his accounts of the slanders against African American politicians during this era, one is struck by the similarities to contemporary accusations against President Obama by his detractors, from the "missing" birth certificate story to the dubious international connections.

The second half of *Black Reconstruction in America* investigates the economic and political situation in the formerly Confederate states, each one a historical case study. In these case studies, Du Bois reveals subtle workings of Reconstruction, including the role of the railroads and the formation of public schools, along with the rise of the Ku Klux Klan, a middle-class organization that often recruited poor whites. Du Bois attributes the backlash during Reconstruction in part to the failure of labor to stand up to the militarized guerilla forces of the Klan. Where labor was weakest, the Klan was the strongest, a fact affirmed in McVeigh's (2009) research on the Klan of the 1920s. Another problem that Du Bois (1935/1998) found was that assumptions were made—including by the abolitionist Senator Charles Sumner— that the South during Reconstruction would fully surrender in exchange for a "civilized" process of amnesty granted by the North:

What liberalism did not understand was that such a revolution was economic and involved force. Those who against the public weal have power cannot be expected to yield save to superior power.... [A]bolitionists failed to see that after the momentary exultation of war, the nation did not want Negroes to have civil rights and that national industry could get its way easier by alliance with Southern landholders than by sustaining Southern workers. They did not know that when they let the dictatorship of labor be overthrown in the South they surrendered the hope of democracy in America for all men. (pp. 591–592)

Du Bois concludes that a counterrevolution of property, formed by this alliance between Southern and Northern white elites, created an embedded civil war that eventually halted Reconstruction and established the supremacy of capitalism. In the wake of the destruction of the project of Reconstruction, what Loewen (2006) identifies as a nadir of race relations occurred between 1890 and 1920. Acts of violence against African Americans and their displacement from communities forever altered what could have been a different path:

> The attempt to make black men American citizens was in a certain sense all a failure, but a splendid failure. It did not fail where it was expected to fail. It was Athanasius contra mundum, with back to the wall, outnumbered ten to one, with all the wealth and all the opportunity, and all the world against him. And only in his hands and heart the consciousness of a great and just cause; fighting the battle of all the oppressed and despised humanity of every race and color, against the massed hirelings of Religion, Science, Education, Law, and brute force. (Du Bois, 1935/1998, p. 708)

David Montgomery (1980, 1989, 1993) was a historian who focused his Marxian analysis on examining the history of labor to the present. He directly challenged the common belief that the working class is naturally more conservative than other classes. His dialectical work also included a commitment to racial equality. Like Du Bois (1935/1998), he viewed race as a crucial component of changing labor during Reconstruction at a time when most historians were limiting their analyses to the impact of just emancipation.

Montgomery's *Workers' Control in America* (1980) presents a history of how industrial workers relied on unions not only for material support and solidarity, but also as a way to fight against alienation of their own labor. Contrary to myth, wages is not the only reason workers join unions; the conditions of labor are essential to maintaining some degree of autonomy, and not just for reasons of safety. Another myth that Montgomery takes on is the idea that manual workers are not able to manage themselves because they are used to specifically defined tasks and hierarchy. Unfortunately, this myth was sometimes promulgated by 1960s activists who viewed unionized workers as conservative and resistant to change. The abandonment of unions as a potential partner for social activism resulted in many of these workers later throwing their support behind Nixon and, eventually, Reagan.

What Montgomery finds is that rather than workers lacking practical ideas for self-management, often their ideas conflicted with employers' concepts of management. For example, when Taylorism was introduced on the assembly line, unionized workers responded by declaring that real science rather than the derivative scientific management should be applied to the collectivization of society as a whole, i.e., they asserted Marxism. Workers would also impose their own quotas, or stints, based on the day-to-day knowledge of what was possible to produce without introducing negative consequences to any member of the union. Of course, employers were constantly putting pressure on worker-established quotas, but they often found it difficult to get them to budge. Work sharing was another aspect of self-management in which no one worker should have to bear the hardest jobs.

Woven into strikes over wages were employer attacks on worker autonomy and the stint system. Montgomery outlines how even in the face of layoffs, workers self-managed to ensure that rehiring was handled fairly and not arbitrarily:

> Organized and unorganized workers alike slowed down, when the word from the shipping room and office clerks had it that a layoff was in the offing...[S]trike settlements seemed to popularize the idea of seniority. Early in the twentieth century the demand of unions that employers should fire all scabs and reinstate all strikers was often compromised after long struggles by reinstating employees (old and new) in order of seniority. (p. 143)

Unions were also instrumental in providing unemployment relief. Several militant unions agitated and won relief for laid-off members. Other unions created relief tent cities and restaurants to provide essentials for workers. Eventually these services were absorbed by religious charity systems, due to a lack of sustained funding. However, this doesn't erase the evidence of the self-organizing capabilities of workers even in the face of hardship.

Montgomery also highlights the Communist Party as virtually the only worker organization that called for full racial equality. Unfortunately, it met much resistance from white unionized workers who by the 1950s had internalized much of the racist and anticommunist rhetoric that employers were all too willing to use. What was once a hallmark of self-management—worker seniority—was subsequently used against African Americans who were new to many urban factories or who had been shut out of hiring. The Communist Party proposed adding 2 to 5 years of seniority to all black workers as a way to even the playing field. This was rejected as "reverse Jim Crow," much as affirmative action is framed as reverse racism today.

In *The Fall of the House of Labor* (1989), Montgomery goes deeper into labor analysis by meticulously tracing the growth of unions in the United States during the peak of industrialization and organizing power from the 1860s to the years before the Great Depression, and by looking at cultural activities inside and outside of formal unionizing. For Montgomery, focusing only on trade unions provides a limited view of understanding the working class:

> The work cultures of factory operatives and common laborers must be studied as well as those of the skilled crafts, if the late nineteenth-century working class is to be understood. The working lives of the operatives turn out to have been fashioned by their youth and the socialization of the large numbers of women among those working youth. Examining their codes and solidarities carries us irresistibly into the neighborhoods. (p. 4)

With this approach, Montgomery's research into late 1800s union organizing explores the tensions between rural and urban roots and conflicting concepts of citizenship, especially during periods of war. Racial dimensions are also explored, as he documents shining moments of solidarity alongside episodes of employers stoking racist fears among white union members.

One of the biggest challenges facing labor during this time was the implementation of scientific management, or Taylorism. Workers in factories had learned to depend upon each other as a team, in light of the dangerous conditions of labor in places such as steel plants. Documenting employee efficiency was a constant struggle because it was difficult to segregate the assembly line in order to collect data on individual workers or departments. One solution the employers turned to was the introduction of machinery:

> The machinery belonged to the company, which sold the workers' output for its own profit in intensely competitive markets. To survive and grow within that market, a company was obliged not only to hold its labor costs as low as possible, but also to introduce new machinery to raise output and eliminate workers. By the end of the century, lifting tables, hydraulic pushers, power-operated tables, and other innovations would reduce the average size of a rolling-mill crew to only five men. (p. 12)

Some of the records that Montgomery reviews indicate that there were workers in the late 1800s who were able to secure a great deal of professional control over the conditions of their own labor. This was sustained by the group solidarity that remained despite the introduction of machines and scientific management. Employers challenged this autonomy by using tactics such as inside contracting with individual workers, where a worker could hire helpers for a cheap wage.

Montgomery discusses several unsuccessful strike actions and their aftermaths. While poststrike supervisory structures remained the same on the face of it, such as promotion based on an apprenticeship system, there were other, more fundamental alterations:

> What had been eliminated was collective, deliberate control from the workers' end. In its place the company cultivated a hierarchy of fiercely competing individuals, held together and secured by the vast differentials in earnings that still existed despite draconic slashing of tonnage rates after the strike, by craftsmen's fear of losing their jobs, and the graft they could glean from subordinates. (p. 42)

The slowly erosion of rights that had been hard won is detailed and presented as a learning lesson from history. Of course, after the Great Depression, union organizing experienced a resurgence, which Montgomery analyzes in other writings. But it is striking how many of labor's gains could be undone in the matter of 60 years.

In *Citizen Worker* (1993), Montgomery explores the ideological side of labor under capitalism. He takes on the complex task of delving in-

to the history of how workers interacted with notions such as democracy, free enterprise, and citizenship, whether they accepted or resisted these ideas in whole or in part. From the beginning of the United
States, elites had an extreme distrust of nonpropertied males voting,
lest they fall into the hands of radical mobs who sought to redistrib-
ute wealth. This paranoia carried over into how to appease the working class while still maintaining economic control, a difficult task in
an agrarian society. In some towns, citizenship was determined by
voting, so the indigent could easily be denied access to work and
housing. This was especially hard for women, who were not able to
own property.

Montgomery notes that voting turnout was the highest between
1840 (after the achievement of full suffrage for white males) and 1896,
with percentages in the upper 70s and 80s:

> It was only between the mid-1890s and the mid-1920s that new literacy tests,
> poll taxes, lengthened residency qualifications, increasingly widespread
> preconditions of full citizenship and the requirements that prospective vot-
> ers register in person sharply reduced the electorate in both southern and
> northern states, significantly offsetting the expansion of the electorate
> through statewide, then federal authorization of women's suffrage. (p. 21)

It is interesting that these efforts to roll back voting occurred just at
the point of increased immigration, worker agitation through unionizing, and the granting of suffrage to African American males during
Reconstruction. Voter suppression has been a common tactic
throughout U.S. history, as carefully documented by Fox Piven and
Cloward (1989, 2000) and Fox Piven, Minnite, and Groarke (2009).

The overthrow of slavery was a pivotal moment in the enforcement and control of indentured labor, creating additional tensions.
Montgomery (1993) relates how during Reconstruction, African
Americans were highly reluctant to enter into contract labor on plantations in the South, for example. Industry found that it could still obtain low-wage labor through urbanization and supporting the shifting
of work from the country to cities. Immigration was also used to employers' advantage later, in the twentieth century, as in the Bracero
work program, which pitted migrant labor against U.S. workers.

Throughout all of labor history, ideologies of democracy, private property, and free choice were readily disseminated in order to build compliance. Yet, Montgomery reminds us that resistance to these ideas was part and parcel of worker solidarity achieved because of, and in some cases in spite of, unions.

Educational Policy Researchers

Since the publication of Bowles and Gintis's often referenced *Schooling in Capitalist America* (1976), the landscape of education has provided fertile ground for theoretical research concerning the policies and practices of schools, from pre–K through adult, public and private. Earlier key works addressing radical readings of schooling include Counts's *Dare the School Build a New Social Order?* (1932) and Illich's *Deschooling Society* (1972), along with works by authors of the free schools movement (Goodman, 1964; Holt, 1967; Kozol, 1972; Neill, 1960), so the field has a rich history of also including anarchist perspectives. Today, contemporary Marxist researchers apply dialectical materialist analysis to a wide range of educational contexts, with a distinct focus on the centrality of social class. Once separated by geographical boundaries (i.e., British Marxists, American Marxists, Global South Marxists, and so forth), within the past 10 years many educational Marxist writers have crossed borders to collaborate with each other on publications and presentations of their work. The body of theoretical educational research that can be considered as falling under the category of "Marxist" is too vast to address here in more than a cursory manner.

Founded in 1989, the Hillcole Group of Radical Educators was instrumental in reviving Marxian inquiry during the 1990s (for an extensive list of authors and publications, visit http://www.tpress.free-online.co.uk/Hillcole.html). Written in the style of the traditional revolutionary pamphlets, *Red Chalk* (Cole, Hill, McLaren, & Rikowski, 2001) lays out the basic tenets of classical Marxism applied to education. The authors distinguish their approach from neo-Marxian attempts at conceptualizing schooling under capitalism by their direct confrontation of capital and the central role of labor, rather than stopping at Weberian notions of social classes. They also critique the inadequacies of postmodernism for its inability to address pressing needs:

> In the long struggle against exploitation, capitalism can easily survive the intermezzo efforts of the postmodern vanguard. While we vent diffuse dissatisfaction with the postmodern left, we do so not because it has annoyingly preoccupied itself for too long with a hectoring and lampooning of Marxism, but because it has reduced the struggle for emancipation to exploring the genealogies of discourses, to identifying relations of power at the level of the individual, rather than understanding the history of class society and ways to transform it.... [O]ne day on the picket line can do more to bring about social justice than all the campus-wide clarion calls for fashioning the self through bricolage out of the detritus of semiotic culture that we can fit between the pages of the latest avant-garde journal. (p. 9)

For Hill (2012), education workers play a pivotal role in the transformation of society because they occupy one of the few remaining institutions that most people experience at some time in their lives. The process of learning is also powerful and transformative if educators are able to locate spaces where they can present an alternative vision of what the world could be like. Unfortunately, it is becoming more and more challenging to locate these spaces when neoliberal accountability policies such standardized testing and merit pay are the norm, and, as Hill describes, "how to has replaced why to in a technicist curriculum based on delivery of a quietist and overwhelmingly conservative set of standards for student teachers" (p. 72). The removal of critical thinking is one of the key ways that capitalism can further utilize the schools, which have always been a means to an end: the reproduction of the workforce. The difference is that under neoliberalism today, the public sector itself is being discarded, with massive cuts to schools, medical assistance, and even basic municipal infrastructure. This makes it more challenging for educators and the community to mount an effective resistance.

A second major volume to come out of the Hillcole Group was *Marxism against Postmodernism in Education* (2002). In the text, Rikowski outlines the potential relevancy of Marx for researchers who examine educational policy:

> For me, Marxist theory affords potentialities for articulating the multiple forms of oppression in relation to people of color, women, gays and lesbians, and other social groups devalued by capitalist society. Furthermore, Marxism expresses, theoretically and empirically, the dynamics of social class as the form of oppression within capitalist society that is constituted by its own development. Marxist theory also allows me to perspectivize gender, "race," and other forms of oppression through the lens of social class. Finally, it articulates the fragility of capitalist oppression. It expresses the scream of refusal, but also gives form to the shrieks of power of the oppressed as they resist and confront capital's insurgence into all spheres of social life. (p. 16)

The central project for Marxist educational researchers is restoring class and labor to the center of inquiry, as they are essential for overcoming capitalism. Paula Allman's book *Revolutionary Social Transformation* (2001) asserts that the role of the educator is key, because in order for radical action to occur, there has to be a simultaneous transformation of both the group and the conditions of education. Allman's work also addresses the element of human consciousness and explores why people have come to accept their conditions as natural or inevitable.

Marxian educational researchers are also critical of abstract notions of "democracy," which can be easily used against people when social conditions become negative. Gibson (2012) views capitalism and democracy not as mutually antagonistic, but as having formed together through history:

> In philosophy, abstract democracy is religion, dialectics without materialism, the dead end of critique, a source of class rule. You suspend your critical thought, agree to one Imaginary Friend (IF) or another, enter an arena run by self-appointed translators for the IF, pay them, accept the hierarchies they created before you arrived, take direction, and adopt the rules of the translators for the IF. (p. 49)

Rather than stubbornly trying to make a classical liberal concept "fit" with a more equitable future (much like leftists trying to make Barack Obama a socialist when he isn't), only to become repeatedly frustrated, Brosio in his *Philosophical Scaffolding for the Construction of Critical Democratic Education* (2000) proposes that educators revisit what they may have once learned in their foundations classes to critique capitalist democracy. Similarly, Ross (2006) advises that social studies reclaim its once radical past as a way for teachers and students to diadialectically understand their existing situation. Weiner (2008) sees bottom-up organizing by the rank and file of teachers unions as another means for changing the definition of democracy, because teachers are among the few remaining public sector groups that stand between communities and the neoliberal assault on working families.

A common criticism of Marxist educational research is that it is all about analyzing problems, not about providing solutions. In one sense this critique is valid, because by "solutions," many expect pragmatic reforms without disrupting profit or privilege. In that case, Marxist educators are not interested in "providing solutions." By documenting resistance movements as well as systematically analyzing the anatomy of revolutions, dialectical materialist researchers are providing important information about where we've been and where we want to avoid going in terms of both education and the larger world.

Social Policy Researchers

Barbara Ehrenreich is best known for her undercover scholarship, first when she engaged in various service-industry jobs (maid, nursing home aid, Wal-Mart employee) in *Nickel and Dimed* (2001), and later when she posed as a laid-off middle-class employee trying to reenter the job market in *Bait and Switch* (2006). She is the author of numerous other books, too, all of which combine historical and discourse analysis with a sharp wit and accessible writing style. Her loyalties lie firmly on the side of the working class, and she is quite outspoken about what she sees happening around her.

In a recent collection of essays, *This Land Is Their Land* (2008), Ehrenreich covers the gamut of headlining topics featured in the mass media, with a focus on the disappearing social safety net and increased privatization as social contexts. Her writing is steeped in class analysis; an example is her treatment of the recent craze for organic and low-fat foods. She sees this dietary fad as an expression of the division of wealth, where those in the top 1% are able to highlight their position by deliberately depriving themselves of higher calorie food types while opting to purchase more pricy organic foods. According to Ehrenreich, the wealthy portray their actions as another consumer choice, as if the poor and working class have similar options but just choose to eat junk food. Ehrenreich views this as yet another way that the poor are painted as financially irresponsible, a notion that she readily deconstructs:

> It's expensive to be poor.... [P]oor people are less likely to have bank accounts, which can be expensive for those low balances, and so they tend to cash their paychecks at a check-cashing business.... [N]ationwide, low-income car buyers, defined as people earning less than $30,000 per year, paid 2 percentage points more for car loans than more affluent buyers. Low-income drivers pay more for car insurance.... [P]oorer people pay an average of 1 percentage point more in mortgage interest. They are more likely to buy their furniture and appliances through pricey rent-to-own businesses.... [T]hey rely on the far more expensive and lower quality offerings of small grocery and convenience stores. (pp. 38–39)

Ehrenreich asserts that rather than vilifying poor people for their "wild" spending habits while turning to multimillionaires for financial advice, we should be studying poor people to see how they are able to get by on so little.

Ehrenreich (2008) also takes on the privatized health care system, which she sees as based on a Calvinist ethos of suffering as a natural part of existence combined with wealth being a sign of God's blessings. She points out that contrary to the myth that anyone can access medical care, the uninsured are charged several times more than the insured for hospital visits; for example, uninsured patients have to pay close to $30,000 for an appendectomy, whereas an insured patient would have to pay nearly $7,000 (p. 147). For the poor and uninsured, the price of access to health care is out of reach The uninsured also often end up paying more because they delay seeking care for financial reasons; relatively small, easy to manage health conditions such as diabetes become bigger, more expensive ones if treatment is delayed. Ehrenreich also provides a clue as to hospitals' resistance to single-payer health care—even though the uninsured make up only 2% of the medical system's patients, they create 35% of its profits (p. 147)!

In critiquing social policies aimed at welfare recipients, Ehrenreich demonstrates that federal funding for marriage classes and the like are based on faulty sociological notions. For example, most low-income women, if they do marry, marry within their social class. The blue-collar sector has seen the greatest loss in terms of the disappearance of living wage work, so the problem isn't that single mothers remain single just for the heck of it—they are responding logically to the lack of decent work for themselves and their potential partners. Ehrenreich calculated how many blue-collar men a welfare recipient would need to marry in order to meet the income level required to be declared nonpoor: 2.3 (she also notes that polyandry is currently illegal in the United States, so that option is out).

In her earlier work *Dancing in the Streets* (2007), Ehrenreich takes on an unusual research topic: mass celebrations and their revolutionary potential. As she explains, "communitas and collective effervescence describe aspects or moments of communal excitement; there is no word for the love—or force or need—this leads individuals to seek ecstatic merger with the group" (p. 14). The primary question that Ehrenreich investigates is, If humans have used public celebrations for centuries as a way to obtain collective joy, then why do we seldom do so today? In looking at the artistic record, she notes that there are countless figures in groups dancing, hunting, or eating, but "no rock drawings of stick figures apparently engaged in conversation" (p. 24). Perhaps we need to tap into past understandings of collective celebrations in order to invoke these experiences today.

For Ehrenreich, the loss of public celebrations and the attending opportunity to lose ourselves in a collective experience with other people has been immeasurable. She traces the decline in festivals with the rise of capitalism as an outgrowth of earlier class societies. The reproduction of the working and middle classes involved separating them through the internalization of separate ideologies. The middle classes had to be frugal and save for the future, to avoid being frivolous, whereas the working classes had to be controlled and acclimated to time clocks and external supervision. Because public festivities often closed the distance between social classes, elites became nervous about their potential for fomenting social unrest. This is a change from the use of festivals during the classical and medieval eras as a way to control the populace.

Ehrenreich also discusses war by looking at the development of the gun and how it shaped views concerning social discipline. This form of discipline conflicts with the looser interactions of the festival or rite. As Ehrenreich explains, people's ability to experience ecstasy on a collective plane was channeled into more isolated experiences, such as those in sports arenas or at concerts where people are often lost in a crowd, which are probably the closest things we have to ancient gatherings:

> Urbanization and the rise of competitive, market-based economies favored a more anxious and isolated sort of person—potentially both prone to depression and distrustful of communal pleasures. Calvinism provided a transcendent rationale for this shift, intensifying the isolation and practically institutionalizing depression as a stage in the quest for salvation. (p. 147)

Ehrenreich concludes by comparing negative uses of group celebrations, such as totalitarian displays of nationalism in parades, and more revolutionary uses of group gatherings, such as what we saw in Tahrir Square. The problem rests not with the existence of masses of people in any one space, but with the identity and intention of the originator of the celebration. Class stratification is antithetical to communal pleasure: "This leaves hierarchical societies with no means of holding people together except for mass spectacles or force" (p. 253).

Like Ehrenreich, Coontz combines historical and current research to deconstruct myths. In *The Way We Never Were* (2000) and *The Way We Really Are* (1997) she looks at notions of the nuclear family, including the views that it has existed since time immemorial and that it is the ideal for proper socialization. In particular, Coontz (1997) takes aim at policies proposed by the family values movement such as eliliminating no-fault divorce, blocking single women from access to sperm banks, and ending access to abortion. A common thread in these proposals is an attack on poor women, who are presented as a drain on society and in need of religious-based intervention. Lying behind these attacks is a larger, privatized ideology of individual morality: If only people would shape up, return teacher-led prayer to the classroom, and stop having sex (unless they are married and want children—all other sexual activity is wrong), societal problems would not exist.

Coontz describes a family values proponent who suggested viewing stigmatization of single mothers as a legitimate public policy. She immediately confronts this argument by asserting that creating public shame around the issue of weight hasn't even put a dent in levels of obesity. Reductions in numbers of smokers was accomplished not by using shame, but through a combination of laws and policies, along with the provision of smoking cessation programs offered in workplaces. Coontz suggests that similar approaches most assuredly would not work to reduce the number of single mothers because the majority of families would be categorized as undesirable according to the values crowd.

Often, family values people, when confronted with how their policies could harm people, will backpedal and offer assurances that each case would be reviewed carefully before lowering the hammer. Coontz finds this highly problematic for several reasons. First, as for the notion of involving government in using a narrow definition of the nuclear family as a requirement for receiving aid, Coontz points out the bureaucratic nightmare that would ensue in determining who was or wasn't qualified for assistance—and this from the crowd who claims they are anti–big government! Second, problems would emerge because power always enters into the picture, as she explains:

> At worst, this approach offers right-wing extremists moderate-sounding cover for attempts to penalize or coerce families and individuals that such groups find offensive. Insisting that everyone pay lip service to lifelong marriage as an ideal while recognizing in practice that life is complicated is like having a law on the books that everyone breaks at one time or another. Authorities can use it selectively to punish the poor, the powerless, or the unpopular while letting everyone else off the hook. (p. 95)

Indeed, whether it is Newt Gingrich being "forgiven" for having an affair, or Bristol Palin's teen pregnancy being acceptable, when it comes to the rich and powerful, family values doesn't apply to them, just to the working class.

Coontz (2000) delves deep into the history of the nuclear family by tracing its roots to capitalism and the postwar conditions that provided the infrastructure needed to maintain a household with one working adult. Often, the nuclear family of the 1950s is bound up with nostalgic concepts that seem to overcome historical reality, producing a full-fledged ideology that continues to impact families today. It has become the gold standard by which families, and particularly mothers, are judged: "The hybrid idea that a woman can be fully absorbed with her youngsters while simultaneously maintaining passionate sexual excitement with her husband was a 1950s invention that drove thousands of women to therapists, tranquilizers, or alcohol when they actually tried to live up to it" (p. 9). Coontz explains that our nostalgia for the postwar nuclear family is a combination of different contradictory ideas. For example, the extended family of the 1800s was just that: multiple relatives and children living under one roof and sharing child rearing by group monitoring. The nuclear family, which began to form in the 1920s, was a rejection of the extended household. Instead, child rearing was consolidated into two adults (well, mostly one), with external institutions such as schools providing educational functions.

For Coontz, the nuclear family is unsustainable because the material conditions that created it are no longer in existence and they aren't likely to return. Family values proponents essentially want the postwar family without the postwar laws and policies that funded it, such as the GI Bill, money for building schools, aid to dependent women and children, and so on. During the 1950s the family also became the expected site for the provision of entertainment and leisure, leading to an explosion in shopping centers, restaurants, travel, theme parks, and all the accoutrements that go with them. Those families without the means to purchase consumer goods were left out of the idealized media portrayals that linger today. Another negative aspect of the nuclear family was its ideological merging with Cold War–era realities such as racism in housing, anticommunism, and sexual and political repression. Anyone attempting to resist the dominance of the nuclear family was viewed as suspect.

Ultimately, the nuclear family represented and continues to represent concepts about what women should be. No matter how gender-neutral the language, statements such as "people aren't committed to marriage anymore" are critiques aimed at women, as they are the ones viewed as responsible for the family's successes or failures:

> The crisis of commitment in America is usually seen as a problem associated with women's changing roles because women's family functions have historically mediated the worst effects of competition and individualism in the larger society. Most people who talk about balancing private advancement and individual rights with nurturance, mutual support, and long-term commitment do not envision any serious rethinking of the individualistic, antisocial tendencies in our society, nor any ways of broadening our sources of nurturance and mutual assistance. (p. 41)

Coontz finds that instead of recognizing that the nuclear family form is unsustainable and unrealistic, society instructs women to find ways to continue to serve as the mediator between household and capitalism within an unfair and unjust system.

Michelle Alexander's book *The New Jim Crow: Mass Incarceration in the Age of Colorblindness* (2010) is an in-depth account of the history of the racially based system of law enforcement in the United States. Alexander asserts that instead of progress on the issue, there has been an intensification of sentencing that has resulted in more African Americans behind bars than ever before, along with increased racial profiling (now applied to immigrants) and the removal of the right to vote. In the opening of her book, Alexander explains how these practices are hidden behind a post–Jim Crow colorblind language because it is no longer socially acceptable to outwardly display one's racism:

> Rather than rely on race, we use our criminal justice system to label people of color "criminals" and then engage in all the practices we supposedly left behind. Today it is perfectly legal to discriminate against criminals in nearly all the ways that it was once legal to discriminate against African Ameri-

cans.... We have not ended racial caste in America, we have merely redesigned it. (p. 2)

For Alexander, the mass incarceration of African Americans also refers to a larger network of laws, policies, and sentencing that go way beyond imprisonment as a form of social control. As economic conditions worsen, it is important for society not only to locate scapegoats to keep wages and social unrest low, but also to extract profit from the most vulnerable (incarceration is big business). The notion that "anyone can make it" is a falsehood, because for some, it isn't a matter of failure of individual will, but of outright prohibition: Those who have been incarcerated are legally barred from "making it." As Alexander points out, there have always been African Americans who have "made it" despite barriers, such as free blacks during slavery. Yet, the existence of successful minorities does not erase the undeniable evidence of systemic racism.

Alexander presents the history of mass incarceration as originating in the slave system, pointing to slave patrols led by lower-income whites allied with the planter class. Policing as an institution has always been a part of disciplining poor people in general and minorities in particular. However, after slavery ended, the older racial caste system was harder to enforce without violating the law, so Jim Crow statutes were quickly created as a way to reinstate the older boundaries of the antebellum era using the justification of "states' rights." Black Codes targeted the movement of former slaves in order to keep them in check by highlighting the most minor of infractions (vagrancy, looking at white women, etc.) for harsh punishments/consequences. Soon, Southern states recognized the social and economic benefits of using convict labor and chain gangs.

After the civil rights era presented a major challenge to Jim Crow laws, the language began to shift from overt racism to "tough on crime" discourse:

The success of law and order rhetoric among working-class whites and the intense resentment of racial reforms, particularly in the South, led conservative Republican analysts to believe that a "new majority" could be created by the Republican Party, one that included the traditional Republican base, the white South, and half the Catholic, blue-collar vote of the big cities. Some conservative political strategists admitted that appealing to racial fears and antagonisms were central to this strategy, though it had to be done surreptitiously. (p. 44)

Tough on crime discourse allows white elites to both appeal to lower-income whites and maintain their ability to turn back civil rights gains. The 1990s brought tough on crime to a whole new level with three-strikes sentencing, mirrored in the schools with zero-tolerance suspension and expulsion policies. All of this occurred against a backdrop of the highly profitable prison industrial complex.

In an interview about the impact of *The New Jim Crow*, Alexander (2012) addresses the killing of 16-year-old Trayvon Martin by neighborhood watch zealot George Zimmerman. Rather than focusing on the guilt of Zimmerman, Alexander advocates that it is the mind-set behind Zimmerman's actions that should be put on trial. This mind-set carries over into police departments and courtrooms, through racial profiling and the positioning of African Americans and minorities as "problems" to be controlled or eliminated. Affirmative action has in many ways facilitated this mind-set by offering "a pathway of opportunity for a relative few at the same time that the system of mass incarceration has been developed" (p. 12).

Alexander also notes in her interview that sentencing is extremely unequal in terms of race; for example, the cultivation of marijuana by whites goes virtually unpunished while the sale or possession of marijuana is a key element in sentencing for African Americans. The drug war itself was originally intended to target African Americans but has ended up harming people of all races as it wages on. Even though tough on crime drug laws do not benefit the majority of working-class whites, their appeal remains, especially among Democratic politicians who feel they can beat Republicans at their own game: "All of this created an environment in which people could feel more and more justified in saying on the one hand, 'I'm no racist,' and on the other hand, 'I want to get tough on them'" (p. 15). Part of the new discourse on criminality is the "black on black crime" meme, which "pathologizes something that is quite explainable given the social and

economic realities of the segregated urban poor" (p. 16). Unfortunately, the black on black meme has been advanced by African Americans
as well, essentially rationalizing the conduct of law enforcement on
the basis of increased representation of African Americans in police
departments.

Red-Green Theorists

Dialectical materialist writing also has been flourishing within environmental circles, often providing a much-needed counterperspective
to pragmatic or liberal ecological discourse. Though they may focus
on different subsets of environmental concerns, red-green theorists
have in common the belief that capitalism is fundamentally incompatible with ecology (Four Arrows, Jacobs, & Ryan, 2010; Hughes, 2000;
Patel, 2008; Wall, 1999, 2010; Williams, 2010, 2012c). This includes the
notion of a sustainable form of capitalism, which, like "clean coal
technology," is a contradiction in terms. Environmentalism without
an analysis grounded in economics, history, and the development of
states and war is incomplete, and will not allow for getting at the root
of the problem of global climate change: "Capitalism is literally a system that is based on the maxim 'grow or die.' So the idea that in any
way that could be sustainable or that they could somehow care about
the resources that they put in or the waste that goes out is an impos-
sibility" (Williams, 2012c, p. 20). Wall (1999), in his study of the an-
tiroad movement in the U.K., views the environmental situation as so
urgent and dire that direct action, "ecotage," is called for, not piece-
meal reforms. Unfortunately, in-fighting among eco-activist groups
and right-wing elements within environmentalism have made it difficult to mount a sustained and effective resistance. Other, related issues Wall addresses include green washing, when corporate-
sponsored initiatives that are merely fronts for the continuation of
capitalism put on the trappings of environmentalism, and connecting
the environmental movement to the needs of the working class, a
theme that Wall later explores more deeply in *The Rise of the Green Left*
(2010).

Marxist environmentalists are also skeptical about the population growth thesis—that the earth is not able to sustain the people that we have, let alone future generations—a concept advanced by what Hughes (2000) terms "green Malthusian" authors such as Ehrlich (1971) and Hardin (1995). Overpopulation, aside from having a racist component (few seem worried about there being too many white people), takes capitalist social relations for granted in formulating solutions: Profit must be maintained at all costs. Williams (2010) points out that the problem with capitalism is *overproduction*, not a lack of goods. Instead of supporting sustainable networks of smaller, local farms that could reach poorer people in a cost-efficient manner, agribusiness has effectively wiped out these alternatives, leaving a nightmare of overrefined foods such as high fructose corn syrup in order to extract even more profit from basic commodities such as corn. We have enough food to feed the world several times over, so the real issue is how we distribute resources (Nestle, 2007; Patel, 2008; Thurow & Kilman, 2009). Ultimately, the problem is the earth's inability to carry capitalism's 1% along with their never-ending consumption and growth—*that* capacity has apparently reached its limit (Angus & Butler, 2011).

Red-green environmentalists also address geopolitical concerns. Abouyoub (2012) views Darfur as a crisis based not just on the conflict, but also on the environmental policy. Most of the media presentations about Darfur frame it as an ethnic clash between hostile "Arabs" and "African" victims, which resurrects the colonial discourse used to divide and conquer the region in the first place. Absent in this spectacle is discussion about the role of the environment; climate change has caused record-breaking droughts, leading to migrations of people and creating scarcity: "The status in Darfur thus seems locked in a vicious circle. Unsustainable overuse of natural resources intensifies the ecological degradation already taking place due to other factors and fuels the competition over resources and access to land even further, feeding into more and more violence" (p. 43). Because the dominant means of survival in Darfur are agriculture and grazing, accessibility to water and land are critical. When these become scarce due to climate change, hostilities intensify, and the dissemination of "clash of civilizations" through the mass media continues.

Red-green theorists also find pragmatic, privatized approaches to the environment such as recycling or eating organic foods to be insufficient (Hughes, 2000; Wall, 2010). For example, Williams (2012c) points out that recycling is often the first step for remedying climate change that is presented to the public via the media, and there's a reason for that: It takes the heat off of production and puts it on the consumers. Williams explains that of all the waste that is produced, only 2.5% comes from domestic sources—the rest comes from corporations. Yet, people are told that they need to change their individual habits, as if that—rather than getting corporations to rethink their manufacture of one-time use plastic bottles—were the solution. As Hughes (2000) notes, such issues are different than other societal ones in the degree of their intensity and universality—everyone is impacted, and individual solutions won't do: "Environmental problems are qualitatively different from other social problems in such a way as to create the need for a new political ideology with distinctive proposals for restructuring the whole of political, social, and economic life" (p. 10).

Red-green theorists also explore the philosophical roots of antienvironmental ideology. Many indigenous religious traditions operate counter to the Abrahamic religions such as Christianity, where humans are placed higher up the chain of being, directly under God (Four Arrows, Jacobs, & Ryan, 2010). This often provides cover for their mistreatment of the earth and living creatures. Williams (2012c) discusses the historical transformation of how the earth was once viewed in religious terms as "mother nature" from the prehistoric age through the medieval era, then seen as out of control and necessitating domination in order to extract its resources at the dawn of capitalism. For Williams, Marx and Engels, though they didn't write extensively about the environment, contributed much to ecological theory through their development of historical materialism and the notion that everything is interconnected and impacts everything else.

Four Arrows, Jacobs, and Ryan (2010) also trace the destruction of the environment to a form of anthropocentrism that holds humans as the only sentient beings worthy of privilege and consideration. The authors assert that much has been missed in progressive educational circles by looking at only human-centered pedagogies:

> Until our collective work realizes and addresses the fact that corporate and political interests are as damaging to nonhuman life as to human life, and that this is equally vital, we will continue to miss the boat. We want progressive education to embrace a different center for its work, from human-based to "creation"-based. By creation-based, we mean making all of creation the operating target for human education, not just human benefit. According to indigenous cultures, all "People" are sacred, but these traditional cultures define "People" as including, trees, birds, mammals, fish, plants, humans, etc. "Grandfathers," whether rocks or frogs or cardinal directions, all teach us how to live in balance. (p. 5)

The authors provide several examples of how animals have been their teachers, opening readers' eyes to a different way of thinking about environmentalism.

In terms of character education, Four Arrows, Jacobs, and Ryan propose a radical reconstruction of what one traditionally finds in schools, which often is based on isolated concepts of individualism and the principle of noninterference. The authors address several areas in which environmental thinking can be enhanced by looking at the world in an interconnected way. Understanding the cycles of nature is one way to learn from the nonhuman world and to determine what is natural and what has been disturbed (by, for example, global warming). Additionally, being open to multiple realities in terms of the world we share with living creatures is also important—it isn't just about us and our needs. Usually when conditions are optimal for animals, they are also optimal for humans, but not always the other way around. Action has to be a part of any of these concepts; otherwise, we get nowhere. The authors conclude by stating, "We submit that if humans could relearn to adopt the idea that every land formation and creature is an imprint of our ancestral consciousness, how different our priorities might be" (p. 17).

Conclusion

This chapter has attempted to demonstrate, with a glimpse into basic dialectical materialist, that the reports of Marx's death in academia have been greatly exaggerated. Rather than being a dust-covered relic from the 1960s and 1970s, dialectical materialism has experienced an interdisciplinary resurgence, both as a critique of postmodernism and in response to the intensification of global assaults on the working class under neoliberalism. As one example, the strength of the Occupy movement (which is flawed in many organizational aspects) is in its direct dialectic, "We are the 99%, they are the 1%." That simple analytical framing was powerful enough to displace what had been, up to that point, the dominant discourse of debt-talk and austerity in the media. Occupy has changed the focus of the conversation, even if the next steps look uncertain.

Marxian research is also highly diverse and interdisciplinary, borrowing from what were formerly distinct subject areas to create a more unified critique of capitalist social relations. Instead of viewing disciplinary boundaries as unmovable, Marxists read widely from a range of topics. This makes it further evident that the central problem we face is capitalism. Issues such as environmentalism have applications to other human concerns such as employment, education, housing, and health. It doesn't take long to realize that dialectical materialism has to work beyond traditional boundaries, including those of race, gender, and sexuality.

Rather than being an isolated movement, theoretical Marxian research can be found at mainstream academic conferences such as the American Educational Research Association meeting and the International Congress for Qualitative Inquiry. There are even special-interest groups addressing related social justice and LGBTQ concerns at the annual Joint Statistical Meetings conference. A quick search of Amazon for books on "Marxism and education" alone reveals 391 relevant results. The academic publisher Palgrave has devoted an entire series to Marxism and education, with nine volumes available in mid-2012 and more on the way. Electronic publishing has made the distribution of dialectical ideas even more feasible, through peer-reviewed open-source journals such as the *Journal for Critical Education Policy Studies* (JCEPS), which has an editorial advisory board of more than 150 scholars. Information about publishing and presentation opportunities are presented in greater detail in Chapter 13. Suffice it to say that as with critical quantitative research (addressed in Chapter Four) and dialectical qualitative research (Chapter Five), there are plenty of opportunities and spaces for those interested in pursuing basic theoretical analyses as part of their research inquiry. What has been presented so far is just the tip of the iceberg.

Chapter Seven

People

Overview

Rather than adhering to neutrality and distance as major ethical imperatives of research, dialectical materialists value advocacy, more specifically, advocacy-in-action, in the service of the most vulnerable in society. Stake and Rosu (2012) explain the many dimensions of advocacy:

> For human beings, advocacy is a default setting. We seek change for the better; we struggle to protect what we have. Advocacy is a plea for what we want and see needed.... [T]he common meaning indicates a speaking out regularly for a condition more than for a commodity. We advocate inquiry and we advocate skepticism. We advocate immediate relief and we advocate for an enduring status. Advocacy relies on bias, pity, reason, love, and hate. (p. 45)

Because it goes beyond simply seeking data-driven results, advocacy can be an effective frame for the Marxist task of not just describing the world, but changing it. At the same time, the kind of advocacy that Stake and Rosu describe is flexible enough to use research for both meeting immediate, pressing needs and building a long-term vision that can move us beyond capitalism. Both are essential components of inquiry in the dialectical tradition.

Understanding the "people" aspect of research means grappling with ethics, on both the institutional and personal levels. Ethics have to be a consideration even before initiating inquiry, yet they are often an afterthought, as if taken for granted. Hesse-Biber (2007) points out that "from the beginning of our research project, who and what we choose to study is grounded in an appreciation of difference. What and who we study has affected our cognizance of our difference and our general approaches to these issues" (p. 140). It is a mistake to assume that if one is conducting research from a qualitative, critical, Marxian, or feminist philosophical orientation, one is automatically protected from exploiting others, and ethics have been sufficiently addressed (Buch & Staller, 2007). In addition to communicating his or her ethics, a dialectical researcher also has to understand how people are impacted differently under capitalism, depending on the dynamics of class, race, gender, ability status, and sexuality. Categories of race and ethnicity are often deployed without a comprehension of the historical forces that created those constructs.

It is also critical to understand that ethics alone is no protection when we are talking about research conducted under capitalism, particularly biomedical research. Recent investigative reporting on the global tissue trade reveals that dead bodies are a big business:

> Inside the marketplace for human tissue, the opportunities for profits are immense. A single, disease-free body can spin off cash flows of $80,000 to $200,000 for the various nonprofit and for-profit players involved in recovering tissues and using them to manufacture medical and dental products, according to documents and experts in the field. It's illegal in the U.S., as in most other countries, to buy or sell human tissue. However, it's permissible to pay service fees that ostensibly cover the costs of finding, storing and processing human tissues. Almost everyone gets a piece of the action. Ground-level body wranglers in the U.S. can get as much as $10,000 for each corpse they secure through their contacts at hospitals, mortuaries and morgues. Funeral homes can act as middlemen to identify potential donors. Public hospitals can get paid for the use of tissue-recovery rooms. (Willson, Lavrov, Keller, Maier, & Ryle, 2012, para. 37–40)

Even though on the surface the tissue trade is breaking no law, and even though all of the major professional associations have codes of ethics, this is a dramatic reminder that the for-profit nature of research always lurks in the background.

This chapter addresses research ethics, beginning with a review of the history and ideology of formal, institutionalized research protocol. Next, as institutional research protocol involves complexity, I identify some issues that can emerge when these models are applied to research scenarios, including maintaining confidentiality, and methodological censorship. Next I address sociological constructs and categories, which include racial and ethnic boundaries that one often uses in research. Finally, rather than rejecting the institutional research model on the basis that it is too confining, this chapter considers that it doesn't go far enough, especially concerning the most oppressed in society, who are often the topic of research inquiry.

History of Institutionalized Research Protocol

Recently, institutional research protocol, specifically the institutional review board (IRB) system, has been critiqued for being overly restrictive and even censoring inquiry (Katz, 2007; Meeker, 2012; Shopes, 2007). Institutional research review committees, like other aspects of implemented policy, on the whole have been slow to respond to the growth of qualitative research forms, yet there have been some practical adaptations and exemptions from the medical model of research for methodologies such as oral history (Meeker, 2012; Shopes, 2007) and action research conducted by classroom teachers (James, Milenkiewicz, & Bucknam, 2008). Even so, due to all of the details involved, many faculty and students find it overwhelming to put together a research proposal to present before the IRB, and members of IRBs have a tendency to overreach by rejecting proposals because they are based on methodology they might personally disagree with, or because of grammatical errors, rather than because of concerns about protecting participants.

Understanding the history of abuses leading to the establishment of institutional protocol makes creating an IRB proposal seem less onerous and more part of a continuum of the legacy of capitalist research. It is staggering to confront the degree of freedom that researchers had prior to institutional regulations (Price, 2011). Most are familiar with the scope of the depravity of Nazi war crimes committed in the name of science, because these were revealed during the Nuremberg trials. Not as many are aware of abuses in the United States, other than the high-profile Tuskegee experiments (1932–1972), in which the United States Public Health Service studied the effects of syphilis under the cover of providing much-needed health care services to African American participants. The participants receiving the care were not told that they had the disease; instead, they were told they had "bad blood" (Jones, 1993). Covert radiation experiments were also conducted on African Americans in the United States, with a little help from some old "friends":

> In 1945, the U.S. State Department, army intelligence, and the OSS, the immediate forerunner to the CIA, recruited former Third Reich scientists, granting them immunity, jobs, and new identities in a resettlement program for Nazi scientists. It was named Operation Paperclip, for the mode of identifying potential recruits—a simple paper clip placed on each of their dossiers. In exchange, the State Department asked that the scientists resume their old habits—working on secret nonconsensual research projects, many of which exploited patients—but this time throughout the United States. (Washington, 2006, p. 229)

Lederer (1995) extensively documents the historical use of nonconsensual research within the United States, from the above-mentioned radiation experiments to research on vulnerable populations such as children placed in state mental facilities. In one 1939 University of Iowa experiment dubbed the "Monster Study," 22 orphan children were divided into experimental and control groups, with each group receiving either positive or negative speech therapy. Many of the children left the experiment with with permanent stutters, causing much psychological damage. There is also John B. Watson's famous experiment on Little Albert, in which Watson used the infant Albert to demonstrate operational conditioning. Albert eventually developed a fearful association with anything related to fur-covered animals. Although the identity of Albert wasn't revealed, Beck, Levinson, and Irons (2009) conclude that he was the 8-month-old child (possibly with neurological problems from birth) of an unmarried woman who consented to his participation in the experiment, thus highlighting further the exploitative networks of unethical research conducted on vulnerable populations.

There are several key documents that emerged within three decades after the Nuremberg trials that attempted to address the public outrage that followed the uncovering of more recent research abuses such as the Tuskegee experiments. The first is the *U.S. Code of Federal Regulations*, Title 45, Section 46 (1991), updated annually, which outlines the protection of human participants, embodied in the "Common Rule," which deals with conduct of research (Mazur, 2007; Smith, 2000). The *Code of Federal Regulations* specifies the creation and maintenance of institutional review boards at research locations, each of which are required to have a minimum of five members, including community representatives. The main role of the IRB is to review medical and social science research in order to protect participants from harm. Vulnerable groups such as children under 18, pregnant women, the differently abled, and prisoners are specified for heightened protection. By 2005, all institutions conducting any research, not just federally funded research, had to have an IRB (Denzin, 2009; Stake & Rosu, 2012).

A second important document in the post-Nuremberg era is the *Belmont Report* (1979), created in response to the passage of the National Research Act (1974). The *Belmont Report* (1979) specifically addresses the issue of informed consent, and conceptualizes the participant as a volunteer: "[T]he extent and nature of information should be such that persons, knowing that the procedure is neither necessary for their care nor perhaps fully understood, can decide whether they wish to participate in the furthering of knowledge" (Mazur, 2007, p. 173). The three underlying ethical constructs in the *Belmont Report* (1979) include respect for persons (informed consent), beneficence (do no harm), and justice (fair treatment and compensation). The National Research Act (1974) also requires informed parental consent for children under the age of 18.

A third significant document is the American Psychological Association's *Ethical Principles in the Conduct of Research with Human Participants* (1992). This document was created to bring the fields of psychology and the social science to the same level of ethical expectations as biomedical research, and it adds the values of trust and fidelity/scientific integrity to respect for persons, beneficence, and justice (American Psychological Association, 1992). Smith (2000) notes that these ethical priorities are derived from Western philosophies that privilege the construct of individual autonomy and seeks to weigh notions of the individual 'subject' in regard to potential harms/benefits of research. According to Fischman (2000), "Treating individuals as autonomous agents means that researchers do not interfere with their choices or encroach on their privacy unless the individuals agree that the researchers may do so" (p. 35).

Informed consent is not just a participant's signature on a document, but a process of carefully outlining, to the best of the researcher's ability, the scope of participation to be expected in the study, along with identifying potential risks and benefits (Mazur, 2007). Price (2011) notes that in the late 1960s, a radical caucus of the American Anthropological Association was instrumental in crafting an ethics code for the field known as the Principles of Professional Responsibility. According to the Principles, member anthropologists were required to ensure that their research would do no harm and would not be conducted or reported covertly, and that funding sources would be disclosed, all key aspects of informed consent. Price points out that since 1990, these requirements have been relaxed, allowing for military and commercial research to be conducted covertly.

Complexity of Institutional Protocol

One of the major barriers to the full implementation of institutional research protocol is badly designed studies (such as selecting sites based on convenience), which can lead to ethical compromises (Sieber, 2000; Walford, 2008b). Often overlooked is a clear rationale as to why a study should be conducted in the first place—is it worthwhile (Mazur, 2007)? Unfortunately, the notion of fitness of research is often put aside in favor of micromanaging aspects of methodology. One problem is that the *Code of Federal Regulations* (1991) defines research as contributing to generalizable knowledge, effectively privileging quantitative methodologies that are not designed for general application (Buchanan, 2009; Denzin, 2009; Torres & Reyes, 2011). The empirical model that is preferred by IRBs also doesn't allow for the unfolding of methodology, a key feature of qualitative research (Buchanan, 2009; Walford, 2008b). For example, it is common for IRBs to request an interview protocol in the research proposal, which might be difficult for the researcher who is planning to conduct open-ended interviews.

Baez (2007) points out that if researchers are critics of society, they need to be especially tuned in to their own role in society, being "attentive to the privilege and authority that such a role carries, and to its potential to exert its own kind of oppression" (p. 20). Researcher self-identification, a component of qualitative research paradigms, also is not typically dealt with in IRBs beyond the basics of listing institutional affiliation:

> Reflexivity is the process through which a researcher recognizes, examines, and understands how his or her own social background and assumptions can intervene in the research process. Like the researched or respondent, the researcher is a product of his or her society's social structures and institutions. Our beliefs, backgrounds, and feelings are part of the process of knowledge construction. (Hesse-Biber, 2007, p. 129)

Qualitative researchers value the personalization that comes with reflexivity, and use this as a way to mediate power differentials between researcher and researched, an established tradition within feminist ethics. However, Hesse-Biber reminds us that often, too much personalization can put a burden on participants and coerce them into revealing more about their lives than they might under normal circumstances. Focusing on reflexivity at the expense of careful study design also can present a false equivalence of power when in fact the researcher still maintains the authority to determine the interpretation of data.

Carspecken (1996) addresses the complexity and nuance of authority in research, using Weber's categories of power. First, there is normative power, where those with less authority submit to those with more authority due to expected norms and customs. Second is coercive power, which is more overt; those with less authority submit for fear of punishment. Third, there are interactively established contracts, which involve subordinates doing tasks in order to receive rewards. Finally, there is a power involved with charisma or charm, where those with less authority act in concert with those who have more authority out of loyalty or a personal attraction. As Carspecken explains,

> If power relations are not equal between the observer and the communities of people affected by her truth claims, then those claims cannot be validated. Distortions in power relations can be much more subtle than the power of one actor to exercise sanctions on those who will not consent to her claims. (p. 90)

In this sense, being an outsider in a research setting can be an advantage rather than a liability because participants might be more trusting than if they shared the same background with the researcher. Outsiders also tend to ask more questions than those who might take the research setting and events for granted (Hesse-Biber, 2007). At the same time, researchers should be careful that in their zeal to share their scholarship with participants they don't overwhelm or alienate participants with professional jargon, or make them feel awkward because they are unable to analyze their lives according to the researcher's theoretical framework (Carspecken, 1996).

"Minimal risk" as defined in the *Code of Federal Regulations* (1991) and the *Belmont Report* (1979) is problematic because it assumes "minimal risk" for participants under safe conditions. Mazur (2007) points out that even in a safe environment, some activities take on different degrees of risk, requiring practical, not just minimal, risk definitions. Simply obtaining a signature on a consent form is no guarantee that participants understand fully the consequences of their involvement in a study (Fischman, 2000). Mazur (2007) asserts that "Principal investigators or members of the research team should not use the phrase 'IRB approval' or 'IRB approved' during informed consent sessions, as if the decision made it okay for the individual to enroll in a research study" (p. 57).

Research, including qualitative methodologies, carries with it the risk of othering through academic discourse. Like power in Carspecken (1996), othering, too, is hard to detect because often it is built into not only the setting that one is studying, but also the research process itself. Krumer-Nevo (2012) describes four aspects of othering: objectification, decontextualization, dehistorization, and deauthorization through the pose of objectivity. Another way of othering is a form of idealization in which researchers refuse to include negative aspects of a group they are studying. Krumer-Nevo describes research at a women's prison in which inmates were perplexed at the researcher's unwillingness to mention in the study that some of them had murder sentences—what they saw as an important omission in the presentation of the participants. Gigengack (2008) addresses a similar concern in studies of street children, in which they are either subjected to institutionalized "pity" discourse or romanticized as "overcomers" through activist discourse. hooks (1996) launches a similar critique of activist discourse in her assessment of the film *Kids* (1995), which she views as more sensationalist fiction than ethnography. Instead of relying on reactionary postmodern framing, Gigengack (2008) makes a sound suggestion for researchers:

> If it is based on intensive and longitudinal fieldwork, good street ethnography will be able to show that, beyond all the coping with poverty, being a street child involves self-destruction. The young street people's victimhood and their agency will thus appear to be two sides of the same coin. (p. 216)

Due to increasing technological access, statutes, legal actions, data sharing, and security breaches, confidentiality and even anonymity is becoming harder for researchers to maintain (Folkman, 2000; Mazur, 2007; Walford, 2008b). Even if pseudonyms are used, a reader can look up the institution where the researcher conducted her or his study, deduce the location of the data collection from context cues, and do a quick Internet search to find employees. Confidentiality also can be breached by sharing study results—those who know the participants often can determine who said what just by using simple logic, or participants might eagerly point themselves out in the study's quoted excerpts, thereby revealing the identities of other participants. Additionally, there may be instances where anonymity "naturalizes the decoupling of events from historically and geographically specific locations" (Walford, 2008b, p. 35). What is special about research settings-as-context can be flattened and falsely generalized, as in the numerous case studies of successful high-poverty schools that suggest that anyone can overcome economic deprivation if they only work harder. Anonymization has encouraged this type of research, making it difficult for other researchers to follow up with these schools.

Privacy is a more complex and nuanced concept within confidentiality and anonymity. IRBs were originally designed to address biomedical research ethics, which involves different concepts of privacy than might apply to qualitative contexts (Buchanan, 2009). Folkman (2000) describes two components of privacy:

> The first has to do with the person's freedom to pick and choose the time and circumstances under which facts about the person and, most importantly, the extent to which his or her attitudes, beliefs, behavior, and opinions are to be shared with or withheld from others. The second has to do with the person's right not to be given information he or she does not want. (p. 49)

It is important for researchers to understand community and cultural norms surrounding privacy so that those can be addressed. Unfortunately, Folkman points out that other than legislation concerning access to information pertaining to children, privacy is not adequately addressed in state and federal laws. Additionally, even if a researcher is able to gain ready site access, this can be taken away at any time, by any participant (Walford, 2008b).

Ultimately, institutional research protocol is limited by its original intent, as Torres and Reyes (2011) explain:

> IRBs are designed to protect the institutional liability and not the public interest and society at large.... [E]xclusive focus on individual ethics allows us to acknowledge only partial responsibility while researchers abdicate their social responsibilities. (p. 177)

Because IRBs are designed to implement research protocol, which is based on classical liberal notions of autonomy and noninterference, not much is addressed in the way of larger societal obligations (Stake & Rosu, 2012). In this way, "IRBs are institutional apparatuses, regimes of truth and systems of discourse that regulate a particular form of ethical conduct" (Denzin, 2009, p. 277). Researchers who feel strongly about advocacy are often on their own when faced with the dilemma of how much intervention or assistance to provide through their scholarship (Buch & Staller, 2007).

Constructs and Categories

Abouyoub (2012), a political sociologist, urges researchers to fully understand what is meant when they use categories of ethnicity:

> In anthropological literature, the term *ethnic group* refers to a population bearing certain traits: that it is to a large extent biologically self-perpetuating, that it shares fundamental cultural values that constitute a field of communication and interaction, and that it encompasses members who identify themselves and are identified by others as a distinct category of population. Anthropological studies have shown that ethnic difference is not based on social isolation and absence of interaction; rather it is the foundation of social systems. In other words, cultural distinctiveness and ethnic interaction are not mutually exclusive. (p. 35)

For Abouyoub, most of the ethnic categories that researchers use, particularly for peoples in Africa and the Middle East, are not neutrally determined, but instead arise from boundaries that are placed by colonial powers, usually as the result of appropriating land and resources. This was the case with the identification of Native Americans, who sometimes were classified as "white" when the intent was to exclude African Americans, and other times labeled "black" for the purposes of marriage laws; most of the time, the classification was "nonwhite" (Deloria, 1988): "When one asks the liberal about minority groups, he unconsciously seems to categorize them all together for purposes of problem solving. Hence, dark-skinned minority groups as categorical concepts have brought about the same basic results—the Indian is defined as a subcategory of black" (p. 171). Most research studies operate within normative racial frameworks, and do not critically examine the formation of these categories. Teranishi's (2007) research into Asian Americans and higher education illustrates the complexities of race and ethnicity: "By reporting these racial characteristics and including international students, we use inflated numbers that exaggerate the achievement of Asian Americans. Such inflations prompt some scholars to describe Asian Americans as overrepresented in terms of earned doctorates; they are actually underrepresented" (p. 41). When Asians are grouped into a monolithic whole, many of the demographic details are lost. For example, there are differences between Asian immigrants and those who have been in the United States for several generations. Yet, U.S. Asians are treated as "perpetual immigrants" by the way they are categorized. There are also critical distinctions among Asians based on their countries of origin as well as factors of social class (those who come from poorer countries often struggle more with literacy skills).

There has been increased scrutiny of how groups are represented in research, down to the terminologies used. The *American Psychological Association Manual* (2009) updated writing guidelines by addressing outdated and current labels for people: For example, instead of the term *disabled children*, researchers should use *children with different abilities*, mentioning the disability or condition after noting that the participants are children. Similarly, the term *low-achieving students* places the attribute first, naturalizing the condition of not performing well in schools, or making it appear inborn; instead, it is better to use the term *students identified as low-achieving*, which properly attributes the definition to institutional forces that have labeled the students according to some criteria, not to the students themselves. Instead of viewing this attention to detail as tedious "political correctness," researchers should see it as a matter of respect. Giroux (2010) reminds us that there are some groups who have virtually no protection against how they are portrayed in the media, such as African Americans who were victims of Hurricane Katrina. Promulgating stereotypes, even unintentionally, can have harmful consequences.

Even setting aside racism, the categorization of groups is fraught with difficulties. In some cases, the people we need to study are the hardest to locate due to economic or linguistic barriers (Sieber, 2000). Even determining who is a "participant" can be problematic in the course of qualitative research—not every person who is a part of a study requires informed consent (Walford, 2008b). In our quest to clearly identify the people we are studying, often we can overlook the fact that categories such as class always intersect with gender and race, making it misleading to simply list a descriptor without commentary (Holmstrom, 2002a). Like race and gender, class is not monolithic, nor is it supposed to be another descriptor of demographic characteristics; instead, it defines the relation of a person to the means of production (Allman, 2007). Terms such as *working class* can be misleading because they suggest that only manual laborers or those making less than a certain salary are working class. Researchers have to be very clear about definitions when they use terminologies. Additionally, statistics can also change the meaning of information about groups, when, for example, one uses the mean to emphasize how well groups are doing when the median is more realistic (Lewontin & Levins, 2007).

Conclusion

Beyond the IRB: A Need for Reciprocity and Solidarity

Even though they compromised by the privileging of quantitative methodologies, power plays, micromanagement, and misapplications, IRBs are essential to the regulation of research, as Mazur (2007) reminds us:

> It will be difficult for the principal investigator or study sponsor to separate the benefit to society in terms of generalizable knowledge from other benefits that may accrue to the involved parties (i.e., themselves). This difficulty on the part of the investigator and sponsor is, by itself, a good argument for the existence of institutional review boards. (p. 31)

Yet, by themselves, IRBs, with their utilitarian focus on principles of noninterference and autonomy, are not sufficient for ameliorating the worst effects of research under capitalism (Denzin, 2009).

Due to the impact of feminism and the growing awareness of the impact of research conducted on marginalized groups, pressure is mounting for institutions to begin to think differently about study design (Brooks, 2007; Stanfield, 2012). Rather than simply creating a list of potential "stakeholders" in the abstract, researchers need to understand how the unique social contexts of people often place them in harm's way prior to the arrival of the researcher (Sieber, 2000). Understanding and being open to these conditions is essential for researchers to begin to benefit participants. Rethinking what is meant by collaboration is also important, as Leavy (2007c) explains:

> The collaborative potential of oral history is not simply a choice of methodology but also carries with it a set of politics and a host of ethical considerations linked to the empowerment of research subjects and the social activist component of feminist research. Collaboration and authority ultimately speak to how a narrative is constructed and who has ownership over the narrative and how it is represented. (p. 168)

A major challenge in this rethinking of collaboration is how to resolve the tension between ceding authority to participants as co-creators of research and retaining a critical, feminist, or Marxian perspective that the participants themselves may not have.

Mitchell Duneier is an excellent role model for researchers attempting to approach reflexivity. For his ethnography *Sidewalk* (1999), Duneier had one of his participants, Hakim Hasan, compose the afterword. Hasan provides a rare glimpse into the role of the study participant, from his own perspective:

> After reading the original manuscript three years ago, I concluded that the events and conversations that took place at my book-vending table could not convey, by themselves, the complexity of the social structure that existed on these blocks. I sent Mitch a long, handwritten letter outlining my concerns. I expected him to think I had overstepped my bounds as "subject"...since I was a subject, how far did my right to theorize go? (p. 322)

Not only did Duneier appreciate Hasan's letter and revisit the research site to conduct more data gathering, he invited Hasan to co-teach an undergraduate seminar that used *Sidewalk* as a course reading. This provided Duneier, Hasan, and the students with a way to democratically interrogate the ethnography's findings. As Hasan noted, "This course marked the beginning of a process whereby the other men and women on Sixth Avenue would no longer be mere data" (p.

322). At the same time, Hasan also learned things from Duneier's analysis that he missed while living day-to-day as a book vendor.

Though attractive to some participants, and certainly those who data collect, relying on the narrative of "future benefits" of research is insufficient. Any research benefits that exist are likely to be distant for participants (Sieber, 2000; Walford, 2008b). But immediate benefits should be built into studies, such as referral to agencies that can provide material or psychological assistance. Another form of immediate benefit could be supporting communities in their activist struggles; often, researchers who work in universities have access and privilege, and are more easily heard. Monetary compensation, too, isn't out of the question. In fact, Fischman (2000) doesn't find it problematic or any more coercive to offer significant compensation to some participants, especially in biomedical research. Such efforts "probably cause no greater risk than the risk that exists in the daily lives of those individuals, and they may even be of some benefit" (p. 41). As Stake and Rosu (2012) remind us, "there is nothing holy about advocacy, but nothing holy happens without it" (p. 56).

Collaborative interpretive focus groups are one way for researchers and participants to move beyond the traditional individualistic protocol model. With interpretive focus groups, researchers meet with participants to share data collected from the study in order to field interpretations, ask clarifying questions, and obtain a more complex form of interaction beyond simply emic or etic (Fischman, 2000; Leavy, 2007c; Sieber, 2000). Sieber (2000) advocates collaborative focus groups as an excellent initial step in order to communicate with those who are going to be participating in the study, promote understanding of the goals of research, and set the groundwork for the future communication of research results. This is important because even if a researcher is able to gain access to a site, she or he may not be guaranteed access across the board, or for the duration of the study (Buch & Staller, 2007). For Fischman (2000), collaborative focus groups can also be an important means of ensuring cultural sensitivity during the process of informed consent, which should include thorough communication of the study's goals.

Currently, existing institutional protocol is based on separating clinical research conducted with participants from the provision of clinical care (Mazur, 2007). This distinction is important because often, study participants are drawn to volunteer in the anticipation that they will receive much needed assistance. For example, pharmaceutical research participants often are recruited from groups who are homeless or in financial or medical distress. Educational researchers find that parents are willing to provide consent to participate in research, thinking they will obtain tutoring and other remediation for their children. The only remedy that institutional protocol can provide is to remind researchers that their informed consent process must be transparent and ethical. Yet, this doesn't deal at all with the clinical care component. Other than some researchers providing immediate assistance or compensation, solutions are not guaranteed, and the policy of noninterference is asserted.

Denzin (2009) proposes that research boards adopt the collective charters that several indigenous groups have begun using as a means of drawing a line in the sand:

> These rights include control and ownership of the community's cultural property; its health and knowledge systems; its rituals and customs; its culture's basic gene pool, rights, and rules for self-determination; and an insistence on who the first beneficiaries of indigenous knowledge will be. (p. 299)

This is vastly different than the individualistic ethos of traditional research, where a small pittance is usually provided to participants and the findings are used in for-profit endeavors. For Denzin, this collective ethics would embody a feminist conception of participants having an equal say about how research is conducted and about the acceptability of findings, and any consequences of the research after the fact should be assessed by the community where the data was gathered. This is similar to Deloria's (1988) assertion that researchers should have to appear before a tribal council to ask permission to conduct their studies, with access granted only upon assurance that money will be provided for the sustenance of the tribe: "Anthropologists would thus become productive members of Indian society instead of ideological vultures.... [A]cademic freedom certainly does not imply that one group of people have to become chessmen for another group of people" (p. 95).

Chapter Eight

Places

Overview: Impacts of Settings

The environment is a critical component of dialectical materialist research, yet it goes way beyond just the physical features of a study's setting to include social relationships that exist under particular constraints, starting with the worker who has to exchange her/his labor power under capitalism (Allman, 2007; Hennessy, 2002). What makes up a research setting is underpinned by this relationship, under the guise of natural occurrences, often commonly referred to as "free choice," or as Slee (2006) explains, "Our decisions of where to live, how to travel, of where to shop—these are not so much expression of an intrinsic preference as they are the best reply to the environment in which we live" (p. 63).

When Marxist researchers talk about context, they are referring to "analysis that ties the ways in which domains of social life are organized and experienced in the field to broader social and political trends in the nation or world" (Buch & Staller, 2007, p. 213). Lewontin and Levins (2007) provide the example of how medical interventions aren't just a matter of pinning individual diagnoses on individual bodies; there are larger systems at play:

> Each person has her/his own network of interactions, some of which are shared by everyone and some are quite individual. The network is simultaneously physiological, psychological, and social without it being possible to isolate each into a separate domain; an event impacting directly on any one of the variables percolate throughout the whole system...therefore the diagnosis of a health problem should include the identification of the network, and the appropriate loci of intervention may be anywhere in the system. (p. 140)

At the same time, people also act upon their environments, which can result in either reproducing and reinforcing the system or changing it altogether. Carspecken (1996) points out that "social systems exist because people generally make only very small innovations when they act" (p. 37). Dialectical materialist researchers are therefore quite interested in key intersections between people and the social environmental contexts in which they live and work. Understanding the research setting in a more complete manner is a necessary task of Marxist inquiry. After all, "[H]ow are we to explain system change as a result of unpredicted externalities if we are not sure what is external?" (Lewontin & Levins, 2007, p. 14). This chapter begins with an overview of Marxist geography, one of the theoretical subfields of dialectics that can provide useful insights for dealing with environmental contexts in research. Next, individualism as a counterresponse to examining social causes is critiqued, followed by a discussion of common racial and gendered contexts that researchers are likely to encounter (family, work, school). Finally, an appeal is made to carefully reconsider the microscopic focus on localisms.

Marxist Geography

Marxist geography, also known as "historical geographical materialism," uses dialectical theory to approach the study of place and the humans who live within it:

> Marxist geography has been committed to applying classical Marxism to a redefinition and understanding of human geography; a redefinition of the classic interests in place and space, differentiation and connection into themes of geographically uneven development, colonialism, and territorial struggle, among others. The way in which contradiction is then given geographic expression has been mobilized in understanding these forms. (Cox, 2005, p. 2)

This macroanalytical approach to geography places at the center of human dynamics the relations of production, not power, culture, or the political economy, as more liberalized forms of post-Marxian geography do. Additionally, Marxist geography views exploitation as an essential and persistent feature of capitalism rather than a site-specific phenomenon experienced by only poorer nations or individuals (Cox, 2005; Harvey, 2000; Swyngedouw, 2006). Dialectical geographers are also likely to question common statistical indices such as population density that do not take into account that urban areas cannot be compared to rural ones in terms of overall impact. Within the existing construct of population density, rural areas are given more weight than urban ones (Lewontin & Levins, 2007).

Based on their research on water rights and urban ecology, Swyngedouw, Kaika, and Castro (2002) outline a manifesto of materialist geography that they feel can be applied to a variety of social settings. First, environmental and social changes impact each other. Second, human-created environments are the result of historical forces. Third, the type of changes encountered and the often unevenly distributed environmental outcomes are not independent of historical and economic conditions. Fourth, the biological world impacts the human-created world, and vice versa. Fifth, development is contradictory—what might be seen as an improvement in the living conditions of some may result in a deterioration of the living condition of others. Sixth, change is never natural or neutral. Seventh, it is especially important for researchers to focus on social power relations, which often determine who can access and who is denied resources. Eighth, questions about sustainability are always political questions. Ninth, the transformation of the environment does not happen independent of race, class, gender, and ethnicity. Tenth, sustainability will be achieved only through a democratically reconstructed environment along the lines of equality of distribution.

For Harvey (2000), "the particularity of the body cannot be understood independently of its embeddedness in socioecological processes" (p. 16). As an example, the work that people do is often tied to their personality traits or characteristics, but the relationship isn't directly causal. Instead, "the type of labor people do puts them into certain social relations, and these relations are institutionalized into sets of practices, cultural agencies, and so on" (Holmstrom, 2002b, p. 366). Historians have concluded from examining population records that the biggest challenge facing people in the late Middle Ages through the Renaissance wasn't other people (i.e., wars); insects, climate, and disease were more significant (Howell & Prevenier, 2001). The environment is not simply a stage upon which these impacts play out, which otherwise remains empty. Researchers should approach settings as constant social sites that have particular characteristics and exist within specific time frames (Carspecken, 1996). Indeed, it may not be possible to observe a setting, even if one is in it; one also has to develop an understanding of what takes place within a specific setting, which involves tying it to larger geographical locales.

Salzinger's (2002) observational study of a maquiladora provides an excellent example of macroanalysis along the lines of historical geographical materialism. In this passage, she manages to capture the connections between setting and workers and how each shapes the other:

> The factory floor is organized for visibility—a panopticon in which everything is marked. Yellow tape lines the walkways; red arrows point to test sites; green, yellow, and red lights glow above machines. On the walls hang large, shiny white graphs documenting quality levels in red, yellow, green and black. Just above each worker's head is a chart full of dots: green for one defect, red for three defects, gold stars for perfect days. Workers' bodies, too, are marked: yellow, sleeveless smocks for new workers; light blue smocks for more seasoned women workers; dark blue jackets for male workers and mechanics; orange smocks for female "special" workers; red smocks for female group chiefs; lipstick, mascara, eyeliner, rouge, high heels, miniskirts, identity badges—everything is signaled. (p. 200)

Salzinger's description weaves together objective accounting and interpretation of what is a gendered space under capitalism. Carspecken (1996) views this type of accounting as an important precursor to forming questions about why a particular environment is the way it is, and why people live/work within it. This moves the establishment of the setting's characteristics into the territory of politics.

In a similar manner, Lewontin and Levins (2007) go into great detail about the unjust system of health care in many countries. Then, they begin to formulate radical questions such as, Why do we spend so much on health care and have so little to show for it? They put forward four possibilities for inquiry: First, we don't actually get a larger quantity of care, we just pay more for it; second, even when some people get health care, much of it isn't good; third, the health care system itself is inherently unequal; and fourth, even though we invest more in disease prevention and scientific advancement, we get sicker and sicker. Lewontin and Levins assert that where we locate the causes of disease matters tremendously, because it impacts the political response. We know, for example, that infant deaths aren't distributed evenly. Even if two infants have the same medical condition, such as asthma, it is more likely to have severe consequence for less affluent households than for affluent ones. People who are impoverished often die from very routine and chronic conditions such as diabetes that are left untreated. As Lewontin and Levins put it, "[I]t is not too far-fetched to speak of the pancreas under capitalism or the proletarian lung" (p. 30).

Marxist geography can also apply to the construction of history, as Hardesty's (2000) analysis of the Canyon de Chelly national monument demonstrates. Hardesty noted differences between Native American groups and white tourists in how the monument was framed:

> People create ethnographic landscapes in their own cultural and social images. When people carrying different cultures come into contact, either living together in or visiting the same geographical region, worlds collide. The social and political controversies created by the collision often involve the maintenance of ethnic or cultural identities. (p. 177)

One of the key ethnic differences between Native Americans and white tourists is the notion of time as documenting history. The Western conception of time often works with horizontal notions and left-to-right progressions, whereas geographic time often works vertically, as with layers of fossils (Howett, 2000). Preservationists need to take these ideas into consideration when designing plans for the preservation of important places.

Francaviglia (2000) posits six different classifications of heritage landscapes, which also relate to how history itself is enacted depending on social context. The first are landscapes that are passively preserved, such as small towns, "found in remote areas or areas of relative economic stagnation" (p. 51). The second are actively preserved heritage landscapes, which involve intricate funding sources and research to support and maintain the site. The third are restored heritage landscapes, such as the Alamo; Francaviglia points out that in many of these landscapes, only the most prominent dwellings are preserved—we don't typically see workers' homes, for example. The fourth are assembled heritage landscapes, "isolated in space and time from those landscapes where progress is evident" (p. 58). These are sites that create a sense of history by their arrangement of objects and features. The fifth are "imagineered" heritage landscapes, created through modern filters, such as Disney's Main Street USA. Finally, the sixth type are imagically preserved landscapes, which include museum dioramas, model railroad layouts, and artistic representations of a site no longer in existence.

> The ultimate goal of preservation is didactic—to convey messages about the meaning of the past. Our preserved heritage landscapes are reminders of what we cherish—and have lost—in our transition from an agricultural and industrial country to a service economy. Heritage landscapes are easy to sell; they enable us to reconstruct, or reinterpret, the past, sometimes as it should have been rather than it was. (Francaviglia, 2000, p. 68)

Limits of Individualism

Although context is given some degree of consideration within mainstream research, on the whole, individualism and its related constructs (motivation, resiliency, agency, etc.) are privileged over notions that the environment presents several constraints on the actions of people. This is in part tied to the function of market ideology, where one is supposed to scrutinize the "bad decisions" of the poor and working class, not capitalism. The diversity seen among humans is transformed into a naturalizing of hierarchy and a further justification for differential access to necessities (Lewontin & Levins, 2007). This reinforces markets as the solution to problems such as "dependency" and provides cover for cutting social welfare programs in order to promote "freedom" and "independence" (Brenner, 2002). Ho's (2009) ethnography of Wall Street found that investment bankers framed events such as downsizing and unemployment as natural aspects of the market, with this consequence: "When conflicts between unequal values and interests are interpreted mainly in terms of abstraction, which in turn is refracted back as a core characteristic of finance, such assumptions further obfuscate the task of grounding Wall Street actors" (p. 37). Individualism is, therefore, the discourse du jour of alienation, as it promotes an atomized conception of the social world as existing apart from one's own self, the one who makes "all the decisions" and is "in control" (Lautensach & Lautensach, 2010).

The assertion of individual uniqueness is held up to counter overwhelming evidence of environmental shaping. It is a common response when confronted with social science, a way to show that "not everyone" experiences the same thing and to steer attention away from systemic contributions. To think in dialectical material terms of social context means making note of repeated events and what they might mean:

> But it does not follow that where there is choice, subjectivity, and individuality there cannot also be predictability. The error is to take the individual as causally prior to the whole and not to appreciate that the social has causal problems within which individual consciousness and action are formed. While the consciousness of an individual is not determined by his or her class position but is influenced by idiosyncratic factors that appear as random, those random factors operate within a domain and with probabilities that are constrained and directed by social forces. (Lewontin & Levins, 2007, p. 30)

Thomas (2012) points out how decision making within the context of deprivation isn't as simplistic as it is often portrayed in the "culture of poverty" framework. Poverty itself has structural features that make it nearly impossible for poor people to make the same kinds of mistakes that wealthier people do without experiencing harsher consequences, just by virtue of their situation of poverty. Those who could benefit the most by "reflecting on future decisions" often do not have the emotional ability or free time to do so.

Whitefield-Madrano's (2012) powerful essay about her experiences with domestic violence illustrates the traps of individualism. She notes that it is very common for women who are victims of abuse to claim that they can "handle it," because domestic violence is portrayed as a private, not public problem:

> The refrain of individual responsibility that underlies this belief has a long history of being one of those antifeminist arguments that sometimes masquerade as feminism. The idea that feminism is equivalent to personal sovereignty comes in handy when a feminist—this feminist to be exact—is in the middle of a hurricane, unable to see anything but the individual drops of rain that, together, compose the storm. (p. 54)

Whitefield-Madrano also recalls that at the beginning of her abuse, she immediately differentiated herself from "those" women, i.e., the ones she saw as weak, dependent on a man, not college-educated, antifeminist. *They* were in abusive relationships; *she* was in an "intense" one. She notes that within the feminist abuse-prevention community there is a reluctance to interfere with someone's autonomy, which becomes a total turning away from someone who can't "handle it" after all. As she explains, "Had my healthy, normal, status-quo self landed smack-dab into the worst of my relationship, I'd have gotten out immediately. But that's not how abuse works, of course. Abuse is gradual, systemic" (p. 54), a conclusion echoed by Shah (2002). Dunbar-Ortiz (2001) and hooks (2001) provide similar accounts of their own experiences with being abused by men, demonstrating that domestic violence is not a private issue and that it has environmental contexts.

Slee's (2006) discussion of asymmetry of information is also useful for understanding the dynamics of market-think regarding free choice. In any social encounter, access to information is not equitably distributed. For example, someone who is unemployed and looking for work is not given the same number of choices or the same amount of information as those who are hiring, thus they have less leverage. The notion commonly asserted by conservatives that people are unemployed because they are too selective is false, because there are always more job hunters than available jobs at any given time. Indeed, some employers view unemployment as a permanent liability and will not hire the currently unemployed, making it clear in job postings that such individuals should not apply (Armour, 2011). In another example, sellers have more inside knowledge about their merchandise than customers do, which allows inferior goods to enter the market because consumers are too nervous to offer top dollar for the unknown. At the same time, Slee explains how retail giants such as Wal-Mart dictate pricing structures to manufacturers, putting a lockdown on any potential competition (where it exists) because those manufacturers are not willing to hold out for a higher price. So, in essence, there is no such thing as individual choice as we know it within the market—most of the decisions have been made even before we walk in the door.

Asymmetry of information applies to the college selection process for minority and working-class students, as Perna (2007) outlines in her critique of human capital theory:

> Traditional economic approaches do not attempt to incorporate the forces that constrain decision-making processes. Human capital models do not assume that individuals have perfect and complete information, but evaluate college options based on available information about the benefits and costs. However, potential students not only lack information about college opportunities, but also have differential access to information. (p. 58)

Beyond minimum funding and student loans, resources for attending college often are not as available to students from lower-income backgrounds; this includes merit-based scholarships, which overwhelmingly go to more affluent students (Kamenetz, 2006). There may also be other constraints such as transportation and family obligations that wealthier students may not have to deal with, and all of these factors affect college selection. Perna (2007) found that besides family expectations, a whole host of institutional forces shaped the selection process, including guidance counselors, curriculum, deficit thinking toward working-class students, and support systems. Social class is also reinforced through the immigration process—20% of Mexicans with Ph.D.s live in the United States, and visas issued to more affluent Mexicans have risen by close to 50% since 2005 (Chacon, 2012). Mexican investors also receive instant visas to live indefinitely in the United States, while less affluent immigrants face a slow, barrier-ridden citizenship process or deportation.

Common Contexts

Allison (2002) uses autobiographical narrative to explore the stigma of social class and sexuality. Here she recalls her experience growing up as "poor white trash," demonstrating how her environmental context began to invade her consciousness:

> That fact, the inescapable impact of being born in a condition of poverty that this society finds shameful, contemptible, and somehow deserved, has had dominion over me to such an extent that I have spent my life trying to overcome or deny it. I have learned with great difficulty that the vast majority of people believe that poverty is a voluntary condition. (p. 31)

Allison explains that it took her until recently to fully comprehend not only how poverty affected her psychologically, but also how those on the outside simply did not see the value in people like her and her family, viewing them as liabilities. As Davis (2002) explains, "the intersection of public and private axes of domination is very much class-determined" (p. 241). Common contexts that researchers need to be aware of include childhood, school, the family, and dimensions of poverty via race and gender, all of which impact educational and workplace settings.

Qvortrup (2008), a researcher specializing in the history of childhood, has found that over time, there has been a retreat from youth-centered social safety-net programs and movement toward support for older adults, which has resulted in a "pauperization" of childhood within the United States. Yet, at the same time, childhood has become highly surveilled and regulated. There are three categories of historical influences on the construct of childhood. The first is regulative—most industrialized societies have instituted an age qualification for full access to adult rights and responsibilities:

> Children do not, either as individuals or as a collectivity, possess rights or powers to ensure distributive justice.... [C]hildren's access to and enjoyment of the environment is limited compared with adults. By giving supremacy to the idea and practice of protecting children in all imaginable ways, one is justifying this solicitous model, irrespective of its encroachments on other

wishes children might have; for instance to desire to have new experiences on their own, or for recognition. (p. 38)

Second, regulations have emerged from norms, another powerful influence on the construct of childhood. These include our assessments about a child's maturity, competence, capabilities, and independence. Qvortrup points out that it doesn't matter if these norms are scientifically valid or not—they exist through historical precedent or in reaction to societal changes. Third, these social norms are not applied equally across the board. When it comes to childhood, generation-centric beliefs come into play and assume structural qualities. We have constructed ideas about childhood, such as developmental stages, which are tied to generation-particular concepts of age, height, and weight.

Historical shifts in how childhood is perceived, combined with media culture, have also impacted the institution of school. Fisher (2009) notes that the decrease in the ability of children and adults to focus, or to maintain attention for extended periods of time, is not an issue of motivation, but reflective of a larger technological shift within late-stage capitalism:

> Teachers are now put under intolerable pressure to mediate between the postliterate subjectivity of the late capitalist consumer and the demands of the disciplinary regime (to pass examinations, etc.). This is one way in which education, far from being in some ivory tower safely inured from the "real world," is the engine room of the reproduction of social reality, directly confronting the inconsistencies of the capitalist social field. Teachers are caught between being facilitator-entertainers and disciplinarian-authoritarians. (p. 26)

Fisher points out the irony that just as traditional institutional supports are eroding, teachers are pressured to use assessment-as-discipline both on students in the classroom and on themselves. This produces an array of paperwork such as annual program reports, development plans to raise standardized test scores, matrices, rubrics, and the like. Data itself becomes representational, and goals soon form around how these representations are managed. Not only has the refinement of technology made it easier for administrators to locate data, but also the sheer amount of data has been increasing at a rapid pace, so "targets quickly cease to be a way of measuring performance and become ends in themselves" (p. 43).

Schooling, in turn, shapes the family. Mayall (2008) discusses how kindergartners and their mothers are impacted by what the school requires. Getting children to and from school on time is one of a myriad of ways that the family is impacted by the institution of schooling. This is one reason why it is important for researchers to consider multiple observational contexts:

> When I first visited the classroom, I was struck by the complexity of the interactions taking place. Many things were happening all at once. Many things seemed subtle, such as eye movements and body posturing that are hard to record. Of course, I also realized that what was taking place in this room could only be understood through observing many other things like other classrooms in the school, the counseling room, the office and teacher's lounge, and the homes and neighborhoods of the students. (Carspecken, 1996, pp. 44–45)

Likewise, the very structure of bourgeois home living spaces has reflected environmental forces, with backyards and dens becoming private, child-centered family areas, replacing front yards and formal parlors and dining rooms where the public was welcomed (Ehrenreich, 2006; Halle, 1993).

The family itself is necessary for the reproduction and maintenance of the labor force, which is achieved by the family bearing increased financial costs and by the special positioning of domestic work, which still falls mostly on women to perform (Fisher, 2009; Holmstrom, 2002b). Current ideology surrounding the family still remains mired in the heterosexual nuclear household model, which is projected backward in forming a historical consciousness about traditional values and mourning what has been lost (Coontz, 2000; Stacey, 2002). Both Stacey (2002) and Coontz (2000) explain that what we think of as the nuclear family emerged from an entirely different extended family form, where work and the home were more closely tied together. The nuclear family came out of the separation of the spheres of work and home, and increased gender cleavage in terms of women being associated with and limited to domestic labor. At the same time, "the ideology of the modern family construes marital commitment as a product of free will and the passions of two equal individuals who are drawn to each other by romantic attraction and complementary emotional needs" (Stacey, 2002, p. 93). This combination of gender-role expectations and relying on the family to meet a range of psychological needs has led to a reactionary polarization of the politics surrounding reproductive rights, resulting in backlash. In the absence of structural social solutions, for the most part, the United States has continued to cling to unrealistic and unreasonable ideologies concerning the family in general and women in particular.

Tilly and Albelda (2002) relate how patriarchal ideologies under capitalism have shaped public opinion along the lines of a double-edged sword. The creation of the federal Aid to Families and Dependent Children (AFDC) program in the United States, for example, was based on the mothers' aid state-level reform movement that marshaled arguments in defense of the family and protection of children. Women with children were viewed as being particularly vulnerable, especially in bad economic times. Yet, less than 50 years later, those same arguments would be used *against* women and children as part of a rationale to cut welfare. Now we have hypervigilant monitoring of the actions of single mothers, down to self-appointed consumer monitors (i.e., other working-class people) spying on what they purchase at the grocery store, and the creation of the welfare "Cadillac queen" stereotype used to divide the working class. As Tilly and Albelda explain, "Public opinion and U.S. public policy have always distinguished between the deserving and the undeserving poor.... [S]ympathy for poor people, especially children, coexists with resentment of freeloaders" (p. 235). At the same time, cynicism about the ability of government to meet the most basic needs has contributed to this overall political climate.

Indeed, Kaplan (2002) explains the connections between privatization and the family regarding how women are positioned:

> What was once called urbanization without industrialization has turned into the feminization of poverty, with the condition of women and children be-

coming more and more precarious…a system of male domination accompanied by the absence of fathers and grandfathers, and the existence of governments that increasingly wish to privatize all social services. (p. 152)

Despite women's increasing participation in the paid workforce and their positions as single heads of households, they remain under the auspices of patriarchy, more so now than ever before. As social services are cut, women disproportionately feel the punishing effects of a shrinking safety net (Brenner, 2002; Holmstrom, 2002a). One could add to the list the rapidly increasing incarceration of African American women, who are viewed as violating the norms of proper femininity and a "woman's place," creating a "continued pandemic of private punishment, connected to the soaring numbers of women being sent to prison, combining to create a picture of the lives of poor, working-class, and racially marginalized women as overdetermined by punishment" (Davis, 2002, p. 243).

Those women who are part of the paid labor force remain underpaid, in terms of both wage rates and their "second shift" of housework on top of their paid work (Coontz, 1997; Holmstrom, 2002b; Smith, 2005). Maclean (2002) explains that if we were to fully equalize the wages of males and females, 53 out of 100 workers would have to switch jobs in order for everyone's financial needs to be met (p. 190). Even though women today are better represented in the waged workforce than in the past, as a whole, they hold roughly only 2% of the higher skilled, better paying positions (p. 190). Additionally, the highly celebrated narrowing of the gender pay gap isn't because women's wages have gone up; it's because men's wages have gone down.

At the same time that gender issues in the workplace are playing out, the racialization of poverty, often linked with gender, is a reality informed by a dialectical understanding of history:

During the 1970s, while affirmative action policy and antidiscrimination legislation was opening up opportunities for higher education and professional/managerial employment to middle-class white women and people of color, good blue-collar jobs were disappearing. Urban renewal and deindustrialization, along with expanding opportunities for residential mobility for blacks who had the means to move out further, undermined the economic base of inner-city neighborhoods.... [B]y the time black urban residents were able to use the political muscle won through their civil rights struggle, they found themselves holding power in cities with a shrinking economic base. (Brenner, 2002, p. 340)

Dyson's (2005, 2006) work fully examines the growth of what he terms the "Afristocracy," where middle-class and wealthy African Americans view themselves as separate from the working class of their own ethnicity, reflected in the public scoldings of the black working class by comedian Bill Cosby and by the black business class in New Orleans prior to and after Hurricane Katrina. In these cases, the black middle class appears to have achieved the most elusive of solidarities—with whites (who celebrated Cosby as a groundbreaking social commentator)—but it is a faux solidarity, allying with white racists in their condemnation of the poor and working class as a whole. Harris (2012) notes that African American women in particular have to engage with a "respectability politics" that is "narrowly defined by professional and personal choices reflecting the social mores of the majority culture—patriarchal, Judeo-Christian, heteronormative, and middle class" (p. 33).

Conclusion: Beyond Localism

A strain of left-libertarian and anarchist writings views microanalysis, smaller scales, and privileging the local as sites of solutions rather than larger-scale, global contexts (Ellerman, 2006; Lynd & Grubacic, 2008; Sale, 2000, 2007). Certainly, localized approaches to distribution—such as smaller farms distributing goods within a smaller radius—are worth considering as some of many ways to improve access to affordable, nutritious food. It is also important for researchers to have a full grasp of the particularities of the environmental context they are studying in order to understand what is happening in that specific setting. However, when the local is detached from the global in terms of analysis, problems emerge:

There is in fact no reason to support, and every reason to oppose, any suggestion that the national and global are on a scale that is less human and practical than the local. This is not to deny the importance of the local and antineoliberal politics, or the importance of the question of appropriate scale for postcapitalist societies. It is to insist, however, that local socioecological struggles cannot be delinked from—and are indeed always potentially representative of—universal projects of transcending capitalism on a world scale. (Albo, Gindin, & Panitch, 2010, p. 120)

First, it is not possible, as long as capitalism exists, to live apart from it or be outside of its sphere of influence, though one can individually resist its more egregious effects as well as possible. Second, certain groups are more vulnerable than others to environmental impacts, such as the poor, women, minorities, and children, due to the impact of patriarchy and racism as they function as aspects of capitalism. Kandiyoti (2002) points out how women's decisions are shaped by a series of patriarchal "bargains" that place limits on their options. Some anarchist-activist movements, such as the Zapatistas in Chiapas, have confronted patriarchy; in their case, by crafting the Women's Revolutionary Law (EZLN, 1994). Despite this important declaration that addresses reproductive freedom, human rights to an education, and a fair wage, Zapatista women are still impacted by larger Mexican policies toward women. Third, the problem isn't government or leaders; the problem is those entities under capitalism. Simply declaring a movement "leaderless," as the Occupy protestors did, does not reduce the impacts of police harassment, sexism, or racism, for example. In some ways, anarchist tactics such as consensus decision making create a form of entrenched minority rule, resulting in stalling action or watered-down proposals (D'Amato, 2011).

For Marxist researchers, the local and the global interact through the labor relations of production. Any setting, therefore, is a reflection of the nuances of these relations in action, including schools, the workplace, and the family. In addition to contextual matters, there are larger, historical shifts occurring, as Kaplan (2002) outlines: "What has changed in the past 40 years in the industrialized countries is that governments are no longer preoccupied with the condition of children and with reproducing the labor force.... What we are seeing today is the collapse of fears about labor shortages in the global economy" (p. 154). We are now facing a world that doesn't need workers, and appears to be able to cope with high unemployment numbers as corporate profits soar. Unfortunately, localism doesn't offer answers beyond coping mechanisms, albeit good ones that at least prioritize people's dignity and respect. Instead, we need a sound dialectical understanding of social contexts and how they sustain capitalist ideology, in order to defeat it.

Chapter Nine

Things

Overview — The Prevalence of Stuff!

For Leavy (2007b), cultural artifacts are a rich area for study, and can represent epistemological struggles involving history, memory, and group identity. As Carspecken (1996) elaborates:

> Cultural products include everything that results from a meaningful act. The act itself could be viewed as a product that can be read in various ways and that affects other actors through their readings of it...the conditions of production; the autonomous possible meanings of the product; interpretations given the product by various cultural groups; and the effect of the product on routine activities of various cultural groups. (p. 185)

Although Marx (1867/2010) was a critic of consumer culture, he was not opposed to using artifacts to illustrate his ideas, including the transformation from handmade to manufactured goods. LaFave (n.d.) notes that because work is alienating (and the products of labor are as well), people often turn to the one outlet remaining — consumer identity, i.e., buying stuff. In many respects, consumer culture, like school, is another way for capitalism to work through institutions to self-perpetuate its ideology. Eagleton (2011) asserts that rather than serving superficial purposes, objects matter because they are the result of human production and energy: "One reason why Marx's theory of history holds good is the fact that material goods are never just material goods. They hold out the promise of human well-being. They are the portal to so much that is precious in human life" (p. 122, loc. 1369–1370).

The accumulation of stuff is also a visible representation of the crisis of overproduction that Marx (1867/2010) outlines in *Capital,* yet, ironically, it is a topic underresearched by dialectical materialists. This might be due in part to the sheer ubiquity of stuff and the fact that simply locating basic information on how much of it exists as a starting point is nearly impossible. Although there are statistics on annual household spending by categories such as food and clothing (Crawford, Church, & Rippy, 2012), and on the amount of garbage produced by households (Environmental Protection Agency, 2010), there is no definitive accounting of the amount of stuff, new and old, that is out there in circulation or being hoarded. It's just there, all around us, ready and waiting to be researched. Much like when we clean out a garage or apartment, we are faced with the dilemma: Where to begin?

The late comedian and social commentator George Carlin (n.d.) addressed the problem of stuff in one of his famous monologues:

> That's all your house is: a place to keep your stuff. If you didn't have so much stuff, you wouldn't need a house. You could just walk around all the time. A house is just a pile of stuff with a cover on it. You can see that when you're taking off in an airplane. You look down, you see everybody's got a little pile of stuff. All the little piles of stuff. And when you leave your house, you gotta lock it up. Wouldn't want somebody to come by and take some of your stuff. They always take the good stuff! They never bother with that crap you're saving. All they want is the shiny stuff. That's what your house is, a place to keep your stuff while you go out and get more stuff! (para. 2–3)

Carlin goes on to lament the process of packing for travel and the systematic reduction of stuff that one has to do; eventually, one is reduced to the basics, a "fourth version of your house" (para. 7). This monologue is a reminder of how humans and artifacts are not easily separated. The love/hate dialectic is there all along.

Stuff permeates popular culture, and has spawned an entire life-coaching and organization industry with self-help books such as *Clutter Rehab* (Wittmann, 2011) and *Decluttering Your Home: The Fast Way to Get Rid of Clutter and Organize Your Life, Volume 1* (Pritchard, 2012). Major holidays center on buying stuff: Christmas, Mother's Day, Father's Day, and Valentine's Day, not to mention birthdays. Retail outlets such as the Container Store devote their entire shop space to receptacles for displaying or corralling stuff. eBay and Craigslist are top-ranked websites for buying, selling, or giving away stuff. Just about every locale has access to a shopping channel. The list of reality

TV shows that deal with the acquisition and trading of stuff (not including the myriad home or vehicle improvement shows, a whole other category involving even more stuff) is long and growing: *Auctioneer$, Hoarders, Hoarding: Buried Alive, Pawn Stars, Cajun Pawn Stars, American Restoration, American Pickers, Picker Sisters, Storage Wars, Storage Wars Texas, Hardcore Pawn, Barter Kings, Operation Repo, Pawn Queens, Pawn Games, Airplane Repo, Treasure Quest, Treasure Hunters,* and *American Diggers. Antiques Roadshow* is perhaps the longest running reality-format show that centers on appraising stuff, and it is one of the most popular shows on public television.

Even the backlash against stuff, as part of the current "simple living" movement, involves stuff. This movement has taken Henry David Thoreau to a whole new level, in directions he probably wouldn't have imagined. *Real Simple* and *Mary Jane's Farm* magazines are filled with ads for expensive organic products, beekeeping supplies, and natural remedies. Upper-middle-class women can sign up to go on "glamping" trips (a hybrid of glamour and camping) or join simplicity clubs. Grigsby's (2004) analysis of the voluntary simplicity movement found that the majority of those seeking less consumption were educated, middle-class white men and women ranging in age from their twenties to postretirement. Many of these individuals are drawn to simplicity because of the impacts of capitalism: stress, alienation from the products of their labor, environmental degradation, and health problems. Yet, what ends up happening is that in their quest to live more simply, they end up being steered to products and purchasing advice.

In their study about the many dimensions of hoarding, Steketee and Frost (2010) found that rather than being affected by obsessive-compulsive disorder (OCD), as is commonly theorized in the media, hoarders more closely displayed characteristics of impulse control disorder (ICD), similar to what compulsive gamblers or kleptomaniacs have. Yet, hoarders do not neatly fit into these categories because of their degree of anxiety and depression over accumulating stuff; in many ways, they merit their own separate psychiatric classification. Steketee and Frost noted that many of the hoarders viewed stuff as opportunity, as a future means of making money or one day stumbling across that lucky find—the central premise of the show *Storage Wars*. Hoarders also don't really care about other people's stuff, just the items they themselves either owned or were about to own, reflecting an intense, inward privatization mentality that the authors connect to philosophical ideas of Aristotle, Hume, Locke, and Sartre.

Steketee and Frost also discuss distinctions between collecting (a more socially acceptable means of dealing with stuff) and hoarding (which comes with stigma). This discussion reminds one of the different ways that those with anorexia and those who are overweight are viewed in society. Both are forms of clinically disordered eating, but anorexics receive far more sympathy, whereas people who are obese are declared lazy. It could be said that the collector, who has objects of value that set him/her apart from the crowd, is much like the anorexic, to be admired for her/his extreme self-denial amidst plenty, whereas the pack rat is viewed by society as similar to the overweight individual. Thought to affect 2–5% of the population, hoarding appears to have some relatable characteristics:

> The boundaries between normal and abnormal blur when it comes to hoarding. We all become attached to our possessions and save things other people wouldn't. So we all share some of the hoarding orientation. The passion of a collector, the procrastination of someone who hasn't taken the time to put things away, the sentimentality of one who saves reminders of important personal events—all these are part of the hoarding story. (p. 14)

Hoarding is ripe for research because it is clearly a recent phenomenon, a product of late-stage capitalism. It is difficult to imagine people hoarding to the same degree in early agrarian societies, for example. Though certainly there are famous stories of eccentric wealthy misers who hoarded during the Victorian era, the phenomenon now has extended to the working class, intensified by the arrival of dollar stores and Wal-Mart with their promises of "bargains." So, in addition to the study of objects themselves (history and ideological content), the examination of how objects are produced and change hands is a fruitful area for dialectical inquiry.

This chapter opens with a description of an approach to researching artifacts, cultural Marxism, including critical discourse analysis. Some suggestions for researchers are provided. This is followed by examples of research that demonstrate the diversity of material culture work that is currently happening in traditions other than the postmodern.

Cultural Marxism

Cultural Marxism refers to the use of Marx's theory to analyze human-created products, from art to texts of speeches to collectibles. Early cultural theorists include Adorno and Horkheimer (1944) and Benjamin (1936), who applied base/superstructure theory to the analysis of art. More recent cultural Marxist work emphasizes other interdisciplinary dimensions such as popular culture, media studies, and visual sociology. The documentary series *Dreamworlds* (Jhally, 1990, 1995, 2007), in which the misogyny in women's representation in music videos is explored and connected to violence and sexual assault, is a good example of contemporary dialectical analysis in this vein. An even more chilling presentation is Hadleigh-West's documentary *War Zone* (1998), about street harassment. The film, which shows clips of Haldeigh-West confronting men about unwanted harassment, captures a variety of responses from the harassers, from amusement to rage at even being questioned.

Critical content and discourse analyses are often employed in dialectical materialist research of artifacts. Leavy (2007b) defines content analysis as "the systematic study of texts and other cultural products or nonliving data forms" (p. 277), which can be qualitative or quantitative in its focus. Here the data studied are not created by the researcher, but exist apart from him/her. Fairclough (2010) distinguishes between critical discourse analysis (CDA) and other related methodologies, in that "CDA views texts as a moment in the material production and reproduction of social life" (p. 304). It is based on these texts that a materialist social critique can be mounted. A major aim of discourse analysis is to uncover what is often are presented as naturalized or matter-of-fact, such as everyday objects that represent ideology steeped in the context of history (Leavy, 2007b; Woods & Martin, 2010). Allman (2007) elaborates on the task of locating ideology within the discourses of artifact/text:

> It is important to consider the general form that these take and why those who disseminate these discourses and explanations have managed quite so easily to convince or persuade people that this version of events is valid.... [T]o be classified as ideology, an idea, explanation, or discourse has to mask or misrepresent either the contradictions of capitalism or the preconditions and/or results of those real contradictions in ways that help sustain or perpetuate them. (p. 39)

Fairclough (2010) finds that even though the media provides more access to products and ideas, usually they express the values of elites. Therefore, according to Ortner (1999), researchers should avoid the temptation of thinking that one can access ideologies by just deconstructing representations within artifacts. At the same time, simply conducting fieldwork is insufficient for understanding how people make sense of consumer products. Both deconstruction and research methodology have to be used together. As Ortner explains,

> Theories of representation, in turn, compel us to think not only about the relationship between a signifier and its referent, but about representations as produced and consumed within a field of inequality and power, and shaped as much by those relations of production and consumption as by the nature of the supposed referent. (p. 84)

By interrogating the images and products of consumer culture, we can obtain a more complex picture of representation (Leavy, 2007b).

Though not identified as a cultural Marxist, Halle (1993) describes his approach to studying how ordinary people purchase and display art items in their homes:

> My argument is that the proper application of the materialist perspective to twentieth-century art demands that we view this art in more than one material context. We do, of course, need to see it in the context of the political and economic structure of modern society—the mode of production. For example, the decline of traditional imperialism in the 1950s and 1960s, triggering growing doubts about Western superiority, was important in the growing attraction of "primitive" art. (p. 203)

For Halle, the modern house is the appropriate context for framing how people make sense of art, not just museums or people's access to art history.

Audiovisual data can be challenging to analyze because it comes in many forms and variations, sometimes exclusively oral (Faubion, 1999). During the process of investigating artifacts, researchers can use preexisting coding categories from theory, or use inductive categories that arise from the artifacts themselves (Leavy, 2007b). Carspecken (1996) presents a useful approach to analyzing material data of any kind. First, it is important to begin with the production chain: How did the object get here? Additionally, researchers should note ideologies that come with the artifact. Howell and Prevenier (2001) find it useful to historically trace the phrasing of texts, paying close attention to significant words. During this initial stage, it is critical to focus on only possible, not fixed meanings. Second, researchers need to find out how people use the artifact, "noting routine activities of the group in relation to their reading of the product. People can talk about a product in one way but act in another" (Carspecken, 1996, p. 186). Third, researchers should look at possible contrasts between the intended, "official" intent of a product/text and how it is used by people. This is important because "class societies also selectively distribute certain forms of culture so that dominant groups remain in dominance" (p. 192). Finally, it is essential for researchers to understand that people are constantly making an effort to use products to meet their needs, which can include dignity, saving face, status, and a range of other psychological strategies. Those too, should be noted.

Examples of Dialectical Materialism Applied to the Study of Things

Examining material culture is not just an abstract academic exercise for postmodernists. Capitalism is always creating an array of new products, most of which reflect deeply ideological assumptions about humans and society along the lines of race, gender, sexuality, ability, age, and, of course, class. We need more Marxian analyses of what is being produced and distributed in an increasingly rapid manner, parallel to the fast-growing economic divide between the very wealthy and the underclass. As a recent example, in June 2012 Adidas was about to release a high-top sneaker, Roundhouse Mids, designed by Jeremy Scott, which featured orange rubber shackles that attached to the top of the shoe. Advertising for the much anticipated shoe carried the caption, "Got a sneaker game so hot you lock your kicks to your ankles" (Solomon, 2012, para. 2). While public outcry caused Adidas to pull production, the fact that these shoes would even be considered for production illustrates the ways in which capitalism works its messages though its products.

In examining the image of these shoes, one thinks about the obvious associations of African Americans and slavery. It seems more than coincidental that Adidas chose this design knowing that a major section of their market is African American males. For many years, advertising has linked major athletic stars to expensive shoes as a way to target black youth (Gaddis, 2012). Then there is the association with prison and the escalating incarceration rate of African American males, as well as chain gangs (Alexander, 2010). Additionally, one is reminded of the wage slavery of the sweatshop labor that produces athletic shoes (Taylor, 2010).

Fawcett and Gupta (2010) note that in the advertising that surrounds products, what is left out, of course, is globalization and the further enslavement of a growing underclass (many of whom are children) in the production of items such as high priced sneakers:

> We don't hear how Western states, the World Bank, IMF, and WTO force and bribe developing world politicians into lowering their economies' defenses, decimating social welfare and workers' rights protections, while prioritizing export oriented production...Where did that process go?... [I]t's one's personal responsibility not to hire babies, another's personal responsibility not to buy cheap clothes. To buy or not to buy. Whether it is nobler to exploit children or let them starve. But don't ask why things are this way or bring that invisible process—the capitalist system—into focus. (p. 72)

The final allusion to slavery these shoes make manifest is the symbolic bondage to consumer society and the need to have the latest product to set one's self apart from the crowd.

The impact of consumer culture in shaping the access we have to materials is made explicit in Rich's (2003) essay about attempting to locate decent poetry books at the mall. In the opening of the essay, she describes the effect of her surroundings on her emotions:

> I enter this mall rarely, but this time I am on a search. A dull, sourness im-
> plodes in me when I'm inside; I can slide toward depression or anger, de-
> pending on the mind I bring to it. Whatever search you come on must soon
> dissipate into mental cacophony or restless anomie. (p. 30)

Even though Rich goes on to analyze why the mall itself isn't particularly exotic or threatening (there are moms with baby strollers, older people, etc.), there is still a sense of being simultaneously overwhelmed at the array of products and still vaguely unsatisfied at not finding what one needs. After finally locating some poetry books on the bottom shelf at a bookstore, she finds that most are volumes of mass-produced poems and maybe two or three of the classics. No books of feminist or ethnic poetry to be found:

> I'm on a search for poetry in the mall. This is not sociology, but the pursuit
> of an intuition about mass marketing, the so-called free market, and how
> suppression can take many forms—from outright banning and burning of
> books, to questions of who owns the presses, to patterns of distribution and
> availability. (p. 32)

Rich's quest is much like trying to find basic items at the store. Even when presented with more than 50 varieties of shampoo, it is nearly impossible to locate the one that will work, even though each brand has at least four formulas, from dry hair to "volumizing." As Albert points out in *Parecon* (2004), do people really need 20 different brands of butter to choose from?

Likewise, Halle's *Inside Culture* (1993) examines artistic preferences within the context of the home. Contradicting previous scholars' top-down conclusions that the museum shapes people's concepts of aesthetics based on status (Veblen, 1899/1965; Bell, 1978), Halle reminds readers that most of the cultural artifacts in museums once belonged to private homes. Halle conducted a visual survey of art in a wide range of New York households by income level, and found universal and particular preferences that suggested a reciprocal aesthetic:

> Many meanings emerge or crystallize in the context of the setting in which the audience views the works (house, neighborhood, and the family and social life woven therein); that the content of these meanings cannot, therefore, simply be deduced from the meanings assigned to the works by artists, critics, corporations, or others; and that these new meanings then have an impact on twentieth-century elite and popular cultural history via people's demand for certain kinds of art and cultural items that are suitable repositories of these meanings. (p. 11)

Halle discusses the historical changes that have occurred in homes and how they are used, which impact artistic preferences. For example, Victorian households made virtually no use of backyard spaces, and placed all of the decorative investment in the front hallways and parlors. The houses that Halle visited may have retained a formal sitting room (if space permitted), but the majority of the socializing took place in the backyard. Halle found that the family photos displayed in homes reflected this shift to informality; most of the photographs featured casual poses and settings, with the exception of wedding and graduation pictures. Unlike in early twentieth-century households, most of the family photo arrangements Halle documented depicted only three generations at most, illustrating a privileging of the nuclear family form.

Duneier's *Sidewalk* (1999), an ethnography of informal networks of commerce among the homeless in Greenwich Village, is an excellent example of inquiry using artifacts. All of the participants in the study sell newspapers, magazines, and/or books, most often scavenged or traded. Their customers are other working-class or poor people, mostly African American, though some are professors and more well-to-do. Duneier explores the tensions that occur as a result of the rapid gentrification of Greenwich Village, weaving in accounts of buying and selling and how these acts shape identity and reveal patterns of racism and economic inequality. In the chapter "When You Gotta Go," Duneier describes how even an essential thing like going to the bathroom is an obstacle for the homeless. Often, the informal policy of urban restaurants is that you can't use the bathroom unless you make a purchase:

> Many people who work and live out on the street believe that they are enti-tled to use the washroom of any establishment in which they normally spend money. Whether they have spent their money at the moment they need the washroom is irrelevant to them. When John said he had been com-ing to McDonald's for 25 years, he was actually giving voice to the common view on the street that this long-term relationship with McDonald's defines his rights as a customer. (p. 182)

Here Duneier explores the nuances in self-definitions of what consti-tutes a "customer." The unhoused men saw themselves as long-term customers because they had spent much of their money at that McDonalds in the past—it didn't matter if they didn't have the mon-ey now, to access the bathroom now. McDonald's employees, howev-er, defined a "customer" as someone who had money to spend right then.

Duneier also examines what the vendors get from selling their items. Many had been addicted to drugs and alcohol, and use maga-zine selling as a way to survive sobriety. Others are still in what Duneier calls the "fuck it" stage, where extreme circumstances com-pel them to make choices that others would perceive as irrational, such sleeping on the street. Usually that is the moment where the men will decide to find a mentor and get into informal selling:

> Just as the "Fuck It!" mentality has a pervasive effect on a person's life, so can the opportunity to take control and earn respect within a limited do-main. Whereas Marvin and Ron had once said, "The hell with you and whatever's right," now they have used the opportunity provided by the sidewalk to become innovators—earning a living, striving for self-respect, establishing good relations with fellow citizens, providing support for each other. For Ron, panhandling led to scavenging and vending, which have given him a trade of sorts and a mentor, who in turn encouraged him to take care of Aunt Naomi. (p. 79)

Duneier's sensitivity and analysis takes material cultural studies to a whole new level. He doesn't romanticize life on the streets or the dif-ficult personalities of some of the participants. At the same time, he provides a glimpse into the participants' strengths gained through the creation of mentoring and survival networks. In a capitalist society that has been resistant to recognizing universal human rights, Duneier concludes, "I am thinking about the sidewalk. Thank goodness for the sidewalk" (p. 80).

Spoken text by politicians disseminated via the mass media is another rich source of data for dialectical inquiry. Howell and Prevenier (2001) provide the example of the public's reaction to the 1960 Nixon/Kennedy presidential debates: Those who heard the debates via the radio declared Nixon the winner, whereas those who viewed the debates on television thought that Kennedy did better. Woods and Martin's (2010) critical discourse analysis of Australian prime minister John Howard's speech from October 2007 located ten themes that borrow heavily from neoliberal discourse, also common in other political propositions: Resources should be used productively in a cost-effective manner, nobody should be compelled, everybody should be treated equally, you cannot turn the clock backwards, present generations cannot be blamed for the mistakes of past generations, injustices should be righted, everybody can succeed if they try hard enough, no opinion should carry more weight the majority opinion, we have to live in the twentieth century, you have to be practical. The authors note that these ten themes are contradictory in many key areas (e.g., injustices should be righted, yet we can't hold present people accountable for the past).

Faubion's (1999) analysis of the 1993 Branch Davidian compound incident in Waco wove together isolated media accounts of the event from numerous sources to create a coherent running script as a form of data. Faubion's words are interwoven with the excerpts from print media to read as a complete story, with his interpretation/fill-in terms in roman font and the media quotations in bold italic font, as in this sample, where he establishes the setting of the incident:

Waco, *heart of Texas, is the buckle of America's Bible Belt. It enjoys one of the highest concentrations of religions anywhere in America, more than 100 at the last count* (Ben MacIntyre, London Times, 3/6/93:14b). It is *the eternal city of the Baptists* (Larry McMurtry, New Republic, 6/7/93:16). But Waco

also has **14 museums, a new zoo and other attractions** (Sam Howe Ver-
hovek, New York Times, 3/6/93:A8). (p. 92)

What is stunning about Faubion's data presentation is that it creates
an odd but immediate collage of how the mass media creates its own
circular narrative that can then be endlessly disseminated, taking on a
life of its own. Faubion explains further: "Though marked with the
signatures of its multiple authors, its stuff is the stuff of redundancy,
of words and images shared among the various media, repeated and
repeated again, most of them resting just on the edge of anonymity"
(p. 92).

Changes in the impacts of technology and the job market are often
framed within generational cohort research (Chamberlain, 2008;
Howe & Strauss, 1991; Tremmel, 2010), particularly research on those
classified as Generation X (born between 1968 and 1982). Ornter's
(1999) interviews with members of Generation X revealed that it
wasn't enough to rely on either ethnographic methods or cultural artifacts alone in order to analyze the shifts that were happening within
this age cohort; they had to be used together. Ortner found that social
class played a large role in how this cohort was portrayed and how
they experienced the supposed technological revolution in terms of
job opportunities. Middle-class Xers, for example, often expressed
anxieties about a lack of class mobility or even a slipping positionality, as Ehrenreich (1990) describes in her work on the declining middle
class. The decline is often presented with reference to the Gen X
"slacker" stereotype, where the loss of job opportunities is blamed on
young people who have checked out of the system.

Educational materials are a manifestation of links between capitalism and schooling. Finley (2012) describes a project she undertook
with classroom teachers to evaluate a commercially produced environmental curriculum with an eye toward arts-based pedagogy. They
focused on materials from Project Learning Tree, a popular line with
educators. What was notable was that the commercial curriculum utilized constructivist, hands-on tactics: "Drawn in by the arts-based
learning, enjoyable activities, and items to generate personal connections among children and curriculum, the students are prepared for a

deeper message" (p. 211). Yet, the message never came. Finley and the teachers noticed that whenever petroleum products were mentioned, nowhere was it stated that these were nonrenewable resources, nor was the resultant environmental damage/costs generated from using these resources addressed. When solar energy was brought up, the curriculum stressed that it was expensive and required expanses of open land. A further investigation of Project Learning Tree uncovered several corporate sponsors, including the American Forest and Paper Association, the Potlatch Corporation, and the Weyerhaeuser Company Foundation. These foundations actively support the corporate clearing of forests for timber harvesting.

Conclusion

According to Gimenez (2001), "Given that our existence is shaped by the capitalist mode of production, experience, to be fully understood in its broader social and political implications, has to be situated in the context of the capitalist forces and relations that produce it" (para. 11). This is true, too, of the material objects that surround us on a daily basis. The rapidity of media information makes it difficult to dissect the mass audience, which has become, unfortunately, a substitute for authentic solidarity (Rich, 2003). It can become easy to confuse release, excitement, or even the provoking of thought on the part of consumer culture with genuine activism and resistance to capitalism.

While they may have similarities in subject matter or a shared interest in popular culture, there are several key ways that a dialectical materialist approach differs from postmodern media studies. First, though both theoretical frames deconstruct the artifact under study by looking at history or interpretations of visual/written text, Marxian research alone connects these to the manner of production. This includes understanding that no matter the message of "freedom" or "liberation" that consumers take from an object in forming their own interpretations, what lies behind an artifact is often rampant exploitation, whether we are talking sweatshop labor or the conditions of the working class who purchase these products. Second, Marxian researchers place limits on the flexibility of interpretations derived from artifacts, whereas postmodernists are more apt to romanticize the empowerment of consumer culture. For cultural Marxists, notions of "free choice" are highly problematic, especially when applied to violence or the sex industry. Finally, there is a question about how much an ally popular culture can really be in terms of political activism. Technology, for example, can be presented as the personification of social organizing, yet we have to remember that most so-called independent media sites are subsidiaries of larger media conglomerates. Even if activists create their own websites, the chances of them showing up within the first 20 pages of a term search are remote at best. Chapter Eleven explores more of the problems of technology.

Not all processes of production involve manufacturing in the traditional sense. Where cultural studies can be of enormous use is in aiding our understanding of how a specific manner of production — that of ideas — functions under capitalism through the distribution of consumer products, as Leavy (2007b) outlines:

> We can learn about the social life, such as norms, values, socialization, or social stratification, by looking at the texts we produce, which reflect macrosocial processes and our worldview...the texts and objects that groups of humans produce are embedded with the larger ideas those groups have. (p. 229)

The example presented earlier of street harassment captured in a documentary can be linked to how women are represented in music videos and commercials. There are many parallels between mass media and what males view as acceptable conduct toward women. At the same time, women themselves are targeted by advertisers to purchase cosmetics and weight-loss products under the imperative that constant self-improvement is necessary, that one is never "good enough." Men, too, are exposed to these advertisements. This then comes full circle as many men feel that they are entitled to comment on women's weight and appearance right out on the street. Even when higher status women such as Michelle Obama and Hillary Clinton are critiqued about their beliefs or policies, inevitably the commentary turns to their appearance (Michelle's booty or Hillary's clothing choices). What on the surface appears to be an isolated, at-omized stream of constant consumer culture is, therefore, a more tightly woven, interconnected web of ideology.

Chapter Ten

Interpretation

Overview—Foundational Ethnographic Methods

Within qualitative research, interpretation will inevitably derive from some form of interview and observation data, and to a lesser degree, from text and artifact analysis. These are considered foundational methods for gathering qualitative data, no matter the topic under investigation. Luckily, there are an array of basic methodological texts available to researchers, from general overviews of qualitative methodologies (Creswell, 2007; Denzin & Lincoln, 2005; Patton, 2002) to specific methodologies including, but not limited to: ethnography (Carspecken, 1996; Madison, 2012; Wolcott, 2008), case study (Stake, 2005; Yin, 2009), phenomenology (Lewis & Staehler, 2011; Moustakas, 1994), grounded theory (Charmaz, 2006; Corbin & Strauss, 2007), mixed methods (Creswell & Clark, 2010; Tashakkori & Teddlie, 2010), narrative (Clandinin, 2006; Reissman, 2008), and oral history (Ritchie, 2007).

Additionally, researchers have at their disposal excellent instructional texts classified by theoretical orientation: feminist research (Ackerly & True, 2010; Hesse-Biber, 2011), LGBTQ research (Meezan & Martin, 2008), disability studies (Siebers, 2008), research with children (Christensen & James, 2008; Greig, Taylor, & McKay, 2007), multicultural research (Grant, 2007; Stanfield, 2011), and critical research paradigms (Willis, 2007), to name a few. There are even books devoted to specific aspects of the research process, such as writing field notes (Emerson, Fretz, & Shaw, 1995), discourse analysis (Fairclough, 2010; Gee, 2010; Paltridge, 2011), coding data (Auerbach & Silverstein, 2003; Saldana, 2009), interviewing (Kvale & Brinkman, 2008; Seidman, 2005), focus groups (Krueger & Casey, 2008), participant observation (DeWalt & DeWalt, 2010; Jorgensen, 1989), online research (Fielding, Lee, & Blank, 2008; Kozinets, 2010; Markham & Baym, 2009), and visual research (Hockings, 2003; Mitchell, 2011; Pink, 2006). Researchers are encouraged to consult a combination of these texts to suit their particular needs, as they are all compatible with dialectical materialism.

Denzin and Lincoln (2005) outline seven historical moments in the development of qualitative research, with an emphasis on ethnographic methodology. First is the traditional moment, from the late 1800s to after World War II, which featured a colonialist, objectivist third-person stance, focusing on "exotic" cultures. Second, the modernist movement, dating from the late 1940s through 1970, extended the foundational methods codified in the traditional movement (field notes, participant observation, emic/etic) in an attempt to make ethnographic work equal in status to quantitative research. Third, the blurred genres movement, encompassing the years 1970 to 1986, featured different paradigms and theoretical frames such as feminism, queer theory, disability studies, postmodernism, and Marxism, along with divergent methodologies such as autoethnography and phenomenology. This was also a fruitful era for ethnographies that examined folk and subcultural groups.

Fourth, the crisis of representation movement, from 1986 to 1990, was marked by a dramatic departure from more traditional ethnographic methods. This was immediately followed by the fifth movement, postmodernism, from 1990 to 1995, which began to codify more experimental methods as acceptable methodological forms. Sixth was the postexperimental inquiry movement, lasting from 1995 to 2000, which more formally introduced social justice as a methodological and ethical expectation. Seventh is the methodologically contested present, dating from 2000, in which qualitative researchers have begun to respond to a renewed attack by proponents of neopositivism and empiricism. We are also beginning an eighth movement, the fractured future, which will be even more concerned with the immediacy of social problems, incorporating indigenous research ethics, and resisting colonialism.

This chapter addresses key aspects of interpretation, beginning with a consideration of data collection and of factors to be aware of in order to lay a solid foundation for dialectical interpretation. The more researchers are able to facilitate participants in providing their own perspectives and accounts during the early stages of a study, the more likely that sound interpretations will result. Next, I discuss using data to support interpretations. Conclusions are only as good as one's data; this means watching for what participants don't say as much as what they do say. This is followed by discussion of some common challenges during the interpretive process, which can include participant resistance, false consciousness, and conflicting accounts. Finally, I remind researchers to frame their interpretations in the context of the big picture.

Dialectical Data Collection Strategies

When conducting qualitative research involving interviews and/or observations, tone should put some thought into data collection as preparation for forming sound interpretations; reviewing at least five or six of the texts cited above would be helpful. A major outcome of dialectical materialist research is praxis, or taking action to change the world, not just describe it. As a result, one's inquiry should be considered a public form of journalism with an emphasis on the role of participants, not "subjects" (Belenky et al., 1997; Denzin, 2009). Future readers can be considered participants, too, so audience needs to be considered as a critical component of inquiry. O'Kane's (2008) explanation of participation is helpful in this light: "Participation does not simply imply the mechanical application of a "technique" or method, but is instead part of a process of dialogue, action, analysis, and change. The successful use of participatory techniques lies in the process, rather than simply the techniques used" (p. 129). O'Kane also notes that facilitating participation can involve using multiple techniques, such as participants creating artwork, role playing, and engaging in scenarios, games, and projects as forms of data. These methods have the additional benefit of being useful for groups with lower literacy levels or language barriers, and for conducting research with young children.

Belenky et al. (1997) describe how "real talk reaches deep into the experience of each participant; it also draws on the analytical abilities of each" (p. 144, loc. 2130). Brooks (2007) found that the traditional question-and-answer interview structure did not work in her research with women. Because many of the participants in her study had not had prior opportunities to share their views in an in-depth manner, it was difficult for them to reflect on their activities and find the right words to use. Therefore, it was up to Brooks to employ feminist methodologies such as interpretive focus groups in order to make participants more comfortable articulating aspects of their lives. Leavy (2007c) also found that homogeneous interpretive focus groups were fruitful in studying white peace activists and their organizing practices, because no one individual participant felt that the magnifying glass was held on him/her alone. Not only did she find that each participant held a different definition of what constituted peace and ways of organizing, she also found that the focus groups revealed the influence of important intersections of race, gender, and class on the activists' perceptions:

> The atmosphere in these sessions was much more comfortable than in the personal interviews.... [P]eople were more open in speaking about racism and privilege when interpreting other white people's voices rather than their own, because there was a distancing from the privilege that provided a safe environment. (p. 179)

The dynamic of a group environment also served to activate participants' memories in a way that was unlikely to have occurred during a one-on-one interview.

When conducting in-depth interviews with an eye toward dialectical interpretation, it can be helpful to begin with more general, concrete questions, oriented in the present (Carspecken, 1996; Kvale & Brinkman, 2008; Patton, 2002). This can also be an important form of verification if one is also collecting observational data, as differences between actions and accounts can occur. Oral history can be particularly effective at accessing the memories and accounts of marginalized groups (Leavy, 2007c; Ritchie, 2007). Participants should also be permitted to formulate their own accounts, so they don't feel as if they are being interrogated:

> This is not like an oral examination in which the respondent must prove that she knows what she is supposed to know... it is more like a clinical interview. By inviting the respondent to tell her story, without interruption, the questioner allows the respondent to control and develop her own response. (Belenky et al., 1997, p. 144, loc. 1729–1733)

Interview questions should be worded so the participant has a chance to create the categories and fill in meanings. This means strategically employing manifest and underlying questions at the same time. For example, in his famous study on the authoritarian personality, Adorno (1969) had several underlying questions based in Freudian theory that he wanted to address in his study but he wasn't about to ask participants directly about their Oedipus complexes, so instead he used a series of manifest questions that were open-ended, such as "Tell me about a childhood memory," and so forth.

In a similar manner, Leckenby (2007) describes how she took several precautions in her research with victims of rape:

> I believe that the high disclosure rates obtained by my methodology were due to my feminist understanding about rape...the use of a large range of questions in the interview schedule that helped to tap women's memories of rape experiences, the inclusion of questions that conveyed a non–victim blaming attitude or bias, avoidance of the word *rape* in all but one of the questions, the exclusive use of female interviewers, careful selection of interviewers who did not subscribe to the usual myths about rape, rigorous training of interviewers and matching ethnicity when possible. (pp. 41–42)

In this way, Leckenby is fulfilling the mission of critical qualitative research, providing rich accounts that include emotion, specificity, and detail, while avoiding stereotyping and generalities (Denzin, 2009). The ability of participants to create their own meanings is crucial when it comes time to formulate interpretations, because these meanings need to be connected to larger social contexts in the analysis.

Maclean (2002) uses dialectical historical investigation to trace women's organizing and workplace activism beginning in the 1970s. Specifically, she focuses on female firefighters in New York City and the impact of their class-action lawsuit. In her historical study, she revealed how gender, race, and class intersected in terms of not only pay, but also segregation of women's paid labor (such as the clerical sector). Taking nontraditional jobs was viewed as a way for women to escape segregation of labor, yet it resulted in a backlash from white male firefighters. By systematically documenting this history, Maclean is also participating as a feminist activist, resisting

> the historical amnesia that has obliterated the workplace-based struggles of the modern era from the collective memory of modern feminism... [I]f not entirely forgotten, these efforts on the part of working women are so taken for granted that they rarely figure prominently in narratives—much less interpretations—of the resurgence of women's activism. (p. 192)

Similarly, Rowbotham (2002) finds that it can be difficult to merge the activist identity with that of the historian who has to maintain objectivity. Even though one's activism can provide key insights into the topic of inquiry, it does not automatically make the research process any simpler or smoother.

Observation can be an overwhelming data collection method for those new to research, and it is probably one of the most difficult skills to master (DeWalt & DeWalt, 2010; Jorgensen, 1989). As a result, beginners' field notes often can be thin accounts, not the deep description that is part of the ethnographic tradition (Wolcott, 2008). Thinly described accounts are not likely to yield much in the way of dialectical interpretations, nor are observations that the researcher composed by rushing to subjective assumptions (such as projecting motives onto participant actions and using high-inference descriptions). This is one reason why it is critical for researchers to go through the entire formal field note process as outlined in Emerson, Fretz, and Shaw (1995), including making jottings while in the observation site, writing up the jottings into a field note within a 24-hour period, editing the field note, and finally incorporating excerpts from the note into the write-up. During the jotting stage, Carspecken (1996) recommends choosing smaller blocks of time during regular intervals in order to obtain a sense of regularity of the environment one is studying. He also recommends prioritizing one's time in order to ensure coverage:

> I take one person in the setting and record everything that person does and says as thickly as possible as a first priority. I record everything other people do and say in interaction with this person as a second priority, and I record everything else happening in the setting as a third priority. Roughly every few minutes, I shift to a new individual as my priority person. (pp. 48–49)

Researchers can also derive dialectical materialist interpretations from working with children (Christensen & James, 2008; Greig, Taylor, & McKay, 2007). Alderson (2008) notes that children often possess a more researcher-oriented mindset than adults do, because they show an interest in every stage of the process, not just data collection. Children are also more comfortable with the ambiguity and partial knowledge that is part of the research process, and will pose dialectical "why" questions rather than foreclosing the purpose of the study. Alderson found that children were especially excited to share the results of their research and follow up to see if their inquiries made a difference or changed things. Yet, children are often framed in psychological discourse as less capable because they are still developing; their progress is compared to adults (Hendrick, 2008; Mayall, 2008). As a consequence, if researchers approach children as miniature adults, they are not likely to gain rich data.

Alderson (2008) notes that "working with child researchers does not simply resolve problems of power, exploitation, and coercion. Indeed, it may amplify them, and so working methods need to be planned, tested, evaluated and developed with the young researchers" (p. 287). Just as feminism uses gender to frame the experiences of women, those who study children use the concept of generation, which has been a factor in the exclusion of children from the formulation of rational thought (Mayall, 2008). One important strategy to use with children is to empower them through participation in the research process, while keeping in mind the developmental appropriateness of data collection methods, lived experiences, and the specific competencies of the children involved (O'Kane, 2008). Methods that work best are simple and open-ended, such as using role play, art or songs, and even tactile props such as stones for indicating amounts or sticks for drawing in the sand (Christensen & James, 2008; O'Kane,

2008). As children complete these activities, researchers can simultaneously observe and interview them, referring to the activity or artifacts that the children are creating. Video and photographs of these interactions and creations can also be considered forms of data in themselves.

Christensen and James (2008) asked children to create a graphic of how they spent their time, using a simple blank circle. Some of the children made traditional pie graphs, while others wrote words in the circle. The original goal of the study was to obtain a sense of how children viewed use of time and how much of that use was determined by adults. An unexpected finding soon emerged related to the role of school, which was facilitated by the open-endedness of using the circle versus a premade pie chart:

> However, in that this skill—doing a pie chart—had been developed in the context of schooling, it was one which, unlike more general drawing, carried with it aspects of the "hidden curriculum" of the schooling process, a factor which, in turn, shaped the way in which the children carried out the task, revealing to the researchers the diversities in terms of educational competencies which arise for children throughout the daily, shared experience of schooling. (p. 2008)

Christensen and James noticed that the children who had been exposed to pie charts in earlier lessons were more concerned with making sure they were drawing them correctly, and would ask the researchers for assurance.

Mayall (2008) also noticed that there were differences in terms of how children in upper elementary grade levels approached research participation compared to children in the younger grade levels. Because the 5- and 6-year-olds had more control over the direction of their in-class assignments, which were developmentally play-centered, they viewed research participation as a simple extension of this engagement, and didn't appear to react much differently. In contrast, the older students, who had been exposed to more teacher-centered schoolwork, viewed research participation as a release from routine, and were more eager to do the activities. The older children were also open with Mayall about being disengaged with school and the type and amount of work they had to do. To facilitate this openness, Mayall encouraged each child to bring a classmate friend along so that the interviews would be done in twos. This also allowed Mayall to make note of the children's cognitive differences and abilities, and how they incorporated the conventions of group conversation, peer relationships, and supportive encouragements that they offered to their classmates. None of this could have been accomplished with a traditional long-format, one-on-one in-depth interview.

Another interesting data collection situation involves studying those in positions of power. Conti and O'Neil (2007) propose using feminist methodologies when conducting research with elites, known as "studying up," mostly as a means of enabling the researcher to engage reflectively with the process of grappling with the contradiction of high visibility/zero access that is part of accessing elites. Ho (2009) explains that while giving participants voice is a reasonable measure to take with working-class participants, it is inappropriate for conducting research with elites. To "give voice" to the powerful without commentary and critique would mean overprivileging their perspectives, because the balance of power is already tilted in their favor. Ho not only documents the perspectives of Wall Street investment bankers, she also contextualizes their actions and statements within the larger dialectical materialist history of capitalist ideology. Researchers who are studying elites have to be creative with data collection because access is the number-one barrier (Hertz & Imber, 1995):

> The ethnography of the powerful needs to consist of interacting with informants across a number of dispersed sites, not just in local communities, and sometimes in virtual form; and it means collecting data eclectically from a disparate array of sources in many different ways such as formal interviews, extensive reading of newspapers and official documents, careful attention to popular culture, as well as informal social events outside of the actual corporate office or laboratory. (Ho, 2009, p. 19)

Indeed, Ho was able to gain access to the world of Wall Street only because her educational background helped her land an entry-level analyst job. Participants were willing and eager to share their perspectives, even in the knowledge that she was researching them, because she shared their educational credentials.

One of the most famous documented attempts at accessing elites was the film *Roger and Me* (1989), by Michael Moore. Throughout the movie, Moore attempts to confront Roger Smith, CEO of General Motors, about his actions on behalf of the company, including layoffs and moving jobs to Mexico. Thomas (1995) notes the futility of this approach in terms of getting past the mahogany curtain:

> What if Moore had cornered Roger Smith? What would he (and we) have learned? Would we really expect a version of Dickens's *A Christmas Carol* — where the CEO of one of the world's largest corporations is struck dumb by guilt and recrimination? Chances are, if Roger had agreed to an on-camera interview, Moore would not have had a film. He would have had a confrontation that tested Smith's ability to manage the situation but provided little insight about Roger, the executive elite of General Motors, or the nature of important people in big companies. (p. 3)

Within Marxist research, uncovering the actions of elites involves not understanding their personal characteristics (greedy, out of touch, etc.), but looking at how the ideology of capitalism operates through what they say and do and the rationalizations they use.

Supporting Interpretations

Belenky et al. (1997) liken the skill of analysis to the reading of literature, where "a good interpretation of a poem is firmly grounded in the poem itself, while a bad interpretation contains too much of the reader and too little of the poem" (p. 39, loc. 1510–1511). Likewise, in qualitative research, interpretations should always refer back to the data, which is the backbone of the study. Dialectical materialist researchers need to engage in a form of epistemological formation by taking the perceptions of the people being studied and extending them to larger theory (Carspecken, 1996). Triangulation, or support of claims using multiple data forms and the perspectives of different participants, is critical for research with egalitarian aims (Denzin, 2009). Interpretation also involves looking for spaces that are silent, or things that are left out (Leavy, 2007c). Researchers should be aware of possible reasons for these omissions, which could include a reluctance to violate social norms by addressing taboo topics, or participants' being unaccustomed to drawing attention to certain topics. These are cases where a solid historical and theoretical background can assist in formulating interpretations.

In quantitative research, evidence in support of validity refers to a study or instrument being able to measure what it is supposed to measure, such as the validity of a standardized test. Qualitative research uses a more multifaceted concept of validity. Torres and Reyes (2011) identify seven different types of validity that can be useful in using data to support one's interpretations. The first type is transactional validity, which refers to the study utilizing data that is rich in description and that has been reviewed by participants for accuracy. For example, researchers should use verbatim transcripts and have participants look these over before proceeding with the analysis. The second type is transformational validity, involving the study contributing to change on the side of the oppressed. A study that only examines the achievement gap but doesn't question the institutions that sustain this gap would not have transformational validity. The third type is outcome validity, meaning that a study should address the problem that it set out to address as well as take stock of who does or doesn't benefit. The fourth type is process validity: Does the study include many perspectives, and address structural as well as affective concerns? The fifth type is democratic validity, where research is conducted with populations not normally considered by mainstream inquiry, as part of a social justice imperative. The sixth type is catalytic validity, where the researchers encourage participant involvement in addressing their own social concerns. Finally, the seventh type is dialogic validity, where the study shows evidence of the researcher reflecting on her/his practices as well as engaging in reflection with participants.

Excerpted quotes from interview data can be a powerful way to support interpretations. Denzin (2009) distinguishes between the documentary interview, which serves mostly surveillance purposes and is used by law enforcement, psychiatry, and journalism, and the dialogic interview, which transforms the personal into the public. The dialogic interview is transparent in terms of how it is produced, whereas the documentary interview often naturalizes accounts of events, presenting a false reality. Krumer-Nevo (2012) notes the power of the dialogic interview as evidence: "This is also an example of the radical power of direct quotations of research participants in qualitative inquiry—they talk to us, the readers, behind the back of their interpreter, and sometimes they know and reveal more than the researcher knows or wants the readers to know" (p. 196). Along these lines, Gee (2010) presents an interpretive exercise using critical discourse analysis of a transcript from an elementary school faculty meeting. He deliberately reveals only a portion of the meeting, and then asks the readers to formulate emerging interpretations. This is repeated until the entire transcript is revealed, and more contextual clues are provided, forcing readers to revise or enhance their conclusions. Through this exercise, readers learn that subtle emphases on words and phrases reveal deeper conflicts than what appears on the surface.

The following passage from Mohanty (2002) is an excellent dialectical materialist example of how interpretations can be supported by data within a theoretical frame:

> I maintain that the interests of contemporary transnational capital and the strategies employed enable it to draw upon indigenous social hierarchies and to construct, reproduce, and maintain ideologies of masculinity/femininity, technological superiority, appropriate development, skilled/unskilled labor, and so on. Here I have argued this in terms of the category of "women's work," which I have shown to be grounded in the ideology of the Third World woman worker. Thus, analysis of this location of Third World women in the new international division of labor must draw upon the histories of colonialism and race, class and capitalism, gender and patriarchy, and sexual and familiar figurations. Analysis of the ideological definition and redefinition of women's work thus indicates a political basis for common struggles, and it is this particular forging of the political unity of Third World women workers that I would like to endorse. (p. 177)

Note how Mohanty draws on Marxian analysis to examine the intersections of race and gender by conducting interviews with majority world female factory workers. She doesn't just stop at the accounts of the workers on the factory floor, but interrogates the domestic sphere, theoretically informed by socialist feminism. Historical overviews also figure into her interpretation, providing the background needed to formulate her analysis.

Carspecken's (1996) overview of the process of data analysis as a hermeneutic endeavor is useful here. According to Carspecken, because humans are naturally communicative beings, they can use various skills in making sense of the social world. Researchers take these skills further by becoming de facto participants in the settings they are studying, yet also remaining outsiders:

> In everyday social situations, one must constantly infer meaning fields from the actions of other people, note the possible intentions of the actor, note the possible ways in which the actor herself monitors all such features of her act, note the possible unintended but motivating portions of the actor's impetus to act, note the possible ways in which other actors may understand the act. There is no direct access to all of this. (p. 99)

In addition to direct quotes, researchers can use observational notes and memos to capture this full range of interactions. Carspecken recommends thick descriptions of gestures, speech patterns, and spacing of bodies, using field notes and diagrams to record what one is witnessing. Quote marks are used to signify verbatim speech, and brackets are used to keep researcher reflections separate from the low-inference terminology used in field notes. These are all data forms that can be used to support interpretations later on.

A major purpose of observational data is to look for what Carspecken (1996) terms "claims to universality," or normative claims made by participants. If a claim is presented, then the researcher needs to make careful note of whom the claim is referring to and why it is being asserted. In this manner, typologies can be a useful interpretive device: "The trick is to use the typology of interactive power to spot the general forms of interactive power, but then to further analyze the situation in terms of cultural milieu and its distribution" (p. 131). Carspecken also differentiates between low-level coding, which is used at the initial stages of interpretation, and high-level coding, depending on greater amounts of theoretical framing: "The higher the level of abstraction, the greater the need to base the code on something other than the primary record alone" (p. 148).

For example, in his study of teachers who worked with students diagnosed with emotional and behavioral disorders and their perceptions about roles, Carspecken found that teachers' various claims to universality fell into distinct high-level coding categories, which he conceptualized as typologies applied to what these teachers should and shouldn't do. He arrived at the following typologies, created from high-level codes during the process of data analysis: the teacher as friendly guide, the teacher who is very busy with other things, the teacher as self-revealing older peer, the teacher as neutral enforcer of fixed rules, the teacher as middle-class progressive parent, and the teacher as no-nonsense traditional parent. Carspecken found that teachers often slid into different typologies, either out of frustration or in reaction to different student personalities. Typologies used as an interpretive strategy are also presented in Patton (2002).

During the interpretive process, conflicts between participant and researcher conclusions can arise. One strategy is to tap into these differences in accounts by either playing back video of observations or reviewing transcripts with participants in person, to obtain their reflections about what occurred or what was said (Carspecken, 1996). Rather than being at a disadvantage, the researcher-as-outsider often is in a good position to see the big picture that participants may miss due to their day-to-day existence in that setting (Howell & Prevenier, 2001). While participant perspectives need to be taken into account in formulating interpretations, Walford (2008b) advises against co-construction of meaning in the form of allowing those occupying higher positions to assert that a particular interpretation be advanced at the expense of others:

> Sometimes participants will ask that they be allowed to see anything that is written and make any changes they feel are necessary before publication. This arrangement should be strongly resisted... [T]o agree to a head teacher's wishes to be able to control publication means that other views are not

heard. Such arrangements automatically give more power to those who already hold most power. (p. 31)

Sticky Situations

Even with the best of planning, researchers can run into confusing or complex situations that impact the ability to make sound interpretations. A major stumbling block is that most participants, like most people living under capitalism, are not aware of their condition, other than acknowledging it in the isolated, general, or immediate terms available to them:

> Language only expresses distortions already present in reality. Nevertheless, even when Marx's science enables us to recognize the relational nature of our material world, the language conventions and concepts, which have developed from human practice and historically specific ways during capitalist history, can make it more difficult to express the true nature of reality, including of course, one's own and others' experiences. (Allman, 2007, p. 33)

As Allman explains, the uncritical response is the default mechanism, because people are for the most part "trapped within the horizon of capitalism" (p. 34). Because they view social relations as natural and given, their actions are likely to reproduce the status quo, which can be frustrating to witness and document.

Simply providing voice to participants is therefore insufficient to ensuring a dialectical interpretation, because "giving voice" shifts the burden of conceptualizing from the researcher to participants who may not be equipped to analyze their condition in situ (Ho, 2009; Leavy, 2007c). Howell and Prevenier (2001) note that in some situations, people are in the grip of *glaubensunwilligkeit*—being unwilling to believe or confront what is happening, especially if some form of trauma is involved. This was addressed in Belenky et al.'s (1997) research on how female college students constructed knowledge. Those who were in the "Silent stage" often had been victims of childhood or domestic partner abuse. They not only perceived authority as all-knowing, they also had learned to anticipate what authority would want from them; therefore, expression and words were not necessary as long as they could determine the wishes of authority, which could be very unpredictable. These women often were viewed by faculty as immature, impulsive, unable to concentrate, or intellectually stunted. Often, the "Silent women" perceived any type of conflict as a zero-sum game: If someone won, someone else had to lose by default. Self-preservation becomes the focus then, taking priority over subjecting oneself to creative risks.

Those women in the "Received Knowers" stage were open to interacting in a give-and-take with authority, but remained interested mostly in official interpretations (Belenky et al., 1997). At the same time, they had difficulty understanding that they were being shaped by others, and viewed themselves as acting on their own free choice, enjoying that they had much in common with others and with authority. Being required to do "original work" was the death knell of assignments:

> For those who adhere to the perspective of received knowledge, there are no gradations of the truth—no gray areas. Paradox is inconceivable because received knowers believe several contradictory ideas are never simultaneously in accordance with fact. Because they see only blacks and whites, but never shades of gray, these women shun the qualitative and welcome the quantitative. (p. 41, loc. 741–743)

It can be quite common to see Received Knowers in participant responses. They may find it difficult to view knowledge as socially constructed rather than as a set of received truths endorsed by authority. Unfortunately, few college environments are set up to accommodate Received Knowers. Belenky and her colleagues found that most of the students who were unable to move on from this stage eventually dropped out, further perpetuating a dependence on authority.

Sammel and Pete (2010) relate that most of their white students follow a colorblind logic whereby even broaching a discussion about race is itself racist, and racism is a character flaw, not socially constructed. There appears to be a taboo about exploring the contradictions of their own experiences being white, and "they have been rewarded [by their schooling] for not seeing difference, not believing the other" (p. 164). Sammel and Pete found that many of their students' views concerning race were tied to a form of meritocracy and "no excuses for failure" thinking. Therefore, it can be very common for research participants to locate prejudice within people, rather than viewing it as being an external matter (Sheehan et al., 2010). This means that when race emerges as an interpretive theme in research data, it is likely that majority raced participants will engage in much psychological maneuvering in order to distance themselves from "bad" people (i.e., racists) rather than acknowledge the structural nature of racism. Researchers need to be attuned to instances of this maneuvering, such as someone immediately retracting, clarifying, or contextualizing a racist, sexist, or homophobic assertion (Leavy, 2007c).

Relatedly, there is also reluctance to acknowledge poverty as systemic, not behavioral, but in selective contexts. Rank's (1994) research concerning the public's perceptions of welfare recipients uncovered some compelling contradictions that are also likely to emerge in thematic interpretation of data related to economic issues. For example, when surveying welfare recipients, he asked whether they attributed their situations to external circumstances, internal factors, or a combination of the two. When reflecting on their *own* experiences of being on welfare, over 80% attributed their situations to external factors beyond their control. However, when asked about *others* who were on welfare, 90% placed the blame fully or partly on the internal characteristics of welfare recipients. Rank found that the majority of the people he surveyed viewed themselves as the deserving poor and others as the undeserving poor. This is much like Ehrenreich's (2008) account of false consciousness:

> I remember talking to a young white woman who professed great enthusiasm for draconian forms of welfare reform—only to admit that she herself had been raised on welfare by a beloved and plucky single mother. That's deeply internalized shame. The ultimate trick is to make people ashamed of the injuries inflicted upon them. (p. 68)

Leavy (2007c) found that when she interviewed Latino/a participants who were recent immigrants about their individual experiences in the United States, they were open about describing racism, job discrimination, and abuse. However, when she asked respondents about their perceptions of structural barriers, including economic mobility, only two said that barriers existed. It would be easy to dismiss these instances as ignorance on the part of participants, but something much deeper is at work here. Dialectical materialist interpretation provides a way to begin to interrogate these key contradictions on the part of participants in order to fully grasp how false consciousness functions on both structural and internal levels to erode solidarity.

Underlying all of these examples is a market-think conception of autonomy and choice. Slee (2006) asserts that a major function of the discourse of individual choice is that it locates consequences entirely within the control of a single person. Once choice is framed in such a manner, then it becomes easy to dismiss the poor as having made "bad choices." Similarly, one can also psychologically distance one's own self from those who make bad choices by constructing exceptions to the rule, as when welfare recipients segregate themselves from the "undeserving" recipients because "my situation was different than theirs," or people deny racism ("I'm not like Fred Phelps so I'm not racist!") in order to save face. Robin (2011) explains faux populism as a project of getting the working class to either locate themselves symbolically with elites or replicate a smaller-scale version of exploitative ruling-class hierarchy, where one positions oneself as better off than someone who is not that far removed from oneself (as, for example, the tyrannical small business owner might). This has enormous interpretive implications for research, and is an important reminder to not take things as they appear or as they are described. Participants may express these views, or researchers may fall into a version of the same trap.

For example, Lewontin and Levins (2007) deconstruct the negatively perceived "choice" of people smoking at work. Rather than judging the actions of workers as "choosing" bad health, Lewontin and Levins assert that often, "smoke breaks" provide one of the few opportunities to escape oppressive work environments, even if just for a few minutes. As they explain it, "people who have few choices in life at least can make the choice to smoke" (p. 315). What on the face of it might appear to be an irrational choice is actually quite rational given the situation. Slee (2006) reminds us of the structural nature of choice in that "most people do make reasonable choices, most of the time. It's just that good choices are not enough" (p. 216). What might look like a bad choice to a rich person is a "lesser of two evils" choice to a poor person. Maybe, instead of bemoaning the fact that individuals don't make good choices, we should be asking (a) why there aren't more choices available for most people, and (b) why the tools for making better choices aren't provided to most people (Lewontin & Levins, 2007).

This ties in to another interpretive dilemma facing Marxian researchers: how to explain participants' apparent lack of resistance to their situations. Activists often work under the (highly flawed) assumption that the worse things get, the more likely it is that people will rise up to overturn the system. Yet, Ehrenreich (2008) finds the opposite: "The worse things get, the harder it becomes even to imagine any kind of resistance" (p. 136). A form of social masochism takes hold, underscored by the knowledge that one can be fired at any moment in an unstable economy. These are transaction costs, or the consequences of choices, meaning that for many people, as these costs increase, their ability to find other options decreases (Slee, 2006). Fisher (2009) describes how people rationalize their shrinking options using the example of a middle managers in higher education:

> In terms of his inner subjective attitude, the manager is hostile, even contemptuous, towards the bureaucratic procedures he supervises; but in terms of his outward behavior, he is perfectly compliant. Yet it is precisely workers' subjective disinvestment from auditing tasks which enables them to continue to perform labor that is pointless and demoralizing. (p. 55)

Garcia's (2012) accessible, point-by-point essay lists the factors that keep people from resisting: few expectations for change, lack of financial security, trained passivity, distractibility, and fear of government reprisal. All of these legitimate and often overlooked factors are barriers to people resisting and should be incorporated into any analysis of people's actions, no matter the context. For example, we could apply Garcia's analysis in trying to decipher why teachers don't overtly resist standardized testing en masse, even though individually they speak out against it. First, we could conclude that many of them don't see legitimate alternatives to testing because few coherent proposals have been put forth, other than the generic "use alternative assessments." The more developed alternative assessment proposals that do exist tend to come from isolated pockets of resistance groups rather than from massive mobilizations that teachers feel will have their backs. Second, teachers also fear being fired, which is definitely a legitimate fear in today's climate of assaults on public sector workers, including educators, especially if one is working in a school that produces lower test scores. Third, both colleges of education and the environments of schools work together to create social pressures to accept standardized testing and its shaping of curriculum, which inscribes a form of passivity. Fourth, small-scale reforms such as professional learning communities and prepackaged solutions to raising test scores create distractions from the bigger problem of neoliberal educational policy. Finally, in addition to the threat of being fired, teachers may fear being blacklisted or permanently excluded from K–12 jobs. As this analysis proceeds, it begins to become apparent that the fault lies with the inability of the left to provide any real alternative, not with the disappointing actions of the teachers themselves, who are behaving quite rationally by not choosing martyrdom.

At this point, researchers should deepen their analysis of neoliberal ideology, which might shed some light on what they are seeing as a perplexing lack of participant resistance. As Allman (2007) notes, since we live in a capitalist society, people are likely to "alienate their potentials" by giving them up, at least partly, or resisting in small, less effective ways (p. 35). Allison (2002) conceptualizes the problem as follows:

> Everything in our culture—books, television, movies, school, fashion—is presented as if it is being seen by one pair of eyes, shaped by one set of hands, heard by one pair of ears. Even if you know you are not part of that imaginary creature, you are still shaped by that hegemony, or your resistance to it. (p. 32)

Even with obvious acts of resistance, we need to be able to distinguish between resistance informed by transformative praxis and resistance that is part of a consumerist mentality, as in Fairclough's (2010) example of students who oppose traditional academic writing: Are they opposed to the patriarchal and classist heritage of academia, or are they opposed to having to exert effort in today's capitalist climate of "hard work is for suckers," as expressed in Robert Kiyosaki's best-selling *Rich Dad/Poor Dad* financial advice series?

A ray of hope in these interpretive dilemmas is that the act of research itself can spur the move toward an alternative, as Brooks (2007) demonstrates through her research on African American women who serve as supportive parental figures:

> As we come to view the capitalist system from the standpoint of African American other mothers we are exposed not only to shortcomings in the system but also to the need for change and new solutions—solutions such as universally affordable, quality child care. In fact, often the very process of enabling women to articulate their own experiences of oppression raises awareness among women and others, about the particular difficulties diverse women face and inspires movement toward change. (pp. 60–61)

Conclusion—The Big Picture

When doing qualitative research, one can easily get caught up in the mechanics of method, whether writing a proposal for the IRB, crafting interview protocols, or creating codes. As Qvortrup (2008) speculates, "losing information in a controlled way is the very idea of research" (p. 67). This aspect of research often provokes anxiety in beginning scholars who are used to finishing one thing at a time rather than working on several aspects of a project at once, with likely setbacks along the way.

Good interpretations are not only limited to one's data, they are also connected to larger theories. These theories provide us with reminders that our senses alone may be deceptive, especially concerning hegemony and the naturalization of the status quo. Even though as dialectical researchers we may recognize these tendencies within society in the abstract, we may be reluctant to identify specific aspects of ideology enacted through the lives of participants (Belenky et al., 1997; Krumer-Nevo, 2012). Walford (2008a) addresses this dilemma:

> A researcher may be able to discover and articulate things about individuals and groups which they cannot see themselves, as well as things which neither the participants nor researcher can see at the outset of the study.... [W]hat people believe to be the reality of their world must be important information in understanding their activities, values, meanings, and relationships and in working out what is going on. (p. 11)

Walford explains that when researchers are able to present often unheard voices of participants to a larger audience, this becomes a political act. Therefore, it is critical that these unique insider perspectives are presented within a full context, and not isolated or taken at face value.

When the big picture isn't considered in one's interpretations and conclusions, one runs the risk of what Krumer-Nevo (2012) calls "othering." This may occur when researchers provide uncomplicated portrayals of human interactions (including single acts of heroism), rely on participant platitudes, ask no follow-up questions when generalities are given during an interview, or fail to address contradictions between what people say and what they do. Dialectical materialist researchers should follow Marx's exhortation to critique everything relentlessly, and that includes one's own research data and interpretations. Qualitative research as public inquiry places the researcher in the role of the watchdog on the side of the working class, not elites. In this situation, research is about presenting compelling accounts that people can relate to while at the same time raising consciousness and promoting action. This type of qualitative research deliberately "exposes complacency, bigotry, and wishful thinking" (Denzin, 2009, p. 122).

Chapter Eleven

Technology

Overview—The Relevance of Technology for Dialectical Research

By 2009, more than 1.5 billion people were using the Internet, roughly 22% of the total world's population (Kozinets, 2010, p. 2). A majority of these users are not just reading materials online, but also interacting with each other: "Not only has it become socially acceptable for people to reach out and connect through this panopoly of computer-mediated connectivity, but these "places" and related activities have become commonplace" (p. 7). Kozinets relates how large-scale surveys of Internet use reveal that roughly 15% of users describe themselves as belonging to an online community of some sort, with the average membership lasting 3 years (p. 14). Most of them are involved with hobby-related communities, with nearly 30% checking in on their favorite sites several times a day (p. 14). These figures exclude social networking sites such as Facebook. Contrary to the stereotypical image of an antisocial computer geek hunched over his laptop in his parents' basement, 56% of those who belong to online communities reported meeting other members in person (p. 14). As Kozinets explains, these online communities cannot be considered virtual in the traditional sense.

Early Internet culture featured bulletin boards, with people exchanging posts about a shared activity or topic by (boyd, 2009). This was part of the Web 1.0 experience, which predates the more interactive Web 2.0 that involves social media sites that have replaced the older bulletin board and web ring formats (Kozinets, 2010). The Internet itself was a project of the Department of Defense before arriving in the commercial sector and going global in 1993 with Mosaic, the first web browser (Fischer, 1999; Kozinets, 2010). Kozinets credits Tim Berners-Lee, who worked at the CERN physics lab in Switzerland, with the invention of the Internet as we know it today. Fischer (1999) describes the impact of the Internet on building communities:

The early 1990s are often spoken of by the computer science community as a second major turning point, marked by a reorganization of the Internet, changes in global competitive structure of the semiconductor and information technology industries, the introduction of new user-oriented tools, and the huge influx of general users to the Internet. (p. 255)

Today's Internet geographies include online groups, forums, chat rooms, playspaces, virtual worlds, lists (often private), rings (linked web pages, organized by interest), blogs, wikis, audiovisual sites, social content aggregations, and social networking sites. Most commercial shopping sites feature one or more of these interactive geographies as well.

Baym and Markham (2009) view the Internet as impacting the following four areas of human interaction: media convergence, mediated identities, redefinitions of social boundaries, and the transcendence of geographical boundaries. Fischer (1999) adds that Web 2.0 requires the simultaneous use of two kinds of knowledge skills—scientific precision/technicalities and social relations mapping. This makes the Internet different than other media forms such as television or even cell phones, which appear to be more a part of the terrestrial social world (Orgad, 2009):

The (seemingly) neat worlds of face-to-face embodied conversation, public speaking, landline telephones, radio, television, and film have all but collapsed into a tangled web of video clips sent over mobile phones, music played over computers, refrigerators that suggest recipes with built-in computer screens, and sites like YouTube where clips of a broadcast television show sit on the same platform alongside homemade videos. (Baym & Markham, 2009, p. x)

Mass communication of this nature begins to form collective memories simply because of its saturation potential (Howell & Prevenier, 2001). Geographic space begins to collapse, at least within online contexts, impacting identities, notions of privacy, shared traditions, and the like (Baym & Markham, 2009).

Rather than the purview of only postmodernism scholars, technology should be seen as a fruitful area for dialectical materialist inquiry. An array of qualitative approaches have begun to form methodological traditions involving technology, including webnography, digital ethnography, cyberethnography, virtual worlds research, and netnography. Kozinets (2010) asserts that we have reached a critical point in terms of technology, where ignoring the role of the Internet means that ethnographers may be missing key components of cultural information. This recalls anthropologists first grappling with the dilemma of how to deal with the arrival of movies and television as relevant cultural knowledge in forming the discipline of media anthropology (Osorio, 2005).

Another reason for dialectical materialist researchers to pay attention to social media is to understand how it is used by elites to further imperialism. A key recent example is the "Stop Kony" campaign, associated with the charity Invisible Children, whose YouTube video against the Ugandan leader of the Lord's Resistance Army went viral. Not long after, one of the co-founders of Stop Kony suffered a mental breakdown, also broadcast on YouTube. After this event, more was revealed about the social media campaign surrounding Kony and Invisible Children, including the charity's sponsorship by right-wing religious groups and millionaires (Berkowitz, 2012). In another case, O'Connor (2012) describes how private groups in Egypt hiding under the nongovernmental organization label have received large grants earmarked for developing social media and advertising campaigns targeted at youth. These groups are part of an overall effort to dampen the activism that has been part of the Arab Spring.

Marxian researchers should also be keenly interested in the ethical issues that technology studies raises, including access to information as a function of civil rights. The cases of WikiLeaks and Bradley Manning are particularly instructive on the rise of the security state and the duplicity of governments manufacturing outrage over individuals who reveal details about atrocities, instead of focusing on themselves as the committers of those atrocities (Colson, 2010). The "risk to security" argument is asserted again and again to build public acceptance of the notion that governments should be allowed to keep secrets. However, that level of confidentiality is not extended to the majority of citizens, who find themselves subject to domestic surveillance as part of the Patriot Act, by which the U.S. government regularly uses databases to monitor information (Conyers, 2007).

This chapter opens with a discussion of some of the divisive or negative impacts of technology, which is meant to provide some counterweight to the notion that the Internet and social media have "totally transformed" reality. Next, the knowledge commons is addressed as an extension of usufruct, or shared investment in and access to information. This is followed by a look at some methodological considerations for those undertaking netnographic research studies, including the impact on ethical decisions. Finally, I argue that while the Internet is part of global culture, it is not apart from it, because its current existence is shaped by capitalist social relations.

Divisions

It is easy to assume that technology's impact on human society has been mostly positive, or that it has created large-scale, irreversible, and radical transformations, as Markham (2009) explains:

> The Internet is certainly globally distributed, which without clarification can seem to imply that it is universal or monolithic technology available everywhere to everyone. Naïve application of this premise leads to oversimplification of technologies that are, in actuality, differentially distributed and have different meanings in different global contexts. (p. 137)

For example, what Kozinets (2010) calls "technological determinism" can disguise the fact that over a third of the world's population still does not have access to the Internet. Instead, technology should be seen as co-determining culture rather than re-creating it entirely. It is important to remember that many of the technologies that now seem outdated were originally presented as revolutionary, such as the chalkboard and the overhead projector, which were once thought to be able to replace books entirely (Ryan & Cooper, 2007). Fischer (1999) relates how the arrival of the personal computer was seen as the solution for leveling the sociological playing field and radically intervening with traditional commercial models that limited access to technology, yet Microsoft and Apple are hugely profitable companies selling expensive goods. Today, the hype centers on the Internet and its ability to connect people globally, but even though there are more free public "hotspots" than before, it is still relatively expensive to purchase high-speed access in one's home.

Social networking itself is heralded as dramatically changing the political landscape. This is the view held by authors such as Mason (2012) who assert that technology is the new means by which activism is occurring, replacing outdated collective organizing methods such as street protests. Mason also sees technology as dethroning older notions of leadership in activist movements, which is in line with his anarchist philosophy valorizing leaderless groups. The problem with this view is that it overemphasizes the role of social media while deemphasizing the continuing need to make the struggle against capitalism the centerpiece of organizing. While technology has provided additional and new tools for activists, the reality is that most people are still members of the working class, relying on a paycheck to survive. They may be fully networked, but they are still caught within capitalism. Technology has not altered that basic social condition.

Rather than neutrally presenting reality as a high-tech consumer-preference popularity contest, the Internet also reflects societal prejudices. Noble (2012) presents a compelling analysis of how women are portrayed via a tool foundational to the digital world—the search engine. Arguing that search engines impact our concepts about the social world, Noble asserts that it is critical to interrogate what rises to the top of Google search results when terms are typed in. For example, after asking her class to type the innocuous phrase "black girls" into Google, the students were shocked to see pornographic representations at the top of the search results. A search for "black women" produced articles in the top ranks about angry black women, or what is wrong with black women. Searching for "women's magazines" yielded highly commercialized and narrow representations of gender at the top of the search results; feminist magazines appeared way down the list.

Noble (2012) attributes many search results to a combination of corporate dollars and public consciousness, where it is hard to separate one from the other:

> Google's search process is based on identifying and assigning value to various types of information through web indexing. Many search engines, not just Google, use artificial intelligence of computers to determine what kinds of information should be retrieved and displayed, and in what order. Complex mathematical formulations are developed into algorithms that are part of the automation process. These calculations do not take social context into account. (p. 39)

Those sites that are able to finance paid advertising are the ones that show up at the top of searches, even if one isn't deliberately searching for commercial web pages. The problem is that when people see a site that is highly ranked, they assume it is trustworthy. Noble (2012) reports that 92% of Internet users 18 and older rely on search engines, with close to 60% utilizing them daily (p. 41). What is incredible is that a majority of these individuals—64%—view search engines as fair and unbiased places to locate information (p. 41). Slee (2006) asserts that search engines represent one of many forms of media consolidation, which is a reflection not of "consumer choice" but of rapidly diminishing alternatives in the quest for the #1 ranking. This illustrates that far from being a straightforward, asocial form of production rooted in engineering and science, technology is all about money and who has it (Hine, 2009).

Another area that technology impacts is the traditional boundary between what is private and what is public (Baym & Markham, 2009). It isn't just large corporations that have access to large databases of private information; now it is common for employers to conduct background checks on their employees even when there is no suspicion of wrongdoing:

> A number of companies are using personal web pages and the Internet to perform background checks on employees. Many believe that web sites provide a more "in-depth" snapshot of a job candidate's individual characteristics, regardless of the information that has been submitted to the company through traditional means with the application form or résumé. Online net-

work sites such as MySpace and Facebook are used to obtain personal information, some of which involves sexual activity, drug use, and other ques-
tionable behavior. (Mathis & Jackson, 2010, p. 236)

Mathis and Jackson explain that because the Internet retains a permanent archive of materials, even if a person is no longer engaged in certain activities, the record remains. There is also the problem of
compromising photographs posted without a person's consent. This
information exists, yet employers do not have the contextual information needed to make fully informed decisions about employee behaviors. Ehrenreich (2001) found that when she worked in the lower-
paying service sector as part of her research on living on a minimum
wage, social surveillance of employees was the norm, much more so
than in her white-collar, professional world.

Access to personal information isn't the only thing that has bal-
looned in scope; the sheer amount of data itself is quickly growing
out of control (Fischer, 1999). Jones (2012) explains the impact on public school teachers of "reforms" such as data-driven instruction:

There's a huge industry in data, in the accumulation of data, in the building
of data systems that nobody uses. Here in New York City we see them laying off people who work with children, and hiring six-figure data consultants to manage and massage the data because they're banking everything on
data. (p. 13)

Data also accumulates so quickly that it soon loses its usefulness as a
measure of progress. Howell and Prevenier (2001) assert that we are
in danger of losing a coherent social memory due to this proliferation
of data.

Finally, forums and social media sites can feature some of the
more interactive components of the Internet, yet they, too, are subject
to shaping by capitalism. It is important not to mistake the enormous
amount of personally created postings and reflections for actual human exchange. Rather than being a democratic site for shaping ideas,
the Internet often "facilitates communities of solipsists, interpassive
networks of like minds who conform, rather than challenge, each other's assumptions and prejudices" (Fischer, 1999, p. 75). Fischer notes

that many of the fiercely defensive, libertarian ideas of noninterference with the Internet have created not a diverse grassroots community of refreshing originality, but instead a bunch of ranting infants, particularly white male ones whose conservative views quickly dominate online spaces. This could be due to the speed with which someone can read a news story and then post their impressions without much thought or reflection. Boyd (2009) concludes the following:

> Just because people can theoretically use the Internet to broadcast their expressions, reach out to diverse populations across the world, or free themselves of their offline identity does not mean that this is what people do or see themselves as doing. People's worldviews—and their neuroses—leak from the offline to the online. (p. 31)

The Knowledge Commons

The intellectual or knowledge commons movement began in the late 1980s as public and university libraries attempted to grapple with the onslaught of information emerging parallel to the phenomenon of personal computers ushering in the digital age (Milewicz, 2009). With public use of the Internet growing in the 1990s, the knowledge commons solidified into an activist movement, employing the hacker's and academic's egalitarian ethics of open access in terms of reproducibility, availability, and no cost to users (Fischer, 1999; Kozinets, 2010; Torres & Reyes, 2011). The main concept behind the knowledge commons is that it is collectively administered and maintained, where no one individual or company profits from this knowledge at the expense of others, resulting in

> real democratic control of the producers, and a society based on the ancient concept of usufruct. That is, anyone can use a resource as long as it remains undamaged for future generations. This is in line with Marx's dictum that we should bequeath the earth to future generations in better shape than we found it; a concept of time entirely alien to capitalist accounting. (Williams, 2012, p. 66)

It is easy to see how an immediate conflict emerged between traditional industry approaches to the distribution of information in the digital age and the knowledge commons ethos, producing a rich territory for dialectical materialist inquiry. For example, Slee (2006) describes how pharmaceutical companies have been applying for patents as a strategy for privatizing biodiversity, often tapping into the resources of indigenous people who have developed medicines and cures for centuries, without their consent. Howell and Prevenier (2001) note that in the early 1980s, financial records held by the United States government were no longer accessible because an overseas company the government had contracted with to produce the technology needed to read these records stopped making the technology. Today, even commercial sites such as Facebook contain strict conditions that may prohibit some forms of academic research using site content (Kozinets, 2010). This is in direct violation of the hacker's ethical code, as Fischer (1999) explains:

> It is an ethical duty of hackers to share their expertise by writing free software and facilitating access to information and to computing resources wherever possible, including the more controversial belief that systematic cracking for fun and exploration is ethically OK as long as the cracker commits no theft, vandalism, or breach of confidentiality. This puts hackers often, and in principled active ways, at odds with industry. (pp. 269–270)

Although hackers have been maligned as criminals by the mass media and law enforcement, Fischer points out that more serious digital violations include financial sector white-collar crimes and the government's use of databases to spy on people (p. 270).

Most of the recent legal developments in the digital era—intellectual property law, including patents, trademarks, and copyrights—have involved software issues (Fischer, 1999). This is due in part to the growth in demand for software after the mass dissemination of the personal computer. Software companies' expectations for copyright protection were thwarted by the ease with which their products were rapidly reproduced and distributed, a problem that the music industry experienced when the free downloading site Napster was created in 1999 (Menn, 2003). What has resulted is a situation where private industries are constantly fighting to maintain previously large profit margins, while accessibility is higher on the priority lists of Internet users. Some online marketing approaches have built on the knowledge commons model by encouraging mass distribution of information and products; on example is the social photo-sharing site Pinterest, where users can post images of items and tutorials that catch their interest. Other Pinterest users can repin these images, further distributing information. According to this "earned versus paid" model, the social media benefits are twofold: Consumers appreciate getting useful information for free, thus making them more likely to purchase items in the future, and they get enjoyment out of interacting on the web site, rather than just being hit with advertising (Evans, 2010). Although Pinterest is starting to grapple with copyright issues, in general, few protest the free mass promotion of products they are selling.

One of the most pivotal legal decisions to affect the knowledge commons project comes from an unexpected place: the model railroad community. The Java Model Railroad Interface (JMRI) is a bundle of open-source software created in the late 1990s that is used by model railroaders to more efficiently run their layouts without having to create an operating system from scratch. The software can be operated from a smartphone or laptop, bringing an enormous degree of flexibility to a more traditional hobby. Along with the software, the JMRI web site has active forums and discussion portals so that hobbyists from all over the world can talk shop and exchange ideas and updates (http://jmri.sourceforge.net/). JMRI adheres to the ethos of the knowledge commons in that all of the information on the web site is free, though donations are accepted. The web site also has an acknowledgments page that lists site updates and recent improvements to the software, which has become a community project. Prior to JMRI, the model railroad hobby was limited to a club structure and used more stationary solutions to operate trains; now, the ability to use portable electronic devices has increased interaction, taking the hobby online to reach a larger user demographic.

In October 2004 JMRI site users noticed that the domain name decoderpro.com had been registered earlier in 2004 by Matt Katzer of KAM Industries, a company that sells railroad software. DecoderPro is the name of one of the JMRI open-source products. Katzer was not a member of the JMRI community, nor had he ever contributed to the development of the open-source software in any way, shape, or form. It was later revealed that Katzer was a habitual cybersquatter, someone who profits off of the knowledge commons by seizing on the communally creative efforts of others in order to privatize these efforts for personal gain (Barrett, 2008). For example, Barrett outlines how previously, Katzer had applied for patents for several other inventions that were not his own. When asked by JMRI about the domain name registration, Katzer replied that

> he was considering whether he would 'be able to take the open source code and turn it into a licensed product so it could be distributed…. If I decide that to released [sic] a licensed version of an open source development effort, what better place to have it then the name of the development effort?' (JMRI, n.d., para. 4)

When JMRI wrote a letter to Katzer requesting the return of the domain name, he didn't reply. A JMRI user, Jerry Britton, made an offer to Katzer to trade another domain name. Eventually, the case was settled, with Britton taking the decoderpro.com domain name with a host of restrictions on how it could be used, including the threat of a $20,000 fine if he attempted to transfer the name to JMRI or even speak about the settlement to anyone. Emboldened, Katzer then proceeded to demand royalties ranging from $19.00 to $29.00 per downloaded copy of JMRI software. JMRI received bills in excess of $200,000 per month.

In 2006 JMRI filed a declaratory judgment complaint against Katzer, citing unfair competition, libel, and patent fraud. Katzer and his attorneys responded by filing motions to dismiss the accusations of libel. Eventually, the case went to court, culminating in a 90-minute hearing (*Jacobsen v. Katzer*, 535 F.3d 1373 (Fed. Cir. 2008)). Because of prior restrictions, the court decided it could not hear evidence that contradicted Katzer's statements about his previous patent activity, and therefore the plaintiff was ordered to pay Katzer's legal fees and the antilibel and antitrust charges couldn't stand. After this hearing, Katzer proceeded to take JMRI copyrighted code, remove original authorship attributions, and sell it as exclusively his own. JMRI filed an amended complaint, citing Katzer's copyright violations, which was followed by another motion to dismiss from Katzer. Incredibly, his attorney argued that copyright did not protect free open-source software. After some back and forth in the courts, JMRI filed a preliminary injunction and a rebuttal to the claim that open-source software wasn't protected by copyright law.

A hearing was held in 2007 to prevent further copyright violations by Katzer. In the meantime, the World Intellectual Property Organization reviewed the earlier case regarding the domain name and returned a decision that Katzer had acted in bad faith, and that the domain name decoderpro.com should be transferred to JMRI. Although this decision was a victory for JMRI, the back-and-forth in the courts continued, taking its toll on the group in terms of financial and emotional costs (which was summarized in detail on the web site, with links to the legal documents). For example, initially, the court rejected the claims of harm to JMRI, stating that not enough conclusive evidence had been provided. By then, JMRI was supported by several other knowledge commons advocates, including the Creative Commons Corp, the Linux Foundation, the Open Source Initiative, and the Wikimedia Foundation. They were able to provide expertise on the intricate maze of copyright law and how it applied to software, and they filed research in support of JMRI's case.

In 2008 another hearing was held on the copyright appeal, with positive results for JMRI. The judge ruled that open-source software was considered copyright protected, just as privately licensed products are. When open-source conditions are violated, the license disappears and one becomes a copyright infringer. After this decision, another series of court filings ensued, with Katzer continuing to fight JMRI's charges up to the point of countersuing the plaintiff for $6 million. This was followed by more legal back-and-forth, culminating in a settlement agreement in 2010. A permanent injunction was leveled against Katzer, forbidding him to misuse JMRI software, including by profiting from it. Katzer also had to release JMRI from any liability for anything tied to JMRI, whose reputation was damaged by the confusion caused by members being charged by Katzer for downloads. Katzer is no longer able to gain royalties from JMRI, nor can he claim copyright infringement. In addition, Katzer had to pay $100,000 to JMRI over 18 months.

This case is remarkable because although we often think about copyright law in terms of protecting private ownership (as in the debate over digitally downloading music), we don't often think about it applying to the protection of *communal product ownership*. If even the model railroad community—a group not known for cultivating controversy—has cybersquatters, it doesn't take much to imagine that there are others profiting off the collective labor of others and then forbidding the original developers to access their own creations or share them with others as intended. It's one thing to have open-source ideas copied and then sold under different names—that happens all the time; but it's another thing entirely to copy the work of others, charge money for it, and forbid access and distribution by the very people who developed it! Clearly the knowledge commons movement will have to continue to deal with challenges to its collective ethos by capitalist predators. Luckily, those who are dedicated to the availability of open-source materials are used to working together in solidarity and mustering the resources needed to mount an effective defense against this predation. Kozinets (2010) addresses the implications of this for research:

> In studies seeking to examine online communities and cultures, this interrelationship of community ethics, power, morality, and legal rights over ownership may well take center stage. If we consider that, in their essences, learning and culture themselves are concerned with copying or imitation, emulation, and enculturation, then these individualistic and private property-related notions of ownership and rights can lead us to the center of some explosive social conflicts. (p. 176)

Research Considerations

In the late 1990s the Association of Internet Researchers was formed to provide guidance to those conducting qualitative and quantitative research online, because of the unique methodological considerations involved with this type of inquiry (Elm, 2009). Whether one is doing a critical discourse analysis of social media sites or actively participating in a virtual community, one must simultaneously consider many elements, including use of theory, conceptions of time, notions of geography, nature of languages, and institutional roles/power:

> Even more than a multisited ethnography, an ethnography of cyberspace presents a topological challenge for a multidimensional approach that is able to bring into sharp juxtaposition the contradictory elements of cyberspace's political economy, cultural elaborations, liberating and subjugating potentials, new information-based sciences, alternative engineering designs, and their social implications. (Fischer, 1999, p. 247)

Those who make the Internet the center of their dialectical materialist inquiry need to be aware that it is not a stable, geographic location in the traditional sense of a "field site" (boyd, 2009; Hine, 2009; Kozinets, 2010). As a result, issues of ethics, access, types of data, and people may not be as straightforward as with traditional ethnographic settings (and even that isn't entirely straightforward).

Ethics

Two major areas of ethics emerge within netnographic research: how to handle the blurring between what is public and what is private, and issues of identity/authenticity. While these are concerns with traditional qualitative approaches too, they can be particularly thorny when dealing with cyberspace. A sound starting point is for the researcher to take the ethical stance of full disclosure when conducting interactive online research. Because netnography involves human interaction, it falls within the purview of protection of human participants. This means that from the very start, researchers take the ethical steps to identify themselves, their intentions, and the nature of the research, with no identity deception (Kozinets, 2010). At the same time, this disclosure should be done in a manner that disrupts the existing online community as little as possible.

Regarding the blurred boundaries between private and public, the maintenance of confidentiality is trickier online than in other settings.

For example, even if cyber-pseudonyms are used, it is very easy for someone to copy and paste a direct quote into a search engine and have that quote tied to someone's real name or online name (Kozinets, 2010). Kendall's (2002) study of an online community she dubbed BlueSky ran into confidentiality issues because participants used forums to discuss her research, both in-process and after her book was published. This expanded the scope of her study way beyond the initial few participants to potentially thousands who knew about the research, thus compromising confidentiality.

The public/private dichotomy also applies to the nature of the information posted and distributed on the Internet. While some could make the case that no one should assume that privacy is sacred once they post something online, things aren't that simple in real-life applications. boyd (2009) captures this dilemma:

> Just because people's expressions on the Internet are public in the sense that they can be viewed by anyone does not mean that people are behaving as though their audience consists of billions of people across all space and time.... [W]hen we look to understand people's practices online, we must understand the context within which the individuals think they are operating. (p. 31)

Elm (2009) points out that many people find it difficult to comprehend the boundaries between private and public on the Internet. Posting gossip to a good friend's Facebook page doesn't "feel" like a public act the way that sharing a web page for one's small business might. Elm also explains that sometimes, public content is not meant to be displayed as such (e.g., a disgruntled ex-boyfriend or girlfriend posts compromising pictures or emails meant for only that one viewer, or unauthorized photographs are taken or altered through Photoshop and posted widely without consent in a form of cyber-harassment). Content is never exclusively "public" or "private," but a mixture of the two, depending on the context.

Because of these dilemmas, it is best for researchers to act as though information accessed online were private, and to obtain informed consent whenever possible, while realizing that the consent process cannot be the same as with traditional research (Elm, 2009;

Kozinets, 2010). Elm (2009) reminds researchers that if they were to approach the consent process in the same manner as in face-to-face research (i.e., by requesting signed consent for every encounter), they would run the risk of spamming most online communities. Kozinets (2010) suggests using "implied consent," where participants would electronically check an "accept" button via email or on a research study web page to which they would be directed. Extra care needs to be taken, including carefully spending time examining potential online research settings for important contextual information, and never assuming that traditional libertarian notions of free will and autonomy are present:

> One may argue that online, an individual has more control, as she chooses what to present, when, and how in an online environment. Conversely, individuals may have less control online, given that disparate pieces of data exist on individuals and when taken together, in ways originally unintended, may comprise a false or distorted image of an individual—the data persona. Furthermore, the researcher may harvest data from an online environment out of context or without consent at all, thereby violating the control over the extent, timing, and circumstances of sharing oneself. (p. 89)

Regardless of these difficult aspects of the online environment, researchers should do their best to maintain as much confidentiality as reasonably possible. Kozinets (2010) describes different levels of identity protection: uncloaked, minimum cloaked, medium cloaked, and maximum cloaked. With the uncloaked option, verbatim quotes are given and real names or real online identity names are used, with the written and signed permission of participants. Often, in this situation, bloggers like to have their work cited, just as a book or journal article author would. Yet, the researcher has to consider whether using the uncloaked option, even with written permission, will harm other satellite participants. With the minimum cloaked option, the actual name of the online community is provided, but individual names/cyberidentities are disguised, though verbatim quotes are used. Medium cloaking is somewhere between this option and the maximum option, where everything is disguised—the online community is not named and all other details are altered, and paraphrasing rather than direct quotes are used. Kozinets recommends treating online pseudonyms exactly like real names when weighing these options.

Authenticity/Identity

Authenticity and identity is a second major methodological area of concern when it comes to netnographic studies. It can be difficult to shake traditional Western notions of the authentic self, particularly in ethnographic forms of research where the whole idea is to tap into the realities of communities and how they function (Baym & Markham, 2009). Yet it is also the case that much depends on the purpose of one's research as to whether confirming identity is even really necessary (Kozinets, 2010). For example, if a researcher was analyzing pregnant teens accessing online forums related to parenting, then it would be important to confirm that participants were, indeed, both pregnant and teenaged, in order to be able to draw conclusions about their experiences. This was the case for Orgad's (2009) study of women who were diagnosed with cancer and their use of the Internet for information and emotional support. It was important to verify that participants in her study were indeed female so that Orgad could draw conclusions about particular issues facing women who were diagnosed with a terminal illness. However, if one was only interested in frequency and purposes of using Facebook, for example, it might not matter as much to verify the identity of participants.

Kozinets (2010) contradicts the notion that people commonly falsify their identities on the Internet, citing data from studies that show that this doesn't occur as often as one thinks. When falsification did occur, usually men did it more often than women, and when women did misrepresent their identities, they did so for self-protection (e.g., disguising themselves as men in male-dominated forums) as well as to have one's posts taken at face value rather than being identified as "female" and therefore disregarded or attacked. In cases where researchers were able to meet participants face-to-face, they confirmed that their personas as presented online were pretty much accurate in the flesh. For Kozinets, then, the issue about altering one's identity is more a hang-up of the researcher and IRBs than a justifiable concern.

He points out that in our daily face-to-face lives we all put on personas to some degree, even to the point of identity falsification. Why this should be a bigger deal online is open for question. Kozinets recommends using sound analytic strategies such as the pragmatic-interactionist interpretive approach, where the focus is on observing participant "acts" rather than zeroing in on their stated identities. At the same time, if participants are indeed inventing alternative personas, that act may reveal much about their own motives regarding self and others.

Setting/Access

The research setting and gaining access is a third important consideration of Internet inquiry. Elm (2009) presents different categories of online environments that can help guide researchers to the best fit. First are public environments, which are viewable for anyone to post or read material. Many news and commercial sites have fully public forums that operate in this manner. Second are semipublic environments, common to what one finds with Facebook, where people have to request consent to gain access to personal profiles if privacy settings are activated. Third are semiprivate environments, which require not only registration but also other formal requirements prior to membership, such as subscription forums. Fourth are private environments, which are hidden from most viewers and restricted to invited guests. Those who are weighing options presented by the different types of sites might also want to consider avoiding sites that have a lot of spam postings, which cannot be treated the same as other forms of data in terms of analysis (Kozinets, 2010).

Gaining access to online communities is a major challenge for those doing netnographic forms of inquiry because the online setting is different than the face-to-face setting in terms of how one approaches these groups. For this reason, Kozinets (2010) suggests that beginning online researchers consider doing "autonetnography," in which they record their own experiences with interacting on the Internet in an autobiographical format. Both participation and observation take on new meanings with online communities. Kozinets also describes how he first approached an online group by using the traditional introductory research letter as his initial forum posting, and how this was a spectacular failure. He had not done prior investigation of the online community he was interested in studying—in this case, a group that had radical views about consumer rights and a distrust of government and academia. One of the community members was highly suspicious of researchers in general, and warned other members in the group's forum against cooperating with the project.

Most participants in online communities tend to resist approaches for research, especially those in groups that are overresearched or barraged with surveys and opinion polls. Kendall's (2009) research participants repeatedly questioned her in the group's forum about her intentions of maintaining relationships after the research ended, making the traditional ethnographic concept of exiting the site much more complicated. Therefore, researchers need to be keenly aware of the online community norms, and should behave like community members. This means embodying the knowledge commons ethos of information-sharing and reciprocation:

> The key to this "offering" strategy is that it offers actual content and communal connection before requesting cultural participation in the form of an interview.... [P]osting insightful, relevant, timely, interesting, noteworthy questions to a particular, properly targeted forum, or directly emailing very polite entreaties to particular people can offer a good foundation that a skilled interviewer can build upon. (Kozinets, 2010, pp. 107–108)

Researchers should act like new members while at the same time being clear that they are conducting research. Kozinets states that academics have much to offer online communities, such as information, web maintenance assistance, and relevant research that can help to reciprocate participant involvement.

One strategy researchers can consider is the use of a research web page or blog that is linked in the forum posts. That way, the researcher isn't taking up too much posting space or running the risk of spamming. Those interested in the project can click on the link and find not only information about the project, but also relevant articles that the group might deem useful. The same can be done when creating Facebook pages or chat rooms. As an example, Kozinets describes how he approached a Star Trek fan newsgroup by first posing a provocative question on their board concerning the connections between Star Trek and religion, along with links to some academic studies. Many of the fans were excited to participate in this discussion and learn more about the research project as a result. They appreciated being invited to comment on the articles and shape the direction of the research.

Types of Data

Data that one obtains from online contexts is unparalleled in its ability to be retrieved and systematically archived (Kozinets, 2010). As such, netnographic data can be categorized into two broad types: online, in the form of text, images, and audio; and offline, where researchers conduct face-to-face or voice over Internet Protocol (VoIP) interviews in person (Orgad, 2009). Online data can range from forum posts to information on how community members link between different content on sites. Offline data can be enormously beneficial for putting into context how people configure their online environments and interactions, as Hine (2009) found by studying the material culture of those engaged in online communities and using Google's TouchGraph browser to graph connections between linked sites and communities. In-person interviews are often employed because concepts such as originality and authorship can make online research challenging, as boyd (2009) explains:

> When people speak online, their words are not ephemeral. Search engines make text, media, and people findable at the flick of a few keys. Hearsay is one thing, but online, you often can't distinguish the original from the duplicate; likewise, it's difficult to tell if the author is really the author....These properties collapse social contexts and change the rules about how people can and do behave. (p. 30)

Kozinets (2010) also finds value in offline in-person, VoIP, or email interviewing, as chat-based interviews tend to result in shallow data.

Within the category of online data, Kozinets (2010) identifies three types: archival, elicited, and field notes. Archival data are obtained by directly copying text from online communities, such as forum posts or YouTube clips. This type of data is not created by the researcher in any way, shape, or form. Elicited data involve the researcher providing some sort of discussion prompt or request to co-create information with participants where there is an interactive exchange of some sort. Field note data are thoughts written down by the researcher that are not likely to be viewed by participants. It is an especially important type of data for online research:

> Reflective field notes become far more salient than observational field notes in netnography. In reflective field notes, netnographers record their own observations regarding subtexts, pretexts, contingencies, conditions, and personal emotions occurring during their time online and relating to their online experiences. (p. 114)

In many respects, the grappling with data mirrors many of the activities that those engaged in Internet communities regularly do, such as classifying by tagging, sorting, and applying taxonomies.

There are several structural considerations for conducting online and offline interviews as part of cyberethnography. Some might find it valuable to post questions for discussion in asynchronous platforms such as blogs or forums. These discussions could be conducted in parallel with or prior to face-to-face interviews (Kozinets, 2010). Synchronous focus groups also could be conducted via VoIP interfaces such as Skype, though Kozinets finds it important to remember that fatigue can set in after an hour. Asynchronous interviews should be used for online-related topics rather than ones that require a more physical presence. Although it originated in the offline world, social network analysis could be applied to online contexts as a way of processing data (Abraham, Hassanien, & Snasel, 2010). Ultimately, "what we are studying is not texts online, but people's interactions through various technologically mediated means" (Kozinets, 2010, p. 113).

People

Kozinets (2010) also relates how various categories are applied to the people who participate in online communities, based on their level of interaction. Involvement can range from silent observation to offering technological assistance and site design services. Hine (2009) finds that taxonomies often form organically within Internet communities as a way to preserve site information for future use. They are often a sign of the existence of a long-term, socially close community. Among Kozinets's (2010) online "types" is the newbie, who is just entering the group and superficially checking them out, perhaps to receive an answer to an interest-related question. Lurkers may do the same thing, only covertly. Minglers view socializing rather than content as the primary purpose of the Internet; they may know several members, but they don't typically go beyond social niceties. Devotees are the reverse—they tend to not interact with many people, but they post daily about content central to the group's purpose. Insiders combine the strong social ties with a wealth of relevant subject matter knowledge. Many of these roles are developmental in that lurkers often become newbies, and later become devotees.

Online groups themselves can also have certain characteristics. Kozinets (2010) found that cruising communities tend to emphasize the social over content, while bonding communities take social ties to a deeper level. Both of these types of communities are not particularly engaged with a central content-based interest. In contrast, geeking communities share a strong interest in a particular topic, with members readily posting articles, links, photographs, and techniques. Building communities combine social and geeking characteristics, and they cultivate taxonomies for future use and longevity. Even a social media site such as Facebook can embody different community types, as there are pages devoted to interests and others centered on political organizing. The task of the researcher is to figure out how all of this comes into play for the site under study, as Hine (2009) explains in her description of the approach she took with her inquiry:

The key guiding principle in my study was to proceed by asking myself why activities that I encountered might be happening and what kind of sense they made to those involved. I read, I interviewed, I lurked, I questioned, I linked, and I searched, all of the time making sense of what was going on. (p. 14)

Hine found that what are often considered "impacts" of technology are highly dependent on specific contexts. Different online communities are likely to view the effects of technologies in different ways.

Orgad's (2009) research on female cancer patients' use of support forums is an excellent example of Hine's (2009) notion of contextual impact:

I thus gained access to an appropriate range of participants engaged in different levels of involvement, in different kinds of online activities in relation to their lives. Researchers may also be interested in studying those who are not online—those who "fail" or refuse to engage online.... Studying this group can also shed light on Internet use and online participation. For example, in my study one of the interviewees was a patient who initially visited breast cancer patients' forums; however, after a short time, she became very critical of these sites and stopped participating in them. (p. 44)

Orgad used face-to-face interviews to go beyond the typical platitudes about the Internet that she found were prevalent in the forum environment. In the personal interviews, participants were more likely to contextualize specific aspects of the Internet to identify which ones assisted them or inhibited them from coping with their cancer diagnoses.

Conclusion

One of the best parodies of Thomas Friedman on the Internet is "The Datsun and the Shoe Tree" (Freetrademan, 2001). Taking off on Friedman's worship of all things globalized and high-tech, the parody embodies all of the metaphors used in defense of the status quo, while exhorting others to "get with it" and adapt to the fast-paced world of exploitation, displacement, poverty, and the knowledge economy in general. It is worth quoting at length here:

I was changing planes at the new airport in Jakarta the other day, on the way to Stockholm from Vladivostok. Three young Bangladeshi boys sat in the passenger lounge, watching The Power Rangers on satellite TV. Their mother—garbed in the traditional sari—talked to her cousin, a migrant worker who sold German-designed Walkman knockoffs in Hong Kong, on a shiny new Samsung cell phone. Sitting to one side of them was a young Chinese émigré on his way to Toronto to work for a software company, and on the other a business-suited Rastafarian making a connection to Bratislava. Meanwhile, a couple of Tuareg tribesmen sat cross-legged in front of the ticket counter, cooking yams over a flaming mound of ticket stubs.

What's my point? I don't actually have one—but opening my columns with strings of clichéd cultural juxtapositions really cuts down my workload. You see, since the Cold War ended, we've gone from superpowers to spreadsheets, Pershings to Pentiums, the Berlin Wall to suburban sprawl, olive trees to Lexuses. Are you ready? Because the whole world is changing. Unless you are one of the eight-tenths of humanity who at this moment are either hungry, illiterate, or field-stripping an AK-47, in which case I'll get back to you in some future column. (Freetrademan, 2001, para. 1–2)

Freetrademan's parody highlights the danger of assuming that technology has changed everything across the globe, including the nature of social interaction and labor. The Internet can be a seductive place that can fool people into thinking that the old categories of social class, gender, and race are no longer relevant. Empowerment discourse predominates in technological settings where people are promised everything from instant financial freedom by starting their own eBay sites to instant celebrity with the right YouTube clip. Indeed, the Internet can seem like a promising frontier where "anyone" can make it.

In his book *Future Hype: The Myths of Technology Change*, Siedensticker (2006)_is more skeptical about the impact of technology, specifically the Internet. He presents the reader with a hypothetical test of relevance—being stranded without electricity—and poses the question, How much impact does the Internet have in that situation? Lacking the basic necessities for sustenance is a reality for the majority of people on the planet. Yet, we persist with the notion that technology is revolutionary, at the expense of employing classic Marxian analysis. As dialectical materialist researchers, we should see technological environments as capitalist spaces that are appropriated in a myriad of ways by users. These spaces are too important to dismiss because they, like traditional terra firma spaces, reflect ideologies and the production of human identities.

critical qualitative research

Shirley R. Steinberg & Gaile S. Cannella, *General Editors*

The Critical Qualitative Research series examines societal structures that oppress and exclude so that transformative actions can be generated. This transformed research is activist in orientation. Because the perspective accepts the notion that nothing is apolitical, research projects themselves are critically examined for power orientations, even as they are used to address curricular, educational, or societal issues.

This methodological work challenges modernist orientations and universalist impositions, asking critical questions like: Who/what is heard? Who/what is silenced? Who is privileged? Who is disqualified? How are forms of inclusion and exclusion being created? How are power relations constructed and managed? How do different forms of privilege and oppression intersect to affect educational, societal, and life possibilities for various individuals and groups?

We are particularly interested in manuscripts that offer critical examinations of curriculum, policy, public communities, and the ways in which language, discourse practices, and power relations prevent more just transformations.

For additional information about this series or for the submission of manuscripts, please contact:
Shirley R. Steinberg and Gaile S. Cannella
msgramsci@aol.com | Gaile.Cannella@unt.edu

To order other books in this series, please contact our Customer Service Department:
(800) 770-LANG (within the U.S.)
(212) 647-7706 (outside the U.S.)
(212) 647-7707 FAX

Or browse online by series:
www.peterlang.com